MW00529174

Goff
on Goff

Goff
on Goff

Edited and with an Introduction by
Philip B. Welch

Foreword by Arthur Dyson

University of Oklahoma Press   :   Norman and London

Opposite page: Bruce Goff at work in his Price Tower studio, Bartlesville, Oklahoma, 1958. Photo by Philip B. Welch.

Conversations and Lectures

This book is published with the generous assistance of the
Wallace C. Thompson Endowment Fund,
University of Oklahoma Foundation.

Library of Congress Cataloging-in-Publication Data

Goff on Goff / edited and with an introduction by Philip B. Welch:
foreword by Arthur Dyson.

    p.   cm.

    Includes index.

    ISBN 0-8061-2868-2

    1. Goff, Bruce, 1904–   —Philosophy. I. Welch, Philip B.,
1923– .

    NA737.G56A2   1996

    720′.92—dc20   96-18190

                                                          CIP

Text design by Cathy Carney Imboden. Text typeface is Berkeley Medium.

The paper in this book meets the guidelines for permanence and durability of the Committee on Production Guidelines for Book Longevity of the Council on Library Resources, Inc. ♾

1   2   3   4   5   6   7   8   9   10

Contents

List of Illustrations   vii
Foreword, by Arthur Dyson   ix
Preface   xi
Introduction   3
One.   Goff's Creative Growth
          and Design Philosophy   17
Two.   Order in Architecture   39
Three.   The New and Different
          in Architecture   79
Four.   Honesty in Architecture   111
Five.   The Idea in Architecture   157
Six.   The Continuous Present
          in Architecture   191
Seven.   Music and Architecture   227
Eight.   Japanese Art and Modern
          Design   255
Nine.   Goff on Debussy   271
Ten.   The Design of the Garvey
          House   283
Eleven.   The New Geometry in
          Architecture   297
Twelve.   Advancing Architecture   307
Index   329

Illustrations

Bruce Goff at work   frontispiece
Goff at his Price Tower studio   175
Goff with Japanese paper
    lantern   176
Goff working on mural,
    Vernon Rudd House   177
University of Oklahoma
    School of Architecture
    corridor, display of Herb
    Greene's drawings   178
Crystal Chapel project   179
Hopewell Baptist Church   180
Interior view, Hopewell
    Baptist Church   181
Ruth Ford House   182
Detail of bedroom dome,
    Ruth Ford House   183
Eugene Bavinger House
    from north   184
Floor plan, Eugene Bavinger
    House   185
Eugene Bavinger House
    from southeast   186
John Garvey House project   187
Interior perspective, John
    Garvey House project   188
Floor plan, John Garvey
    House project   189
Bruce Goff composition,
    "Squircle"   190

All photographs are by
Philip B. Welch, courtesy of
Theresa Welch.

Many people mistake buildings for archi-tecture. Architecture, however, is about the workings of the human mind. Any good architect knows the difference; only excep-tional architects note it for the benefit of others. Phil Welch was one of these.

Foreword

By Arthur Dyson

The contents of this book represent a harvest of encoun-ters with architecture through his lifelong friend Bruce Goff. The mechanics of these moments are recounted in the introduction. Phil's words do not tell you, however, what an outstanding architect and educator he was himself. He preferred to concentrate on letting his friend do the talk-ing. His modesty also prevented him from telling us how much he was admired and appreciated by Bruce Goff.

Phil Welch, for example, would tell you how Goff seemed to enjoy a spiritual rapport with his clients. Through his good architectural offices, so to speak, an equilibrium of freedom arose that allowed people to share new ideas and create fresh personal expressions of the human heart. The results of this architecture challenge our thinking and lift our spirits. That was Phil's motivation in preserving the process by which they were achieved. This book invites you to join in the raw creative moment.

Although Bruce Goff was a wonderful writer, he pro-duced very little written material. He chose the more immediate verbal delivering of a master bard. His buildings materialize stories about his clients. The language in which they are written is architecture. They speak of dreams, aspi-rations, character, and personal mythologies. The materials specified by this kind of architect are subtleties of con-sciousness, images of both heart and mind, that suggest the infinite range of human endeavor rooted in everyday life and culture. Here a choice in architecture has the potential to echo in a structural outcome the beauty of inspirational work with creative passion.

Aesthetic reaction inspires the known to go beyond itself to new discovery, a mysterious and magical result of arrangement in the prosaic world. At a time when much of the architectural profession aimed at safeguarding and preserving the strictness of regimentarianism, Bruce Goff sought to develop a stream of architecture based on truth and honesty, even if it seemed to go against the safety of accepted values and comfortable familiarity. This, too, was the dedication of Phil Welch.

Listening to the words of Bruce Goff is a psychological, even therapeutic enterprise. The mind is forced to move from static, fixed conventions to the fluid dynamic of poetry—the language of the soul. This book will help you understand the philosophy of Bruce Goff, his objectives, and his approach to his work. At the same time, Phil Welch will be standing with you, guiding your attention to this cause or that result. After all, it was he who had the insight and willingness to bring these pages to us. Perhaps the greatest legacy of this book is the apparent truth that good architecture makes for good companions. Phil Welch and Bruce Goff always loved making new friends.

When I arrived in the summer of 1950 to teach on the faculty with Bruce Goff at the University of Oklahoma's School of Architecture, I realized very quickly that Goff's style of communication was unique. It became apparent to me that he would not put into writing his concepts of architecture or his philosophy of design. He was a living example of Gertrude Stein's "continuous present" in that there was no beginning or end to his process.

Preface

When giving lectures, Goff would start talking on a vast variety of subjects and keep talking in depth until whatever time was available ran out. His knowledge of architecture, art, music, and most world cultures was immense, and he delighted in sharing it with anyone who was interested.

I discussed with Goff whether he would let me record his thoughts so that we would have a record of them for future reference. Tape recording being only a few years old at the time, he was agreeable to experimenting. This book, *Goff on Goff*, is the result of our efforts. It opens a path to his thoughts.

In the beginning our method was to go up to the third floor of the stadium (the school of architecture at the University of Oklahoma was under the football stadium) and find a quiet spot. After setting up the equipment, I would ask him a question and he would start to speak on the subject, continuing without interruption until he saw the tape was about to run out; then Goff would summarize and complete his thoughts . . . as the tape ran out of the recording head.

Goff would occasionally deliver lectures to the entire school, and I would record these as best I could. These lectures were more difficult: I did not have control over the distance between him and the microphone, and the sound was not so good.

Three of the lectures presented in this book were delivered outside the state of Oklahoma, and they broaden the range of the material. The Illinois Institute of Technology lecture, "New Geometry in Architecture" (#9), was delivered to a technical conference on building that was attended by more engineers than architects. Goff made a plea for creative architectural design. The Wisconsin presentation to that state's chapter of the American Institute of Architects (#12) had much humor and some major points to professional architects about how to educate the public about architects. Goff's comment was direct: Build more architecture, not just good buildings. Coming from one of the period's finest architectural designers, it was outstanding advice to the profession.

The event recorded at the University of Santa Clara (#6) was an unusual presentation. Goff was the architectural artist in residence on the campus during a spring festival entitled *The Continuous Present*, and that, too, was the title of his lecture: "The Continuous Present." Over the years, Goff referred many times to Stein's essay, "Composition as Explanation," in which she proposed the idea of the continuous present—the idea that there is no beginning or end to any composition; the composition flows along continuously and tunes in for your time and during your time. Goff developed this theme in a beautiful manner in this talk. It was one of his finest lectures and was delivered to a very friendly audience.

When I first invited Goff, in the 1950s, to do the recording sessions from which these lectures and conversations have been taken, I could not have anticipated that the tapes would wait in careful storage until the 1990s, when I would be able to put them into a form that could be shared with anyone interested in Goff's philosophy. The Graham Foundation, awarding me a grant to do this book, made the work possible.

Transferring Bruce Goff from audio tape to print involved more than simple transcription of the material: it required an understanding of his concepts, designs, and philosophy. There were a few times when a small portion of the tape was not quite audible and assumptions had to be made as to what exactly he meant. In these cases, my personal knowledge of Goff enabled my interpretation to reflect his thinking. This did not happen often, and every effort was made to keep his discussion as close to the original as possible.

After duplicating the tapes to microcassette, I sat down at my computer. On the wall I placed the photograph I had taken of Goff in 1958, when he lived in the Frank Lloyd Wright Price Tower in Bartlesville, Oklahoma, sitting in front of the Klimt landscape he was so proud of. He wore a white sport coat and a black shirt with gold thread woven throughout—a typical Goff outfit. For four months, the two of us sat there while he told his stories and conveyed his philosophy and sense of humor. The voice on the tapes was fresh and full of insight, penetrating and fulfilling; it was as if the events were happening now. I had not thought one could relive the past in such a powerful way, and this wonderful experience reminded me of how enthusiastic we all were for the future of architecture.

***

Technical information. The tapes transcribed in this book were recorded over a period of years on a 1950s Wollensak

reel-to-reel tape recorder using a seven-inch reel by 1/4-
inch 1.5 mil. acetate recording tape. The tapes have been
little played over the years and in most cases, at the time
of the transcription in 1994, were still quite clear.

The tapes will be deposited in the Bruce Alonso Goff
archives in the Architectural Library of the Art Institute of
Chicago.

Goff
on Goff

Introduction

My interest in Bruce Goff began in 1948, when an article about his work, "Pride of the Prairie," appeared in *Architectural Forum*. I wrote him in 1950 and met him shortly thereafter, beginning an association that continued through many years. In this introduction, I would like to present some historical background on Goff, mostly by way of a series of vignettes that give insight into his growth, development, and methods. These personal memories expand the material presented from his recorded tapes. I make no interpretation of his philosophy: the purpose of the book is to allow Goff to tell us about Goff without interference.

When I first met Goff, in 1950, I had graduated in architecture from Stanford and was working for Frank Lloyd Wright. After witnessing the destruction of war as an infantryman in World War II, I found that creative design had become the driving force in my life. But my schooling had not taught me how to achieve individual expression: it seemed to be an unpredictable process. Although there were many books on the subject, they really did not have the key to developing one's own creativity. Studying with Bruce Goff changed all of that. He introduced me, and hundreds of other students, to the process of how creative design grew within each of us and how we could learn to be part of this natural process. His method has been introduced, in turn, by many of his students to their students and to many institutions, creating a network of design methodology that covers the United States and many other countries. Rarely does this network credit its source.

Goff's method of teaching creative design could be another book. This book, *Goff on Goff*, taken from the audio tapes I recorded in the 1950s while I was a student of his, gives an insight into his architectural philosophy and demonstrates how he allowed his own creativity to flow into his buildings, designs, and paintings. The material is as pertinent today as it was when he delivered it.

Goff's creative work evolved through so many different styles that it is difficult to identity his finest work. I feel that the buildings designed between the late 1940s and 1958 represent work that embodies some of his most significant architectural output. He had done many fine designs prior to this period, but the early 1950s brought about a revolution in inventive concepts and creative thinking without parallel.

This book includes photographs that I subsequently took of some of his major work initiated during this period—the same period the tapes were being made. The Ford House, at Aurora, Illinois, his Quonset rib masterpiece, was under construction in 1950; the Bavinger House at Norman, Oklahoma, designed in 1950 but not built until 1956, was a breakthrough in innovative interior space, room relationships, site relationship, and the use of materials; and the design of the Crystal Chapel in 1949 for the university in Norman, Oklahoma, with its glass roof and side walls, opened a unique vista of religious glass structure, incorporating original concepts for religious space. In addition to the great clarity of the building and the siting, the chapel embodied new ideas about how to use water for both growing plants and cooling a building's interior. The basic design vocabulary of the chapel and its educational wing inspired subsequent designs by other architects.

Other photos show the Garvey House, in Urbana, Illinois

(1952), which was such a new design that nothing has paralleled it to this day: it was a great loss when the aluminum manufacturer backed out with its major support (see note, page 283). Joe Price studio—designed in 1953 but built starting in 1956 over a period of several years—redefined the concept of a bachelor's house. And the Hopewell Baptist Church in Hopewell, Oklahoma, is included in this series as a demonstration of what Goff could do with a very limited budget, still delivering an innovative solution. The church was built by the congregation, using discarded materials from local oil fields.

In addition to his architectural designs, Goff created many paintings, and both his architecture and his paintings reflect the same design thrust. One painting from this period demonstrates his use of the squircle—a device used also in the design of the windows for the Garvey house.

EDITOR'S PERSONAL NOTE
Within 150 miles of where I was raised are some of the world's greatest modern buildings. Kewanee, Illinois, is 90 miles from one of Wright's greatest houses—the Dana House, Springfield, Illinois; 75 miles from Sullivan's Grinnell Bank, Grinnell, Iowa; 150 miles from Wright's home, Taliesin; and 150 miles from Oak Park and Chicago, where are to be found the masterpieces of the Prairie School. Two blocks from my house was a Talmidge and Watson house, incorporating all the Prairie characteristics except the horizontal, which was lost in their emphasis on verticality.

In Kewanee there was a Carnegie Library with a wonderful head librarian, Miss Currey. When I was twelve years old, she was kind enough to let me take out any book in the library that interested me and not worry about its being from the so-called adult section. One of the books that aroused my attention was Sheldon Cheney's *New World Architecture*. I took it out many times to look at the photographs it contained of wonderful buildings. I particularly remembered Wright's Taliesin for its natural use of stone, its low, broad, shingled roofs, and its low angles to the ground; it left a lasting memory of the kind of house I would like to have. There were also photographs of Bruce Goff's Boston Avenue Church, a design that inspired me with its powerful, clean, vertical forms and beautiful stained-glass windows. Ten years later, after World War II, when I decided to become an architect, I recalled Cheney's book. Within two weeks of my decision to become an architect, I was at Taliesin West speaking with Frank Lloyd Wright. I had no idea where Bruce Goff was at that time. This was March 1947.

I had enrolled in the architecture program at Stanford University and visited Wright to see about joining his fellowship after my graduation. He said to join him when I was done at Stanford. However, when I graduated, the Taliesin Fellowship was full and I would have to wait. I moved down the California coast to Carmel and worked for an architect specializing in schools and hospitals— excellent training for my future work with Frank Lloyd Wright. Monterey, nearby, was planning to build the first community college in the country and our office was assigned the job. The office needed a field superintendent, but no one could be spared except the young new draftsman just out of college. The first phase involved assembling old barracks buildings, trucked down on trailers from Watsonville, California, and the office thought I could handle the job. The project started out with 1 sheet of working drawings and no specifications; by the time we finished, we had 165 sheets of working drawings and a giant volume of specifications.

All during this time, I kept in contact with Frank Lloyd Wright. After we finished the college, I visited Wright at Taliesin in Wisconsin and arranged to meet him in San Francisco to discuss supervising a job for him. I met him at the St. Francis Hotel, during his visit to the V. C. Morris Shop, then under construction. (Vere Morris was in the room with Wright when I arrived: I asked him when he was going to build the house that Wright had designed for him, and he replied, "I can only afford one monument at a time.") Wright gave me the working drawings of the Walker House for Carmel, California, and asked me to look them over and report to him in the morning what I thought about supervising the job. Having just finished the community college, I knew all of the contractors and subcontractors in Monterey and felt that I was well prepared to do the job for him. I accepted the assignment.

Returning to Carmel, where I was living at the time, I met Della Walker to review the schedule with her, applied for the building permit, put the job out for bid, and prepared to get underway. We had received a good bid from an excellent contractor and obtained the building permit when Mrs. Walker decided to take a trip. Everything was put on hold. When she returned, she asked Wright to put a back door into the kitchen because she didn't want her maid going through the main part of the house. Wright didn't want to put a door in as it would mean moving the house back from the edge of the cliff, spoiling the land-and-sea relationship. After several weeks of discussion Wright gave in and gave it to her as a birthday present. I redrew the plot plan, moving the house back three feet from the cliff ledge, and applied for the building variance. We had everything all lined up when Mrs. Walker decided to take her nephew around the world as a graduation present. Everything was again on hold. It was the summer of 1950.

Architectural Forum magazine, in its March 1948 issue, had published an extensive article on Bruce Goff's recent work, entitled *Pride of the Prairie*. I was reminded of seeing pictures of his work in *New World Architecture*, but had not known his work had evolved in such wonderful, creative directions. The magazine said he was in the San Francisco Bay Area, so—the work at Carmel lagging—I went looking for his office, and the architectural offices I visited seemed to think he was in Berkeley. I found a professor who told me where he thought he lived, but when I got to the address all that was left were some Goff designs painted on the walls. I went back to Carmel, discouraged.

Several days later there was a knock at my door and a young man introduced himself as William McHugh, a Taliesin apprentice, asking if I were working on the Walker House. Bill was from Wright's Fellowship and deeply into organic architecture. In our conversation we discussed the Goff article and he informed me that Goff was chairman of the School of Architecture at the University of Oklahoma. Bill was planning on finishing his architectural education in Oklahoma studying under Goff.

My dealings with Wright had been stop-and-start for ages, our only communications consisting of two-line telegrams and no feeling of contact with the person. I wrote a letter to Goff telling him my background and asking if I could work for him, as the Wright project was moving so slowly. I sent him some of my published photographs. Within ten days, I received a three-page, handwritten letter, very understanding, open, and encouraging. He asked me to go to Oklahoma, to the university, and teach while I studied for my masters in architecture. I wrote back that I would be honored to be part of his school.

Several weeks went by and I did not hear again from Goff. The beginning of the school year being near, I was concerned and decided to go visit him and see what was happening. At that time, the School of Architecture at the University of Oklahoma was in a deserted World War II navy air base. I found the former barracks building that housed the architectural school, and Jerri Hodges, Goff's secretary, mentioned who I was and said I would like to see Mr. Goff.

Inside the building, Goff had strung white string in the hallways, along the walls and ceiling, in geometric patterns, with round fishbowls of water containing philodendrons hanging in the space. The display areas were covered with architectural student work of the most fantastic designs and ideas.

Jerri sent me to the end of hall, where Goff was waiting. He was in a small office, hung with large, silver snowflakes and sheets of translucent plastic. The two side walls were covered with his abstract paintings. It was difficult to relate the cordial Goff I saw at his desk with the fantastic architecture he had been producing throughout his career. He was just like his letter—warm, friendly, and interesting—and he greeted me as if we had known each other a long time. He told me that he was just writing a letter to me to say they had cut his budget and would not have the position he had thought to offer me; but he had an idea. He asked me to wait so he could go over to see the president about the matter. After about an hour, Goff returned to say he had received additional funds, that I should go back to California, pack, and get to Oklahoma in time for the start of classes in September. The position was to teach two design classes the first semester for $1,250. In addition, I would use my G.I. Bill to take a full load of classes from Goff, in design, and Mendel Glickman, in structure. Glickman, Frank Lloyd Wright's engineer, was on the faculty at the school.

I was very nervous about my first day of teaching a design class. My background was in architecture and photography, with a strong engineering emphasis, and I had never taught a class. Nothing had prepared me for teaching a studio at the University of Oklahoma's School of Architecture directed by Bruce Goff. I sat nervously in his office waiting to get my instructions on what I was to do. After a short, friendly chat about the weather, he said, "Let's go meet your class." We walked down the hall, past all of the great student work, and into one of the barracks classrooms where about thirty-five students were taking second-year design. "Well, here we are," said Goff. I asked, "What am I to do?" He replied, "I don't know, you are the teacher. It's your class," and he walked out, leaving me thunderstruck. It was my introduction to Bruce Goff's famous hands-off policy when working with people. He never told students what to do; he led them back to their own sense of self and let them work it out from within. It was a profound lesson to learn, and I have applied it ever since to all my teaching.

When Goff was in his office it was always with the doors open, so it was easy to go ask questions about resources, discuss how he developed his ideas, or just watch him as he painted on poster board with tempera and talked in his low-keyed manner. We always felt he was present to assist, but really his main assistance was to stay out of our way. He did his advising by example, and occasionally by lecture. When answering a question, he was more apt to pull a book from his extensive library and say, "Why don't you look that over and see how the Balinese have done it, or how the Egyptians solved that problem."

There was a great sharing in the school following Goff's example. Everyone felt that the school was unique, unusual—which it was, in architectural education circles at the time. Everyone prized that quality and it created a great camaraderie: I have not seen its equal in any architectural school since. I have taught at six other universities, all tightly structured and goal-orientated, and in none of them did I find the unity of philosophy or the carefully balanced curriculum of Goff's regime. It was an outstanding school, and it produced so much first-class creative work that nearly fifty years later the student designs are just now beginning to look like some of today's architecture.

Goff thought highly of Gertrude Stein's writings and would quote from them often. He had Stein's "Composition as Explanation" copied and passed out to the students. Her work, "The Continuous Present," was one of his favorite essays. We all realized that Goff spoke most of the time in the "continuous present" manner: there was no beginning or end to the conversation. Ask him a question and he would start discussing the subject without any notes or references. He would talk about it as long as there was time available, whether it was five minutes or five hours. If the subject came up several days later, he would pick up from the paragraph in which he had been speaking and continue with the conversation, seeming to tune into a larger continuum as he shared his thoughts. Well read in most world cultures, he did not restrict his views to Western civilization, in either philosophy or aesthetics, and this extensive world view expanded his students' horizons in many directions.

As I have already noted, Bruce Goff was a warm, friendly

person. After I left the faculty at the University of Oklahoma, we continued to exchange letters and to telephone and visit each other whenever it was possible. While I was the chairman of the Arts and Architecture Department at the University of Santa Clara, California, he was always available for advice and suggestions. He wrote letters with ideas for new music that my wife and I should be hearing (my wife was a ballet dancer, and he often mentioned new musical compositions that would be interesting for her choreography); he also sent us records he thought we should be especially aware of.

We had developed an artist-in-residence program at the University of Santa Clara inviting major artists from various creative fields to spend two weeks on campus to give the students a broader exposure to what was happening in the arts. We invited Goff to be the architect-in-residence, which he was happy to do. We put up a large exhibit of his work, arranged for a major lecture at the end of the visit, and gave him the run of the architectural studios. He stayed at our home during his visit, giving us time to catch up on all his latest activities: in fact, he was just part of the family. This relationship was not unusual and everyone who knew Goff had a similar relationship with him. He was always open and friendly. Anyone who knew him for a short time felt they were a friend of his.

Anyone could go into his office at the University of Oklahoma anytime and discuss any subject, from architecture to personal problems, and he would try to help. As chairman of the School of Architecture, he did whatever was necessary and possible to support his students and staff.

Many times I took my four-year-old daughter to the School of Architecture and he would come out to meet her and play with her. His favorite game was to try to get her to see if she could find the people he called the Ik-Nicks who lived under the stairway in front of his office. Once I showed him some of her paintings and he asked me to mount a show of her work. She picked out about forty paintings and crayon works and after we matted them he hung them in the School of Architecture gallery. He even sent out a news release to the local papers. My daughter still talks about the one-woman show she had when she was four years old.

More Memories

Goff's record and book collection was extensive. He had been collecting records since 1920, and thus had a thirty-year inventory of modern classical music. His book collection followed many paths, stemming from his range of interests in the modern movement—in architecture, painting, sculpture, and literature. It included many cultures, with a special emphasis on so-called primitive cultures. He shared this material with everyone who indicated interest, always wanting people to grow creatively; always wanting them to have the broadest exposures. His office was so filled with recordings and books that little room was left for him to work in. His home was a storefront, with shelves and shelves of records, books, paintings, and reference materials.

A major exposure to Goff's music collection was his wonderful habit of playing records at the end of every day at the school. He always had the latest hi-fi system, which in the 1950s you had to assemble yourself. Goff would walk through the architectural labs about 10 P.M., gather up a few students, and go to the lecture hall, where his equipment was installed. We would have a concert of music that could range over the entire spectrum of classical and folk, with the lights low so you could meditate on your own. Many architectural fantasies were created by the students while listening to that nighttime music. This was one of Goff's most important contributions to the students' creative growth: he not only introduced them to the world's greatest music, he also created the environment where students could bring this rich diversity into their daily lives.

Another forum that stimulated education was the hallway gathering. The school boasted two public areas with a few chairs where people could gather and chat between classes. These areas had a high-energy level: it was here that students would discuss, at various degrees of heat, the philosophy of architectural design. Many times Goff would stop by while one of these exchanges was in progress and listen with interest or sit down and join in the discussion. On occasion Goff would be so interested in the discussion that he would spend the entire afternoon on the issues.

Goff arranged the layout of the school to have the beginning design classes outside his office so that he was always seeing the freshmen and getting to know them (the upperclass design studios were at the other end of the building, and upstairs). As a result, the discussions outside his office were composed of the new students, giving Goff the chance to stay in touch with their ideas and directions of growth. Goff always said the pressure in a good school was from the bottom up, not from the top down. Many times I heard the fifth-year students say they wished they were just arriving at the school because so many new and good things were happening and they would like to participate with a fresh view.

When the Vernon Rudd House in San Mateo County, California, was completed in 1962, Goff visited from Kansas

City (where he had relocated his office) to work on and in-
stall the murals he was creating for the house. One mural
consisted of small mosaic pieces of glass and small, glazed
tiles.

In 1964 I photographed Goff putting in a second mural
in the living room on a three-foot by twelve-foot vertical
panel. The panel was covered gold paper and on it he had
spray-painted a graceful design in purple. Small, green-
glass beads were glued to the panel and there were also
snowflake cutouts in silver. The Rudds were great friends
with Goff and there was a great deal of joking going on:
Goff would just quietly smile and add another piece of
mosaic to the mural while the activity continued around
him. For me, as photographer, it was a good session of
portrait-making, showing Goff creating a design and cap-
turing his manner of working. I photographed the house
with a Nikon perspective-control lens, showing the house
in its original brilliant colors of bright orange with deep-
blue trim—looking like a Chinese pavilion floating on the
side of the hill in the dark-green pine trees.

Another project that afforded me insight into Goff's relationship to his work was the Ford House in Chicago.
When this building was under construction in 1950, I saw
the working drawings in Goff's office and asked him questions about the design. I felt the house was very elegant and
graceful, the way the Quonset ribs burst from the ground
in circular form and met in a termination and accent at
the top of the roof with a pointed chimney. The sections
through the structure confirmed this wonderful interplay
of curves and dome-like volumes within. When pictures
of the house were published in *Life* magazine, I was disap-
pointed: the colors in the magazine were garish and didn't
seem to fit the design. I felt the colors made it look almost

like a nightclub, not a home, and I went into Goff's office to discuss it with him. I made my points and asked him why he had used those colors the way he did. His reply was that this was Mrs. Ford's house and the colors fit her. His disappointment was that they had photographed the house from a helicopter and it showed the roof from above. He said he would never design another house without designing the roof as seen from above.

A few months later, I was in Aurora and saw the actual house. To my great surprise, it looked wonderful. Sited on a large lot, with green grass, trees, and blue sky, the house was as I had seen it in the drawings and sections—a beautiful dance of Quonset ribs defining wonderful, spherical spaces for living. The color that had been exaggerated in the printing process was not at all like that when seen onsite. The house had a quiet repose, with a few accents to give life and interest to the design. This taught me a lesson in architecture: don't judge a structure until you have actually seen the building.

One

Goff's Creative Growth and Design Philosophy

I used to start designing in the early days with no problem to solve at all, just trying to exercise, you might say. I did many sketches that had no reason to be except as exercise. Lots of these problems I set for myself without any idea of ever having them built. Sometimes they got built anyway. I suppose all of that doodling and exercise was good for me in the beginning because it got me curious about forms and ideas. When I first saw Mr. Wright's work in 1916 or 1917, I was extremely impressed. In fact, I couldn't eat, sleep, or think of anything but Wright for about three years. It was quite a surprise, and it was something I wanted to see and needed to see, and I recognized it immediately. It was purely an accident that I even saw his work.

In the first case of seeing Mr. Wright's work, I had started working with old man Rush, in the firm of Rush, Endacott & Rush in Tulsa, Oklahoma, and what he called the basic principles of architecture, which was a matter of tracing Greek columns on linen and inking them. I didn't enjoy

This recording session was done on the third floor of the architectural school in Norman, Oklahoma, on March 11, 1953. Only Goff and I were present. I asked him to talk about how he arrived at his design solutions, how they developed, what took place within himself, and how it all happened. To answer these questions, he went back to the time when he was a boy and gave a personal history of his design development. It was a story he told many times, but I believe this is the most complete account of it.

that. One day while I was working on the Corinthian Order, Mr. Endacott, the engineer of the firm, came in and wanted to know what was wrong with me. I told him I didn't like it and he said, "What in the hell are you doing it for?" I told him the old man told me to. He said, "Well, hell, you will never get any place that way, what do you care what the Greeks did three thousand years ago. It's what we are doing now that counts for us." He said, "Come back in the drafting room here and see what is going on." I said, "What about the old man?" He said, "To hell with the old man." That was the first seed of revolution probably.

I went into the drafting room, and he set me up at a table in the back corner. The twelve draftsmen were so busy with work they didn't pay any attention to me. I was a little kid in the sixth grade at that time. I was a little bit afraid I didn't know what I was getting into. Mr. Endacott said to design a house. I asked what kind of house. He said the kind you like. He just left me with that. I had never heard of Mr. Wright or anything about modern architecture or anything of the sort. Probably I had been interested vaguely in things that were influenced by things that had been influenced . . . perhaps, I don't know. Anyway, I had a taste for casement windows then, opening out with broad eaves and flat roofs with low chimneys. Houses that stayed down on the ground. So the house I designed was pretty much of that feeling, without any idea of making a modern house. I thought I was originating something of my own. I didn't copy it, but as soon as I got through with it the draftsmen in the place got curious. They came over and wanted to know what I was working on. I showed them, and they all said, "That looks like old man Wright's stuff." I said "Who is he?" They said, "He is a crazy old nut up in Chicago." They got me on two counts; one was, here I thought I had originated something and they said it looked like someone else, and the other was they said that he was crazy and this design looked like his work so that would mean the design was crazy, too. It bothered me considerably. Almost everyone that would see my work would say that or something very similar. Even representatives of manufacturers who used to come through the office occasionally to interest the firm in new materials would say the same thing. I finally got extremely curious about who this Mr. Wright was. I asked Mr. Rush, who was the senior member of the firm in his late sixties, who this Mr. Wright was. He said, "He is one of the greatest American architects; if you had his feeling for form and Sullivan's feeling for ornament, you would really have the American architecture." This was his theory. Well, it was not quite true, but anyway, it was more open-minded than most architects of the time were. At least he recognized that Wright was somebody.

I still didn't see any of Mr. Wright's work or know any more about him. Usually, if I found someone from Chicago I asked them who Mr. Wright was. They would reply that he was that crazy old guy that had such a way with the women. All they knew about him was scandal. They had the stories all mixed up about the tragedy at Taliesin. This bothered me considerably, because I was being identified with a person who was supposed to be crazy.

One day I noticed that whenever Mr. Rush designed anything he went over and opened a cabinet that he always kept locked. He would pull out a dog-eared magazine and would peek in it and look carefully around to see if anyone was watching. Then he would go over and draw like mad. He would put the magazine back in the cabinet and lock it. This secrecy intrigued me, so I watched my chance. One day he went out for lunch and left the cabinet unlocked, I stayed on and got into the jam. I looked into this magazine. It was the March 1908 issue of *Architectural Record*. It was the first comprehensive showing of Mr. Wright's work anywhere. It was the first I saw. Of course, it knocked me for a loop. I was dumbfounded to see the things in there that I liked so intuitively, actually built, with photographs of them. It was amazing how wonderful they were. I was so entranced that I didn't realize that the noon hour had gone by and that Mr. Rush had returned and caught me looking. I thought the jig was up. He smiled and said, "I knew you would find that sooner or later." I suspect now that he planted it. Anyway, I did find it. It was such a revelation to me that I was completely bowled over and I couldn't eat, sleep, or think of anything but Frank Lloyd Wright for several years.

I borrowed the magazine and took it home and read the article "In the Cause of Architecture," which I think is still one of Wright's best expositions of his work, particularly of his earlier attitude toward architecture. That was my bible and I could have recited every word of it then. I never copied any of his work, but I couldn't help but feel the impact of it. Every line I drew looked as if I had copied it straight out of the book, while I really hadn't.

Finally the chance came along to do the actual work. The firm didn't like to do houses; they did mostly commercial work. I was given a house to do when I was in the eighth grade. The client approved my sketch and the house was built. One day when I was out at the site looking at it, giving it the last once-over before the people moved in, a carload of folks came by, and they all started laughing at it and making fun of it. I couldn't see what they saw that was so funny about it. It disturbed me a lot, because young people hate to be laughed at worse than almost anything. They usually don't feel too secure, and when someone starts making fun of them, or laughing at them, it undermines their self-confidence considerably. It worried me a lot. I got out in front and looked at it and tried to see what was so goofy or funny about it. I knew it was different, but I didn't think of it as strange or peculiar. It just seemed different to me.

It bothered me a lot. I went back to the office and Endacott, who could always tell when I was in trouble, wanted to know what was the matter. I told him what had happened and he said, "Hell, don't let that bother you, just remember as long as you are in the trenches doing what everyone else is doing no one will notice you are there; they will just accept you and there won't be any trouble. But the minute you get out into no-man's-land they are going to start shooting at you from both sides. He said, Brother, the way you're headed you're going to need a good tough hide, because you are in for it. What do you care what they like or don't like, the people you did it for like it. You know you have done your best, so what else matters? The other people are not going to live in it. You couldn't have the same thing for dinner, or the same kind of clothing, or the same kind of show, or the same kind of life, or anything else. Everyone has a different opinion on all of this, just as they do about buildings. You couldn't build a single building anywhere that would please everyone, it would be physically impossible. So why do you worry about it?"

It was good advice, just at the time I needed it. I have always been thankful for it, because from that time on I have never really cared what anyone thinks about my work so long as I know it is the best I can do in solving the problem: that is the owner's problem and other problems that are involved in the solution. It has never concerned me since then whether anyone laughs at the design or doesn't laugh at it. It was a big turning point in my life right then.

Not long after that another thing happened. I was reading an article by Mr. Wright and he was complaining about his imitators. He said form's the man and man's the form, and you let his forms alone, that you should develop your own forms. That seemed directed at me as I knew I was directly influenced and inspired by his work. I got to wondering, if they were not forms like Mr. Wright's, what kind of forms would you have?

I started a conscious search for some other way of doing things. I then ran across the work of Eric Mendelsohn—his sketches particularly. I began to see there was more than one way to skin a cat. The design didn't have to follow the old classical work, which I had learned to detest in my youthful arrogance. I could see other ways of designing through Eric Mendelsohn's work—through the work in the Bauhaus, and Le Corbusier, as I grew into it—and particularly through Oriental architecture, through work in Japan, China, Siam, the South Sea Islands, Egypt, and all of the places that had done wonderful things—that there wasn't just one way to design. They were all doing organic architecture and still it was different in each case. That taught me a valuable lesson—that it didn't all have to look alike. There could be many faces or appearances to architecture.

Music was teaching me the same thing. Along with all of this I was learning music. I had started out by detesting music and thinking anything called classical music was snobbish, high-hat, longhair, and something that I should avoid because it was snobbish and overintellectual. A high-school friend of mine, Ernest Brooks, was a very excellent pianist who had tried to get me to like Bach, Beethoven, Brahms, and Chopin. When he would use the word classical it would just go against my grain. I would shut my ears and not even listen. There was something about it that didn't interest me. I had never heard any modern music and the popular music didn't seem to interest me. So I was practically illiterate musically to start with, like most people are.

One day, a strange thing happened. My friend didn't know any modern music but he always bought the records that came out by his favorite pianists. Alfred Cortot had recorded *The Fountain* by Ravel. The process of buying what just came out in those days was pretty safe, because not much came out except the old warhorses. This was a joker in the deck, even though Cortot had recorded it; it was a piece of fairly recent music. My friend was completely baffled by it. He couldn't make head nor tail of it, but he had bought the record mainly because Cortot had played it. He thought it would be a good joke on me to play it for me. He did, and much to his amazement I took to it like a duck to water and liked it immediately. It seemed to do something to music that Wright had done in architecture. It gave me something to hear that I had been wanting to hear. It seemed very magical and very beautiful, fanciful, not at all like the expected thing happening all the time that I had heard in other music. In the old classical music I always seemed to know what was coming next and anticipate it so it wasn't any fun. In this music there was a surprise all the way along. There was a freshness and beauty that just got me. I was so thrilled over it that my friend couldn't understand why I was so taken with it. To him it had no rhythm, no melody, nothing. No harmony or anything that he had been taught. I had to have the record, and that meant I had to go without lunch for several days to save up the two dollars to buy it. It was only on one side of a twelve-inch record, on a very poor old acoustic record. I did get it, and I played it and played it and played it. Each time it seemed more wonderful than before. Then I began to realize that there was a kind of music that was not like the old music.

I was beginning to see the same kind of thing in reproductions of paintings in *Broom* magazine and *Vanity Fair*. All of these things were creeping in on me gradually and I was naturally curious. If I have any redeeming quality at all it is curiosity, and I have always been curious: trying to discover and find out what is going on. I was naturally very intrigued with music then. I wanted to know more about Ravel.

No one knew anything about Ravel around there then. My friend's teacher didn't know anything about Ravel. I went down and looked in the big encyclopedia on music in the library. There wasn't even a mention of him anywhere. I thought that was ridiculous. A man who could write a piece like *The Fountain* must be important. It was just stupid that there wasn't anything about him in any of the encyclopedias. Of course, there wasn't anything about Wright in any of the books then either. I knew that I could expect that, but it seemed strange that there wouldn't be something in the music books. I asked the librarian, and finally with her help I located an article in a magazine which referred to Ravel as merely an imitator of Debussy. That made me furious. I didn't know who Debussy was, but my hero was being accused of imitation and I was ready to defend him. Then I was anxious to know who Debussy was. I was a little antagonistic toward him at first because I didn't think he could possibly be as good as Ravel. I looked through the music catalog and found a few things by Debussy. I wasn't able to hear these records before I bought them because the old lady in the shop would play them for you, and she naturally intimidated you to where you couldn't really listen. I saved some more lunch money and went down and just bought these pieces outright: *The Girl with the Flaxen Hair*, the two *Arabesques*, and the *Prelude to the Afternoon of a Faun*, all old acoustic records.

I took the records home and I don't know just what I expected, but I expected anyway to be thrilled by them as I had been by Ravel's *The Fountain*. Then I realized it was a big disappointment, because while *The Girl with Flaxen Hair* sounded tinkly and sketchy, not much to it, it didn't make me mad or glad. The two *Arabesques* would flow along with nothing particular happening, like water through your fingers. The *Prelude to the Afternoon of a Faun* had me completely baffled. Of course, it was a very obscure sounding recording. I had nothing to take hold of there either. It was for orchestra, and the medium sounded strange. I felt that I had kind of missed on that. It didn't do anything to me. Then I would go back and play *The Fountain* some more.

I had quite a sizable investment at that particular time in those Debussy records. So I thought if there was anything in them I was going to get it. More and more I felt naturally impelled to listen to them. It made me sort of angry that I couldn't understand them, because I knew that was what was wrong. I didn't blame the pieces so much as I knew I just wasn't getting it. It would go in one ear and out the other. I kept listening every once in awhile. Then gradually, I don't know just when, a strange thing started to happen. *The Fountain* began to lose a little of its luster and brilliance, through familiarity probably, and the *Faun* in particular was beginning to gain. I got to where I wanted to hear it more and more. Even to this day, I can't say I really understand it; that's good, because it still preserves its mystery. I did begin to catch on to it enough to realize that I should never trust my first impression of something. It was rewarding me more and more, and it still does, every time I hear it.

I realized then that snap judgments about art, or anything else, were invalid, that you had to earn the right to like them or dislike them. Many times they were not the sort of things that would come out and knock you down; some things you have to make an effort to grow into. So that was a good lesson for me, and fortunately at that time there were a few things available on records and I was able to grow along with the recording industry in a way, so that I could absorb the things as they came out. Nowadays it is very difficult, because so much is dumped on us all at once that it's hard to know what to listen to or what to listen for. I feel fortunate in that respect.

At the same time then I was exploring painting. I was trying painting myself, and wondering why paintings had to represent things. I didn't know anything about Kandinsky or others who were trying to get away from that. I myself felt that when you put some paint on the paper it was beautiful in itself, that it didn't need to tell any story or represent anything. I was playing around with color and I was interested in music, and finding out more about architecture as it was going on in the past and in the present. All of these things were having a terrific influence on me. Some of it was very obvious and some of it was not so obvious. I drew a great deal and made many sketches. I tried lots of ideas. Some of them were pretty bad, a lot of them are bad, but all part of the wasteful process of growing.

I began to be very discouraged, because it seemed that I didn't have anything of my own to say. Everything I said was something that someone else had already said. I went through that stage where it seemed that I had nothing to offer and I wondered what else could you do. Everything was already done it seemed to me. I was pretty disturbed about that, and still, in seeking something of my own I knew I was going to be blamed for being a radical or freak of some kind, because I could see that everyone else in music, and painting, and architecture, who did try had that to face. So I was prepared for that. That didn't bother me. It did bother me a great deal within myself whether I had anything to say or not and whether it was worth all the strain and pain of doing it.

Then I had an opportunity to do some fairly good-sized jobs. I did a fourteen-story building, a large warehouse, and a church. I definitely tried in those buildings to not show Mr. Wright's influence. Probably you could trace it in through some features, but I was under the influence of other things. Like the verticality of feeling about democracy which was very prevalent right then and that was married into what I was trying to do, too. The feeling and striving for monumentality was there. Trying to make architecture out of building was there. The fact that it succeeded enough to interest other people gave me some encouragement, but it was never what I really wanted. It was thought of as original by most people, but I could see certain influences in it after I got through with it. In general, it was regarded as fairly original. In my painting I think it was more original at that time, too, because I had less to go by then.

Eventually I kept working and got into trying all sorts of things, many of them familiar. I had many limitations of cost and other restrictions. Probably nothing I had done previous to the Unseth house in Park Ridge, Illinois, in 1940 could be called very much my own. There were touches of it in the Colmorgan house in Glenview, Illinois, in 1940, and maybe even in the Cole House in Park Ridge, Illinois, in 1939. There were still many remembrances in all of it. I think that one of the freshest statements that I was able to make in the early days was the Unseth house and followed right after with the Triaero house, Fern Creek,

Kentucky, 1941. I was just beginning to feel a way to do something of my own and then the war came along and I was plunged into that.

I then had to work with very limited materials and restrictions to try to do something in the service.* My chapel at Camp Parks, California attracted a lot of architects. I liked it much better than my big church in Tulsa, Oklahoma, because I knew I had done more with less. Even so, I still didn't feel I had a very definite stand. But I did have, for the first time in my life, a chance to think a little bit rather than just keep working. Many hours in the Aleutians were spent just thinking about architecture and the principles of design and so on. I was completely removed from most of it. I couldn't even look at most of it in books, magazines, anything else. I was up in the Aleutians pretty much by myself. I was very hungry for it, of course, but at the same time it gave me time to pause and get my bearings as to just where I was and what could be thought of as important things in design.

I think that period was very valuable to me for that reason, because sometimes you can be so busy just working on the thing that you don't realize what you are working with. I began to see several things very clearly. One was that in architecture there are no limits to forms, colors, and textures that you feel you should use. Feeling was the important thing; that you should actually feel something about your problem. You should try to find some kind of order through the problem, and in the solution of the problem, that would be distinctly of that composition, and not some other one, so that everything seems to belong, no matter how varied or contrasting, and that any materials

*Bruce Goff's architectural projects while he was in military service include buildings for the U.S. Navy in the Aleutians in 1943 and for Camp Parks, California, in 1944.

were fair, old or new, that we had to reevaluate them to use them in ways that seem fresh and valid for us, even brick or stone or wood or any of the old materials. Then I also realized that just using materials for material's sake wasn't enough because that could be an end in itself. We should be able to master materials enough so that they would be in the nature of the thing, but not the answer. Just as in a person: the person is made up of bones, skin, muscles, and all that, but that is not the important thing about a person to us, even though those features are all honestly expressed in the design of the person. The thing that interests us about the person is something else that transcends all these physical properties. That is what I felt about architecture, and I still do.

I was also going through another change of attitude. In the earlier days, like many young people, I felt that things were of very sharp contrast—that there was right or wrong, or good or bad, or ugly or beautiful, or very opposite things with very clear-cut divisions. I could have told you exactly where they were. I knew whether it was right or wrong or if it was good or bad, and I didn't hesitate to say so, either. I think that is another virtue or vice of youth, whichever way you want to look at it. Gradually I began to realize that it wasn't quite so clear cut as that. Sometimes it was hard to say where one idea left off and the other started in opposites that way. Then the question was, does it just break off that way or does it sort of merge one into the other, or shade into the other. Then I thought for quite a while, that's what happened, that it went from one extreme to another. That there was a gradual shading in between and you would choose your point rather arbitrarily where you wanted to say it was one way or the other. That was the second stage of my development.

The third stage, that I am in right now, is that I believe they are all composed of the same thing. Any opposites are contained within the same thing. We see them or understand them according to the way we wish to or are able to. That is why the same thing can mean different things to different people. We are apt to see what we want to see, or hear what we want to hear or are able to understand in anything, such as the opposite ideas of simplicity and complexity. Or we try to make a differentiation when we think of it or talk about it, but actually, when you analyze it, almost anything that we think is simple is very complex, too. And anything that we think is very complex is often fundamentally very simple if you can understand it that way. I think that has been a big help to me to realize that. For one thing it has made me much more tolerant—I hate that word—or much more understanding, I would say, of things that I don't necessarily care for in architecture or painting or music or anything. Even people; I realize that they have good in them and not so good in them and it doesn't bother me now like it used to. It used to bother me when I would find inconsistencies in Mr. Wright. I would hear what he said, or read what he said, and then I would see what he did and I couldn't understand how he could do some of the things he did and be consistent. I know now he is consistently inconsistent. That is one of his great strengths, that he is able to approach things from different points of view. He isn't stuck even with his own philosophies. He is able to, as he says, "take a holiday now and then." The general direction is certainly there, but it's enriched with a lot of different approaches.

All of these ideas were fermenting when World War II was over and I realized even before the war that if we were going to have architecture we had to have architects. If we were going to have architects we had to have schools or places where they could be trained and developed. I didn't believe in just saying there was no use in such a thing. I had done some teaching in Chicago trying to get some ideas across. After the war I had the opportunity to come here to the University of Oklahoma and go further with teaching and the developing of architects, and I feel it is as important for me to do that as to do work. I like to do both, but they are all part of the same thing again to me.

Following the war, I was able to approach work with a better understanding of what I was trying to do. I had had a little more time to think about it and I realized that we had to be able to think of things in ways that hadn't been thought of, even by Mr. Wright or anyone. There was a job to do and it was necessary for someone to do it. The next thing was how. I began to think a great deal of possibilities of architecture, what hadn't been done, as well as what had been done, and to look not into the future, but into the present more, to try to see what we were not utilizing of the present. Actually, very few of us live in our own time, and I realized that I wasn't living in my own time much, either. I was very interested in things that weren't even of my own time, even recent things were still not of my own time, because our own time is moving so fast.

Inquiring into these possibilities and probabilities and so on, I began to realize that in the planning of a house, for instance, we were no longer sitting around the fireplace hearing grandpa tell stories. We no longer should have big living rooms and big dining rooms and little boxes for bedrooms. It seemed to me that even in Mr. Wright's work that there was a great deal of attention given to the entrance and to the living area and the dining area. But the bedrooms and other parts of the house were all boxed up pretty much as necessary evil. I wanted to think of the house as a more continuous thing; not necessarily wide open all the way through, but where you would feel that it was all important and that there were no leftovers, no backs, and no unfinished building parts. I became more and more interested in that idea. I wanted to practice it some way. I tried to think of ways to make these necessary complications in a plan seem simple, so that they would fall in with the organization of the whole scheme. So you could tell it was part of the same house.

Then other problems of design, the matters of balance, proportion, scale, color, texture, and all these things we study now—I made a very self-conscious effort to think of those things. I know I had been using them all along, as anyone does who designs anything, but I had never really considered them very much as abstract ideas or principles. I became more and more aware that while the important thing is the feeling we have about all of this and the way we express that through the work—that knowing more about the things we are working with gives us a more scientific attitude toward design. We realize it isn't the hit and miss process that a lot of people think. There is a science to it that's undeveloped as yet—probably as much of a science as there is about mathematics, but we haven't formulated it, or tied it down. Probably that's a good thing so long as we understand the basic principles that are involved that are not personal or timely.

I began to realize that the principles about balance were true for the Egyptians or Mr. Wright or anyone; they didn't belong to anyone except when they used them. The same applied to rhythm, or modulation, or counterpoint, or contrast, or incident, terminal, and climax, or any of these things as ideas; they didn't belong to anyone. Neither did

geometric forms. The square didn't belong to anyone or
the circle or the triangle. They belonged to everyone who
wanted to use them. Our only obligation was to use them
in our own way and not try to remember how someone else
used them. That gave me a new kind of confidence that
gave me a clear way to see and understand things for myself. Because then I wasn't worried about how Mr. Wright
used squares or triangles or how someone else used them.
It was important as a matter of investigation in analyzing
their work. When it came to my own work I realized that
was unimportant. The important thing was, how could I
use them?

About this time I was beginning to realize more and more
the importance of an article by Gertrude Stein, "Composition as Explanation," where she talks of composition in
the "continuous present." I began to realize that things had
no beginning or ending really. We tune in on them even
in a design or a problem of any kind. There is no place
where you can say the problem really begins or really ends.
Even when the client has decided that he wants to build a
house, that is not the beginning of the problem; the problem started long before that in many ways. Even after the
house is built, it isn't the end of the problem, because he is
going to live in it and someone is going to be affected by it
and it's a continuous performance all the time. That made
me realize some other things, that it wasn't a cut-and-dried
matter. It was a continuous performance and only a part
of a continuous performance of larger dimensions. On the
one hand I could see the International boys and the purist,
so called, who were after abstract things that I could appreciate. They were saying that architecture was not organic
but that it was synthetic and that we combine things together because we are human beings and we try to arrive

at impersonal, anonymous kinds of solutions because no client and no problem is going to stay the same. So we put a static solution to it so that it will be nondescript enough to take anybody. I could realize, even though I had considered some of Mies Van der Rohe's work very beautiful, in matters of proportion and cleanliness and the nice use of materials, that there seemed to be something very dead about it, too, that didn't account for human beings. It was an abstract exercise and beautiful just to look at, but not to live with, or to be with, or to grow in. It was a museum piece. I could realize there was a danger in too much abstraction.

You can have architecture for architects' sake or you can have architecture for people. The same thing goes with music. You can have music in which only musicians can appreciate the fine points of the game, and you can also have it so it wouldn't mean a thing to people in general. I am assuming that the people in general are making an effort to understand, which isn't always true, but if they did make the effort there would be something there for them.

It seemed to me that I had to choose between being purely abstract in my approach or in trying to deal with people in a way they could understand if they wanted to. I chose the latter course. Even in doing that I still bear in mind the abstract principles, too. I do realize that the clients aren't going to live forever and that they're going to demand certain things that may be personal idiosyncrasies, but still the solution is going to have to outlive them. I don't see why it can't do both. I have been criticized for considering architecture as an opportunity more than an obligation. I don't think that is quite right. I consider it both, and certainly always an opportunity.

When someone asks me to do a house for them, I first of all try to understand the people I am doing the house for and try to get some feeling about what sort of house they would like or what they would feel at home in. I have never yet built a house that I would like, for instance, or that I would feel at home in. I don't know whether I ever could, even if I did one for myself. People have accused me of doing just what I like. Actually, I have never done anything that I like yet. But I have done things I hope my clients will like. Usually they do. When they think they have the best house I ever did, that is a sign that I have succeeded in that part of it anyway. That's okay as long as they don't feel that there is just one of them that's the best.

First of all I try to get some feel about the client, what kind of people they are. There is a great deal difference in them and that would determine my approach. If they were a very quiet and reserved and retiring kind of people who are afraid of attracting any attention I would naturally go much easier with them than someone who wants a shocker. I get them all the way in between. Some people want to put their foot in the water and not get wet, some don't even want to get near the water, and some want to plunge all the way in. I think you have to gauge pretty much what you do by that, to start with, and to try to understand that.

The property of course comes into account: what the site is, what the climate is, what the neighborhood is like, or the country's like, the landscape, the seasons, the kind of weather you have—all of that comes into it. Also the way you would approach the property, where you can park, how you would drive up to it. We almost always drive to the property now rather than walk. What would be the natural way and the easiest way for a car to approach this property. How are you going to accommodate parking for the clients and their friends and guests without cluttering up the streets, which are usually inadequate. I think that's an important first consideration.

Then, of course, the money involved is always a consideration. We have to try to gauge what we do for these people in view of the budget and almost always they want more than they can afford. We have to be very mean and step in and say you can afford only this much so you can only have this much. Whether they have a million dollars or five thousand dollars, it's the same problem. They have to realize that the amount of money isn't always a guarantee of good or bad results. You might have a low-cost house that would be more successful architecturally than the very expensive one with less restrictions and limitations. Sometimes these very limitations, as Mr. Wright has said, are your best friends. I think that you would naturally try to give them the most you can for the money, maybe too much sometimes. You do have to consider how they are going to get the money, too; whether it is something they borrow or something they have or how many strings are attached to that. That will naturally limit you or loosen you up one way or the other.

Then we have the problem of materials and construction and labor. What kind of people are available to build this in this locality. What kind of materials are feasible, what would be available, and what looks good with the site and the other buildings around, if any: what methods are good to use there or could be used there—not necessarily the ones that have always been used but what are the possibilities.

Thinking then of circulation, how you would approach the lot, how you would want to move through it, of sight and sound control, the amount of spaces for people, the sense of space whether it is intimate or open, the kind of construction that would be best to solve these spaces and conditions. I am beginning to realize more and more that the space through the building is just as important as the materials in the building. I started out the same way most people do, thinking that architecture was the building, the physical part of the building, the walls, the roof, the floors, and so on. Then I got to realizing it was not only that, it was the space inside. It isn't all just one or the other; it's the space inside and the space outside and the shell and the materials, too. I think we have a three-way manner of thinking about that particular part of it. We have to consider the outside space, too, which is a little harder to think of the way the building works with the space it's in, than to just think of the space within the building where the boundaries of the space are the physical part of the building.

Where you start is a problem very difficult to answer, because you could start with anything really. You really just tune in. There is no beginning to this composition and no ending. I think when I started out originally I used to draw a floor plan, and then I would draw elevations. I thought that was the organic way of doing it. By drawing the floor plan I would be working from the inside out and I'd know pretty much the space necessary and all that. Then I began to realize that I should work through sections too. Good design usually wasn't a matter of extruding the plan and just putting the lid on for a roof. It was a matter of thinking of more than one thing at a time. The design didn't start anywhere or end anywhere. It is like which was first, the chicken or the egg. Then I could see it didn't really make any difference where you started. Whether you started with the elevations if you had the plan in mind, or if you started with a section if you had the elevations and the plan in mind. No matter where you started, you had to keep in mind all the other things going on. That is very difficult to do when you are just starting. You have to let the right hand know what the left hand is doing all the time. You will find though that usually when you are on the track of an idea that is a really good idea, you begin to sense the order in that idea. You can be pretty sure that things will fall into place pretty well themselves. You discipline this falling-into-place process, you might say, through your own reason, intelligence, and through the solutions of the problem. You begin to realize they all will naturally fall into place if you let them.

That was another big step in my development, when I realized it was better to not force designs but to get on for the ride and go along with them, and try steering them in certain directions, rather than just sitting around waiting for inspirations to hit you hard and then fretting over things. I think most people worry the life out of designs. They take the life out of them by sweating over them too much. Actually a lot depends on our understanding the order within an idea so that we can go along with it instead of imposing a lot of things on that idea. If you can think of each building as an idea and work spontaneously that way and then try to direct it, organize it, and perfect it after you get it going, it seems to me that is a more logical and beneficial way to approach it.

And that is the way I try to do it.

Two

Order in Architecture

Tonight the subject I wish to discuss I believe is of great interest and very important to an architect, of all people, or to any artist. It is one that most artists are accused of not having any idea about, and many of them don't, I must admit.

It is the idea of order.

What do we mean by order? I think that we have heard of the five Orders, so called, of Greek architecture. Actually, the Greeks never called them that; they were named this afterwards. Even the five Orders are not all Greek, either.

The Greeks had several ways of doing things that were called Orders in attempting to keep a design unified, or related, through all of its parts. Practically all the great artists, of all times, have been very conscious of this idea of order. This sense of order implies many other ideas, of course. One is the idea of unity. I think we should just write down some of these words. First, *Order.* And some other related ideas: *Unity*

Goff gave this lecture to the entire School of Architecture on September 23, 1953. It was the beginning of a new school year, and he was discussing the idea of order in architecture. He developed the theme in great detail and used some outstanding examples, referencing Wright's designs of the Larkin Building and the Unity Temple and the Larkin Building's relationship to the Johnson Wax Building. It is one of Goff's best talks about the design process, both with regard to his own work and to Frank Lloyd Wright's method of designing.

would certainly be part of order, wouldn't it? Discipline of some sort. Mr. Wright once said, "The thing that most people don't understand about my work is that each building has an idea." I think when he said that he meant a sense of order. That each work would have a sense of order about it.

The Japanese have words for this, too: *edaburi,* which

means, as nearly as you can say it in English, the formative arrangement of the branches of a tree. In other words, the sense of order in the design of a particular kind of tree that you would find in the arrangement of its branches. If you were speaking of the *edaburi* of a willow tree, it would be quite different from that of an oak tree or a pine. This sense of order isn't just in the differences of the kinds of leaves; it carries through the textures, all the way through. Think of the kind of textures that would be in the willow tree in the leaves and the limbs. Think of the difference, the *edaburi*, of a jack oak tree. In nature you will find that almost everything has its own kind of order. I suppose everything has, even if it is imitative for some protective reason.

We can say that order, unity, discipline all go hand in hand, part of each other. In art, it is necessary to have some feeling that the order that exists in this particular composition is self-sufficient and self-sustaining. It is not good enough to be just a part of another kind of order, or a piece whacked off the same bolt for a dress pattern. That could have an order, of course, that is running through the bolt of goods. Each individual composition that we do wouldn't be as valid if it were only part of the order of a whole group of work, as it would be if it were self-sustaining in its order.

I think that is one of the great weaknesses in modern architecture today and in many other forms of modern art. That too much is done "in the manner of some kind of order" that is not reasonable with the work at hand, the one that is being considered. Too many people are interested in doing something, "in the manner of," or trying to follow an order that is extraneous, or foreign, to the natural order that should exist, the dominant thing in the solution to the individual problems.

We find, then, too many painters trying to arrive at their

style. Now *style* is a word to consider in relation to order, I think. Style can exist as an overall thing where we are trying to work within formulas, or limitations, as expressive of some abstract idea that would apply to all sorts of things. Or a style can come out of the nature of the solution to individual problems. Of course, after a man's work is pretty well accomplished, like Mr. Wright's, some people will erroneously refer to it as the Frank Lloyd Wright style, which is wrong, because there is no Frank Lloyd Wright style, but most of his buildings would have style. We could say that some other great architects have more sense of style as an overall style. It is more important as an overall thing than as a solution to individual problems.

I think that each work of art, then, should produce its own style, should have its own style, just as each person has his or her own style—his or her own *edaburi* if you want to compare a person to a tree. What is the idea that is in each thing we do? Do we have an idea, or do we just concoct something, or manufacture something? It is easier to do that. You can arrive at a formula or a way of doing something that is passable. I think that most artists work hard to get a trademark or a style that is definitely recognized as theirs. In doing so, they sacrifice the nature of the problem at hand to arrive at something that will be sort of an overall idea that can be used on any occasion, or for any purpose. I think that tied up with that is the idea that we must surpass other people, too. Debussy once said, "The struggle to surpass others is never really great if disassociated from the noble ideal of surpassing one's self, though this involves the sacrifice of one's cherished personality." Now the cherished personality would be the trademark. Naturally, you're going to have to change your trademark if you are going to do anything in art. You can't arrive at something, then sit back and keep stamping it out from then on. Some people do, but you can't continue to grow in your art if you do that. You have to sacrifice this cherished personality in order to accomplish this matter of having each thing you do have its own order and its own style. In doing this, we naturally seek freedom; we have to be free to change. Freedom is a very important asset, as we all know. Just being free isn't enough; you can be free and accomplish nothing by going off in all directions, just like the man in Leacock's story who jumped on his horse and rode off madly in all directions. He was free, I imagine, but that doesn't get you any place.

We have to discipline our freedom. As Debussy said, "We must seek discipline and freedom, but not in the outworn traditions of the past." We have to look into freedom as a means to change and to grow and to find the kind of order that we feel exists in each thing we do. We also have to discipline this freedom to do that. We have to accept limits of our own and we have to strive to accomplish something that will add up to an idea, or several ideas, that will add up to an idea if you want to multiply the idea into a larger form. What comes out will have a sense of order and unity with freedom and discipline.

I think there are very few things done by man that have this sense of order. A sense of order does not necessarily mean you have to design with a straitjacket or a frugal restricted design diet. It can be very rich and can be very complex at times and still be ordered. You can have an ordering chaos, if you can hear the order in chaos, or see it, or feel it. It is possible. It isn't always the thing that looks reposeful, serene, clear, pure, and all of that. It often is, and I think in general we are more apt to consider it more ordered if it does have clarity, purity, and is restricted to certain limitations. It can also be very rich and very complex with many ideas working together and still have order.

We often hear it said that the structure of old works of art is greater than the structure of contemporary works of art, but not architecture. Architects can see it when they are talking about architecture, but in music and the other arts we often have modern architects who are advanced in thinking about structure but get fouled up in thinking about structure in other arts by holding that work done in the remote past is the most ordered structurally. Sometimes that's because we are not trained to see the kind of order that exists in some of the most recent work. It would be like saying in architecture that there is no structure existing in architecture since the old days. It would be ridiculous for you to begin to say that. There is a new kind of order to structure now, just as there was a new order to structure then. Today if we regard the structure of a piece of Bach's music or Beethoven's music as final in the way of structure, we are just burying our heads in the sand, because the kind of structure in more recent music, of the better work, is in a different form, just as the kind of structure in the Golden Gate Bridge is different from the county bridge here in Norman, Oklahoma. There is a great difference. It may be that we are not able to perceive the new thing as structure because sometimes it is so free and integrated with other ideas that we are not able to perceive it as structure. But it is there and don't think it isn't. In the best work it exists in a very profound way.

I think it is interesting that some of the people who have been accused of having the least sense of form and structure in their work have really given that the most thought of almost any element in their work. Debussy, for instance, was very conscious of sculpture and form in his music. He would never let it go until he was certain of that even if it meant holding up publishing a piece that he really needed to have published to make some money. He waited until he had the right idea. He worked with it and strove to protect the structure and form always. Someone else came along and congratulated him for his abolishing form, structure, and melody. One time he was congratulated at a big banquet, given in his honor, for abolishing melody and he said, "I have abolished nothing; my music is nothing but melody." Everyone laughed, they thought he was making a joke. Now, of course, we know he wasn't.

Just because a structure doesn't stick out like a sore thumb doesn't mean there is no structure there or just because it isn't obvious or overly obvious, you might say. In architecture, for example, if you knew how to design a building, and you made a point of a beam or a column, or whatever it was, to the point where it was the dominant idea, you had a sense of order in structure. You can have it in form, in texture, in scale, and all these ways we think about building. You can have it so integrated with the whole concept or the main idea that you are not so conscious of the parts. When we see an oak tree, we are conscious of the order of that tree in general, aren't we? Very few of us dig into all of the botanical differences that exist between an oak tree and a willow tree. They are there all right, but we aren't so concerned about that unless we are a botanist. We are more concerned about the general kind of order that goes through it. That's the way with architecture; unless we are specialists we are not so worried about all the little details. But being specialists in architecture we should be very concerned about how this order prevails through the entire composition and how it is characteristic clear through. That doesn't mean that you wouldn't have variety, or contrast, or change in that design. It means whatever change, or variety, or contrast you have, it would still add up to a kind of order that would be characteristic of that particular design.

If you take a concrete example, the Johnson Wax Building of Mr. Wright, you will realize right away that the kind of order that exists in that design is quite different from the kind of order that existed in the Larkin Building: both by Mr. Wright, and both for similar purposes: both were administration buildings for manufacturers, and both built primarily of brick and concrete. But what is the difference? One is for a soap company and one is for a wax company. It isn't just soap and wax, is it? Both are clean designs so I guess we could get by on that.

Think of the kind of order that is in the Larkin Building and the kind of order that is in the Johnson Wax Building. There is an interval of time that's made a difference for one thing, isn't there? A lot of water has gone under the bridge since 1904–05 when the Larkin Building was put up. Not only for Mr. Wright personally but for the thinking of the architectural world. The newer building has the benefit of the experience of the former one and the advantage that age would give Mr. Wright, as well as the disadvantage. We have then two kinds of order for very similar purposes.

The Larkin Building sense of order is more of a squarish type. The corners are sharp and there is very little in the way of modifying members. What there are are very abrupt modifications of form or transitions of one form to another. The planes change abruptly, always with a very angular quality. There is a sharpness to it, a clearcut kind of feeling all the way through. It is businesslike, and certainly American as we think of American pioneering, looking forward, democratic, the biggest and bestest, and all that. It's all in that building. It goes up higher than its neighbors. In those days democracy meant going up higher; now it means going out horizontally.

The Johnson Building is quite a different design, looking at it from the standpoint of democracy. It is more horizontal even in spite of the tower. Even the tower is horizontal. The approach to the Johnson Building is much more inviting, much more democratic in the sense that it sort of lures you into it before you realize it, and at your own scale. You don't go through big iron gates anymore, as you did in the Larking Building. That was part of the order in the Larkin Building, security, and being monumental in a grandiose sort of scale. The Larkin Building isn't, in general, as personal in scale, is it? There are personal elements in the scale; by that I mean a person isn't thought of as much in the scale of the Larkin Building as he is in the scale of the Johnson Building.

Naturally, the way you get there is different. You used to go to the Larkin Building by streetcar or taxi or bus or something, maybe even horse-car or carriage in those days. Now we go to the Johnson Wax Building by car. So the entrance is that kind of order of transportation. We are invited in at our own scale, a low, broad carport; the steps we go up are very few; whereas in the Larkin Building we went up a lot of steps to impress us when we went in. Big stairways were the rage in those days, in courthouses, city halls, and capitol buildings. Anything important, you had to go up a lot of steps to get into. Nowadays you walk in at your own level. The Larkin Building was certainly more friendly than most of that time, but that's because they had some of the first glass doors, with remarkably small members to hold the glass. Not at all practical, of course. Today we have a much glassier treatment to the entrance to the Johnson Building.

Much broader expanse of glass, with steps that are lower, broader, and fewer. Before you know it, you are into the place. You are confronted with an information desk, just as you are in the Larkin Building, but here the information desk is more like furniture. In the Larkin Building it was heavy and monumental, made from brick and heavy, cast-stone top, with a very large-scale design all around it; whereas in the Johnson Wax Building you are greeted with natural wood, rubber floors, highly waxed, of course. The woodwork waxed to a fare-thee-well. Everything was waxed there except the concrete.

We have then this big room in the Johnson Building where the people worked. We had a big room in the Larkin Building where the people worked, but the rooms are different. Where the room in the Larkin Building had a tall nave running up through it, almost like a cathedral, with galleries around the sides for the slaves to work in, in the Johnson Wax Building we still have the top light, and the people are all working together on the one main floor— a much more social kind of arrangement. There are all sorts of comparisons and differences, but I think you can say that the Larkin Building would be the order of democracy of that day, and the Johnson Building in the order of democracy today as Mr. Wright interprets it in both cases. This order has come through the way the building is used, and the way it is approached. See how much more human the scale in the Johnson Wax Building is than the Larkin Building. The Johnson Wax Building is not trying to show off its bigness like the Larkin Building was. It is accepting the fact that it is not the biggest building in the world. It is making the most of what it is. Over and above all of this is the feeling that prevails through the building aesthetically, as part of this design of course, and you can see how considerably it follows through in both cases. In the Larkin Building all of the moldings are square, blocky sort of moldings with very wide projections. The differences are quite sharp and sudden, as I said before. The ornament in the building is applied more, with special places like the tops of the piers, where the ornament is in block forms of abstract type of decoration. The light fixtures are ornamental, reflecting the abstract plan. We also have in the Johnson Building the ornamental feeling of the caps of the columns, but it is not quite the same idea of ornament that we had in the Larkin Building. It is more integral with the form of the column than the ornament in the caps of the Larkin Building, which look more like they are applied to the column, rather than being of the column, as they are in the Johnson Wax Building. This indicates a great advance in the handling of ornament, I think.

The nature of the materials themselves becomes more ornamental in the Johnson Wax building. The slightly concave texture of the brick, the glass tubing, all carry through a circular kind of order that probably started with the idea of the column with the big circular top. Maybe you could stretch your imagination a little and think of it as the circular motion of waxing. I don't know if Mr. Wright consciously did that or not. I hope he didn't. Anyway, the Johnson Wax Building is more like the circular motion of waxing while the Larkin Building is more like a cake of soap. Those examples may be too obvious.

The circular motion that you find in the capitals of the columns in the Johnson Wax Building is carried through in many parts of the building, including rounded corners, where the columns naturally make the corner by following the wall right around the column. The circle gives you a good way to make a transition from the rectangle. If you remember the plan, it was a big rectangular building; and where the columns are placed near the corners, the corners of the rectangle are rounded. Where the building comes up higher, where the offices are, we can take off from the circles then either at right angles, and rectangles, or we can go on the diagonal, or the bias, and get into forty-five degree angles. You will notice if you examine the section that the glass tubing is circular. In the plan the stairways are circular, and the elevators are circular. The whole feeling that goes through the building is basically of a circular motion. Even the brick is concave; even this is part of the big circle. So this building, while it has forty-five degree variations, carries the circle theme even into the furniture. The chairs had circular seat and circular backs. The Johnson Wax Building is pretty much on a circular theme established by the columns, but basically working within a rectilinear idea of form.

The Larkin Building has the sense of order of square forms all the way through, even into the furniture. That sense of order that carries through could be compared again in other cases of Mr. Wright's. I am speaking of very familiar samples. You might look these up to refresh your memory. Take the squarish order that exists in the Larkin Building and the squarish order that exists in Unity Temple. Both by Mr. Wright. There you have a very delicate point of difference in order. Both the Larkin Building and Unity Temple have a similar kind of order, with the same base and section. The base is the variation of the old Greek stylobate base. The base is a modifying member to the ground and then the wall comes up from the base in a straightforward manner. The caps come straight out from the wall, without any further ado, and project out with a stone edging and then continue straight up. That is constant in both the order of the Larkin Building and Unity Temple. The tops of the piers in both buildings are related, too. They have square sort of block ornaments, or caps at the top, with repeated rhythmic devices so that series of squares is all related in an abstract design. One is made of brick and one is made of concrete.

Why is it that one is a temple or church and one of them is an office building, outside of the fact they are used for that purpose? Is there something in the design itself that would make that difference of order, the order of a religious concept and the order of a working-place concept? Both are very closely related designs. Both buildings are lighted from the top, aren't they? So you couldn't say it was the holy light from above that makes one religious. Nothing like that. It is in both buildings.

The Larkin Building is taller than Unity Temple, so if there is anything about aspiring vertical lines, it should be more religious than Unity Temple, shouldn't it? Why is it then the order of Unity Temple seems religious to us, and the order of the Larkin Building doesn't? That is slicing it pretty thin. I don't know whether we could say exactly. It is the feeling that went into the designs, that comes out of building, that we respond to. I think the feeling is above the materials, above the forms, above the structure, and that's why it is so difficult to analyze in this particular case, because the forms and methods are so related in their order. And still the feeling which has transcended that has come through, in both cases, over and above all of this. We see an order that is related to the purpose of the building, that has made it that way. How that has been done physically is an interesting question. We need to think about that a little bit.

The approach to the Larkin Building is more direct. You go through the gate and the walk leads you directly up the steps into the entrance. In Unity Temple, you go around behind a wall that shelters a terrace before you go into the public space. This leads into the religious part of the building, or into the social part of the building on the other side. What is it that makes it religious—or what do you think it is? If you are thinking of the order of religious feeling that goes through a Gothic cathedral, you might have difficulty thinking of Unity Temple as religious. Still I think that everyone knows it is a church even without having a cross on it. There is not a cross anywhere. Still it is in the nature of the building, in the order of it. Inside of course, in the Unity Temple, you have the feeling of gathering around the preacher. Even the different levels of the main hall are not high above where the preacher is and are not far removed from him. The seating is fairly close and intimate, which would be a more democratic kind of feeling in a church than the long rows of pews reaching up into the distance to the altar and the priest. This is a more friendly gathering place in that sense. The space is cheery, well lighted, and doesn't fit back behind big piers and big columns. There is no hocus-pocus dim lighted, soft organ music sort of atmosphere about it; it is all out in broad daylight, very clear. It would be even harder to get a religious feeling that way. It would be much easier to get it through the order of aspiring lines, for instance, if we think of heaven as up. I think we would have much more feeling of mystery in dimly lit places where you can't see everything at once as you can in Unity Temple. So he didn't have those tricks of the trade to help him, but it is in there somewhere: this feeling of a religious order that carries through it, that differentiates it from the Larkin Building. I think it is something that bears a lot of thinking about, because it shows you how finely divided these kinds of orders are. It is not just a matter of in one building everything is round and in another building everything is square, or in another building everything is triangular, or something like that. It is much deeper than that. It comes out of the feeling that you put into it. The kind of order that is in your feeling: it's about what you are doing. It is the basic idea that is in it. It defies analysis many times, as most mysteries do, if they remain mysteries. We can feel that without actually knowing why.

I talked to the janitor in Unity Temple not long ago while he was painting—he was sort of a jack-of-all-trades. He was fixing up the building a little bit and he asked me if I was interested in the building. I said, "Yes, we are looking at Mr. Wright's work here." He said, "I don't know why people are so hopped up over this building," and I asked him why. He said, "Well if you had to wash these windows you would know why. These are the awfulest windows to wash in the world. The architect didn't even consider how you were going to wash them." He was complaining about the glass around the top of the auditorium that was all fixed, and in order to wash the windows you had to take a ladder up to the first ledge, then have a stepladder from there to get up to where the windows were, and that was pretty rough. The ones that bothered him the most were the ones that were set back in the little narrow slots, in between the corner piers and the wall. They were about six inches wide and back about twenty-four deep. He said when he put his ladder against the wall, the windows were about twenty-four feet high, it was easy to reach the windows up near the top, but as you got down near the bottom you had to have long arms, or some type of pole. He didn't think Mr. Wright was so great. I suppose from his standpoint he had a legitimate gripe, but naturally he was more concerned with the physical aspects of the design. In fact, he was so concerned with these details that I doubt that he was ever aware of the

rest of the design. We can often overlook this other quality, because of our concern with physical matters. But it's
there, it's in the building, and it's still in the building after
all these years, since 1906. It still has its mystery and it is
still a religious building.

One time the preacher complained to me that too many
people came there just to see that building; he wished more
would come to hear the sermon. I told him that the building
was a sermon. He said he had never thought of it that way. It
is a building that you can't help feeling is a religious space, a
special kind of space, different from one used for commercial purposes. Now how do you achieve that? What is that
kind of order that exists in the space inside? Mr. Wright said
it was the first time he was able to have the continuity, or the
flow of space, within the interior that satisfied him. That
may be why it is the kind of space it is, and that makes it
religious, and you can recognize that. No matter what your
own religion is, or whether you have any, it still seems religious. It seems very ancient in one sense, like something as
old as the druids, and in another sense it seems very new. It
is still very alive and still very mysterious. Why that space,
and why that particular kind of design, would seem religious, and the Larkin Building wouldn't, is a mystery; part
of it might be due to the fact that we know that one is a business establishment, and we know one is a church, because
they have a sign on it that says Unity Church. But I don't
think you have to have a sign on it, in either case, to know—
because you can sense it through the order of the design
that goes through it. This order of design not only carries a
consistency of language through all the parts, very related
in this case, but it also carries an order of feeling through
it that dictates the forms and the structure in the space.

I think that is the important lesson to learn from it, no

matter how finely we try to analyze just what gives it that difference. We know it's there; we feel it there when we are in the buildings. Maybe we will never know exactly why; I hope we don't. But we can sense it, and we can realize that the creator of both, being the same man, had two different kinds of feelings of order when he did both jobs. The Larkin Building and Unity Temple were done very closely together in Wright's lifespan—-only two years apart. Still, with very similar language he said two different things: one a beautiful fine place to work and one a very fine place to worship. He was successful in transmitting his feeling over and above the language he used to create two kinds of order of that kind. If you think that is easy, try it; it isn't easy at all. It is natural if you have enough feeling about what you are doing. It will naturally result that way. I don't know if Mr. Wright was conscious of every reason why. I know he must have been conscious of some of the reasons why, but he was certainly conscious that each problem has its own order and its own idea. If he tried to feel that through the whole design, and even using similar language as he did, he was able to arrive at two kinds of feeling through the building that were suitable in both cases. Both buildings are disciplined and ordered. They have unity and clarity.

This quality of clarity is very important in a sense of order. If things are all mixed up and confused, if the parts of the design are so involved with each other, so tangled up in each other, they lose their identity. Or they become confused and they lose their sense of clarity. I think the sense of clarity is very important in establishing order. Clarity would mean that every part, or every idea in it, would be clear in its own right. Even where there is a clear statement, each time, it's still a part of this overall order, and the overall scheme.

Now this sense of clarity is very difficult to achieve, unless we are clear ourselves. Sometimes it is very self-conscious. I think that in some of the contemporary work it is overdone to the point of being too obvious. For instance, we say we want to have our structure clear from our walls. We often bend over backwards to show that the column and the wall have nothing to do with each other. Le Corbusier has laid down his five points of architecture to insist that the structure be independent, or clear of the rest of the design; that the facade be clear and independent of the plan, that each facade be clear and independent of the other. That would be taking clarity and overdoing it to the point where you might sacrifice a sense of order by having the parts so independent that they don't seem to relate to each other. It isn't enough just to be clear. You could have each part in a piece of music very clear and still it might not blend with the other parts you hear. You have to have clarity instead of muddy orchestration, or muddy ideas, or something of that sort. To get a good sense in the design, to get a good order, the sort of discipline you wish, you still would need to have a feeling that the parts are clear and they are all working together. I think that is where a great deal of modern design falls short. Many of the parts are clear, but they are not always working together. In Wagner's music the parts are not always clear, were working together to make a big pile of sound, weren't they? Quite often it is sheer volume and mass and brass and bigness that puts it over. And still the music does add up to a big mass of sound, whereas sometimes when things are so dreadfully clear, they don't always add up. There is such a thing as bending over too far backwards as well as forwards. We can be clear and still lose our sense of order, or we can be clear and our sense of order will benefit from it. I think we should always consider everything we use in a building—the structure, the materials, the space, anything aesthetic—from the standpoint of clarity. We should know what every bit of it is doing. We should also know how to order all of this clarity into a complete whole, so that what comes out adds up to more than just a lot of clear parts. Now that is one thing that is very difficult to accomplish and I know you very seldom see in student or professional work, where you feel it is the same order carrying through all of the design. Sometimes it's the body of a crocodile with the head of an ostrich and the wings of a dove. You see, it can be all sorts of incongruous combinations, and you can usually get by with it nowadays because it is considered even more modern if it looks irrational. I don't think that we should be too finicky about looking irrational, because sometimes the truest things may seem irrational, when they are not. On the other hand, when we strive for effect, which I think we should always do, I think that we must realize that these effects have to have relationship with each other. In nature, the effects have to have relationship with each other. In nature, the effects are ordered. We don't find a willow tree having oak leaves. You don't find a hummingbird with a great big bill like a parrot. Everything carries through its own kind of order and form, color, and texture—with great variety, too.

We need to strive more and more to arrive at this kind of feeling of order, clarity of parts, unity of parts, so that the discipline carries through the whole thing, no matter how free the discipline is, or the composition, so that we arrive at something that is distinct in itself and has a reason and a law of its own for being. I think there is entirely too much mass production going on. It's too easy to set up a kind of order that can be repeated, ad lib and ad infinitum, to carry on the same rubber-stamp process, no matter what you are doing. You can see it in art, you can hear it in music, you can see it in architecture, and literature. Someone makes a success with some particular work, and then he is stuck with it, and he keeps repeating it, and the public is stuck with it. Then the change is very marked if this man makes the least bit of change. Maybe he has got all his disciples to paint their steelwork black and then he can make a big change and paint his white. Then all the disciples can paint theirs white and a terrific change has come about, the difference between black and white. Those are pretty fine differences I think.

I do think that we have to be always on the search, on the lookout, for the real reason that exists in what we create. Architects are unfortunate in this respect. We have to manufacture art, more than most artists do. We have to concoct it, and we have to make it out of synthetic materials sometimes; even our feeling has to be synthetic at times. That means then that we have to be able to understand order very quickly, and to perceive it, and to realize it easily, so that what we do will have this kind of unity, and kind of reason or drive that goes into our work. It can't always come from an inner impulse in an architect's work, like it can come from the inner impulse that causes a composer to have to create a piece of music, because it is in his system, and he has to get it out. Or a writer to write something he feels very deeply must be said, or a painter to put down what he thinks is so important to do at that particular time. The architect has to have inspiration through order more than anyone else. Now I know painters are commissioned to do work, and composers are, and all that, and they can work very well within those limits if they are great artists. The freest form of all of this art is in the kind that has to be because it is a necessity. There is a reason that drives peo-

ple to do what they do. We have to do it; we are part of our
time—that's part of the drive, we are part of our art. The
changes that have to come about through our art will come
about through us as mediums that interpret our art to our
society. We have to try to understand the kind of order that
is in nature and all of its phases in art.

We can't always design something exotic. You have a
hamburger stand to do, then we have to put on our hamburger suit, and do a good hamburger stand, you see,
regardless of whether we have any deep convictions about
hamburgers. We might also have to do a church, whether
we are religious or not. Maybe we would have to do a house
whether we have a family or not. Maybe we would have to
do many things that are outside of our experience. Maybe
we detest playing golf but we have to do a golfclub. We
should be able to. We should find the kind of order that
would be suitable for that purpose. In our case it will take a
little more seeking, and working, unless it just happens to
coincide with the happy day that you might get up out of
bed, feeling like doing that very thing, which happens very
seldom. Usually people are contrary enough to want to be
doing something else, anyway, from what they are doing.
It's natural human obstinacy to always think that the grass
is greener on the other side. If you have a particular job to
do, you can imagine how much more fun it would be to do
some other kind of job. That's human nature. I think that
in architecture we have to accept this challenge, this opportunity to do something in each case, and we have to regard
it as an opportunity. What has been held up as a bad thing
in modern architecture was expressed by Mr. Wright—that
he looks at architecture as an opportunity. This has been
said in terms of derision—that he is looking at it as an opportunity to show off Frank Lloyd Wright. I think that is

very unjust. He can't help being Frank Lloyd Wright. He is Frank Lloyd Wright, and his work is going to be part of Frank Lloyd Wright. I think there is nothing wrong with recognizing any job as an opportunity to do something that amounts to something in architecture. It has it's own kind of order, and own reason for being.

Mr. Wright, I think, has taught us more than any other architect, the importance of finding the order in each design we do. It isn't necessarily his style, or his kind of order, but the principle of that which is so important for us to know. We shouldn't be satisfied with our trademarks. We must sacrifice our cherished personalities and work for something bigger and better than we are. As individuals we are apt to feel we are the most important thing in the world. Maybe to ourselves we are, but I think we can't but know the truth if we stop and think about it. As Voltaire said, "We are very pleasant atoms." We are only a very small part, after all, no matter how great and creative we may be, of much bigger schemes.

Architecture with a capital A is a big force, a big possibility, bigger than any architect who ever lived and always will be. It is always challenging us, and as architects we always seek to find architectural solutions to these problems. We can never say that we are architecture—that anyone is architecture. Architecture is bigger and more impersonal than any of us. Architecture is only a minor part of another bigger order. You see these orders keep growing bigger and bigger, until we can no longer conceive of them. And they grow smaller and smaller to where we can't conceive of them. There is no beginning, and there is no ending. Only in our limited frames of perception and understanding is there a beginning and an ending. There really is no beginning or no ending that we can conceive of. So when you think of things in those terms, you can realize that we are very pleasant atoms. We are not so much, after all, and we must realize we must be humble toward architecture, or toward our art. We must respect it very very much in order to do good work with it. We can't feel that just because we do it it is the greatest thing that ever happened, even if it is. We have to realize that there is more to it than us, and there always will be. That's not meant to sound frightening, but to get you to stop and think a little bit about how broad this thing is we are working with. How it is not of any time, place, or people, until people make it so. Otherwise it exists as a principle and an idea bigger than any. It is no worse off because the Egyptians, the Greeks, the Goths, and the Japanese found as much as they did. There is still plenty there and more where that came from.

That leads us to think of possibilities. How many of you have thought of the possibilities as we can conceive of them. Tremendous even as we can conceive of them. What we have achieved within those limits is very, very little. It makes you angry when people think you have gone off the deep end, when you haven't even gotten near the deep end. You realize that the worst is yet to come; that if this is scaring them, what is going to happen when some of the things that are bound to happen and have to happen, do happen? It's going to be a massacre, because they are going to happen because they have to happen. Like I told some of you the other day about Schoenberg, who was accused of doing such awful dill-pickle music, and why did it sound so bad, and why did he write such awful stuff? He replied that someone had to be Schoenberg and he was it. Someone has to be an architect, and you are it, if you are going to do things that architecture has to do for our time, place, and people. Because you are part of our time, place, and people.

Sometimes you will be scared yourself. You look at what you are doing and think, my gosh, did that come out of me. No kidding, you will. Sometimes you will think it is wonderful, and sometimes it will make you feel very repulsed. Just as we can think of our own time in two ways. It could be considered the most exciting and miraculous time that ever was, or it could be considered the worst. It depends on your point of view. Maybe it is both—probably is.

As architects, we are going to find the order of our time, place, and people in the big sense through this, and we are going to realize in the specific sense it's through the individual work we do. That will break down into smaller individual cases through all the parts of the work we do. You see the whole thing is related in a big order, everything from the hinges on the door clear up through the whole building. Through the entire results of that order in that job; through the order in your work, through the result of the order that causes that to be of your society, and your time, and your place. It is all part of the big order, and believe me it is a big order, too. We have to feel that. We have to realize we are part of this. We are not just little individuals doing something strange and peculiar always. We are trying to find out what part of this order we are, and what part of us will be suitable for this particular calling. We are trying to find that part of all the facilities and possibilities in design, in materials, in structure, and all that are suitable to make this kind of order.

This feeling of order that we have, or this idea, where this thing can be carried through: that's very important. It is more important than what shape something is, or what color, what texture, what structural principle, or what scale, or any of that. Those are all tools that a good architect can use. He should know them forwards and backwards, that's for sure, because the more he knows them the freer he is to find the kind of order that he wants. He isn't going to be mixing up orders and have the leg of a giraffe with the trunk of an elephant. He is going to be able to put the kind of order together that belongs together, and not irrational concepts of things that don't go with each other, even if he wants an order of irrationality. We must not forget there is an order to that, too. So in this idea of order, I don't think that we must have a deadly monotony that prevails through a given piece of work, that everything has to be square or everything has to be round. Or that everything has to be brick, or concrete, or some material, or that only one kind of structural principle can be used. Nothing like that. You can have great variety. The more free you are to understand the order in all these things, the more variety you can have, the more richness and fullness of expression. You can do many things of interest in your creative work if you under-stand the many phases that exist in this particular kind of order that you are working with. It is the sign of an ama-teur when it is all alike, almost always, if everything is the same. It is easy to achieve order that way. I think real ge-nius is to be able to orchestrate your kinds of order, to make an order, so that you can have a great deal of richness, and variety, and interest carrying through the design, so that it isn't just a repetition of one theme over, over, and over. So that gets into higher mathematics.

Don't be discouraged if you can't achieve it right now; it will probably take a lifetime even to get close to it. Hokusai, the great Japanese painter, made the statement one time, that I think is very great, when someone asked him how it felt, at the age of seventy-some, to be such a great painter, and recognized by so many people as a great painter: he said, "Well, when I was sixteen I showed an aptitude for drawing, and a little later I could draw well enough to be accepted as an apprentice by a great artist. When I was in my thirties I could please my friends. However nothing I had done before I was seventy was any good." He was seventy-six when he said that, but it wasn't quite true. He had done some wonderful things before he was seventy. In his way of looking at it, it didn't count. He was only then beginning to perceive the order in nature, and his brush was beginning to be able to express it slightly. He hoped that by the time he was ninety he would be able to express the mysteries of nature and the order that he felt should exist in art. He said, "If I could only live ten years more, then I would be able to make every line and dot breathe with life." You see that requires a very humble spirit. It is not quite like the one that says, "There need not be another me for five hundred years." If you know who I mean. Hokusai was really a great artist, with a great capital G, because he realized there was still a long way to go. Unfortunately, he missed it by six years. He lived to be ninety-four, but he came awfully close. I think it is to his everlasting credit that he had that attitude and that idea. He was always seeking more, even when he had achieved so much. He was still growing, still a boy. That's why I said the other day that when you grow in art, keep growing in art, or keep growing in anything else—that's what separates the boys from the men. Not the other way around. Hokusai was still a boy at ninety-four. He was still growing. Think that over; most people want to grow up to be a man.

This feeling that we need to achieve—we need to understand order that is bigger than ourselves—is very strong. We need to express it through our work individually and collectively. It is a great birthright that a creative artist has, and we need to respect it. Every one of us has it in various ways. It is nothing so rare, but most of us quit using it after a while. It is the thing that will make architecture, rather than "just a building." We do not have to have any kind of order in "just a building." It could be a good building, do everything a good building should do, but still it wouldn't need to have one bit of order, would it? It might, accidentally; maybe the fact that the columns are twenty feet on center will give some kind of order, but that would be about all, maybe. It wouldn't necessarily have the kind of order we are talking about. But a work of art, or architecture, should. If it does, it becomes classical in the finest sense of the word. We understand the order for a long time to come, whether we understand it the way the creator did or not. There are many kinds of order that can exist in this one order, and then we can understand those kinds of order in our own ways. I am not sure we understand the order in Egyptian sculpture the way the Egyptian sculptor did. But we can understand it in our way. We can understand that in any great work of art. Well, this could go on and on. I would like to stop for a few minutes and see if any of you have something to ask about the subject.

Question: How is our sense of order related to our present-day culture?

Goff: Our sense of order is certainly related to our present culture—it always is. Our sense of order will change many times on account of that. Something that would be considered orderly in one time might be considered disorderly in another, and vice versa. Jackson Pollock's paint-spilling jobs might be considered very disorderly by many people today. But many people today can see an order in them, too, you see. I think that the kind of order that we can understand in one of his paintings is part of our time, in the sense that it couldn't have been part of the last century. Where we find an order in it now, whether it exists there or not, we search for one, or look for one, where previously it would have had to be in it to start with.

In that light, I believe that everything we do will express in many ways the general feeling for order of our time. If we are living in a disorderly time, there will be a disorderly order, and if we are living in a peaceful time, then it would probably be a peaceful order, or a more controlled kind of order. I think in our time we can't help but feel much more freely about order. It is coming at us from all directions, you see. We have to limber up our attitude toward order a great deal. We have to understand that no matter how confusing all of this activity is, that it is all part of some big order of some kind, no matter how noisy, and how hectic, and how wild it may seem in relation to something that has a more reposeful kind of order, reflecting quieter more peaceful times, maybe. But it is an order of our time. And naturally it's going to affect us. It is going to make us go along with it or rebel against it. We will find artists who enter into it with great glee and have lots of fun throwing paint around, and slashing things together that don't belong together, and making them go together. We will have others that will set themselves against all of this and want to reform it and want to find a voice in the wilderness, the same old idea again. They will want to get their bearings in all of this chaotic kind of order. If you notice the work of any artist, in relation to the way he lives, you will find that his work is almost a perfect seismograph of his way of living and feeling.

If you could take the life of Frank Lloyd Wright as a diagram—it sounds very hard and cold-blooded—but if you could graph it so you could see the happier and more pleasant times of his life, and the more depressing and more hectic times of his life, then if you could put another graph of his work superimposed over the first graph, I think that you would find that they would coincide very closely. Consider the Imperial Hotel, the biggest job he ever did. Greatest opportunity of his lifetime: the most money to spend, in a country that he loved very much, in a culture he respected a great deal. The biggest opportunity that he would ever have. Still, we can't find the peace and serenity in that building that we find in the Larkin Building, Unity Temple, or the Johnson Wax Building, can we? Why is that? It is from inside him, and the way he felt, and the kind of order he was living in at that time. A perfect example of what happens to a very sensitive artist through his work and what is happening in his life. Why was the Midway Gardens so gay? Why was that building so warm and friendly? It still had a great deal of repose, calm, and quiet about it. Still, it was happy, wasn't it? You can read happiness in every line of Midway Gardens, because Mr. Wright was happy. Why is the Imperial Hotel so tragic? Because his life was tragic at the time he designed it. You can't get away from it, it just shows clearly. It isn't always easy to see because sometimes a great artist can cover it up pretty well, but it's there. It exists in everything you do: the way you feel can't help but show. That is the kind of order that you mentioned in your question, *of your time*. It will naturally react on a person's work as well as his personal life. The feeling of your own time is going to come into that.

Mr. Wright has a calm self-assurance now of age and achievement, but his buildings no longer have the serenity that he had when he was young. Why is that? Usually you think serenity and repose come from age, you see— maturity. But here, in his case, the earlier buildings had more serenity and repose than they do now. It's not his fault he has matured, and he has learned a lot in his lifetime, no doubt. But why is it less reposeful? Because our time is less reposeful. That's why I say the kind of order of our times does definitely influence what we are doing whether we are aware of it or not.

Question: How would you define *order*?

Goff: *Order*. We have been talking about it all evening and I guess we should try to define it. It is hard to define, like a lot of other words. You take the word *beauty*. What do you mean by beauty? We say something is beautiful or ugly. Just what do we mean that would make a difference? The definition would be both subjective and objective. I think *order* would simply mean, in the way I feel about it at least, that sense of belonging together. A feeling of continuity, of grammar, or language, or means, so that you feel that is part of the same composition, belongs to the same composition, and not part of the order, say, of another composition where each one can have its own kind of order. Now the word *order*, I think if we tried to pin it down to a definition, might be a straitjacket definition and I would hesitate to do it. I think it is a sense of something rather than a formula. Just like beauty: we have a sense of beauty, but we can't say this is it, can we? We can say we think this is it, and still we are not sure that it is it for everyone. A sense of order will vary with individuals, too, just as beauty will, but that's the subjective term of the idea of order. The objective kind of order would exist for more than ourselves. So that is why I think it is both subjective and objective. I think in general we would mean by order that it is the working together of the parts so they belong with each other.

Question: Do you think this sense of order in architecture is possible in group work?

Goff: It is certainly very difficult in our time, anyway, where our backgrounds are so different, and our reasons are all so different. I can understand why in a time when the feeling is so much related through people, like in the days of the Egyptians or the Gothic cathedrals, or the Japanese culture: there couldn't help but result an order that would be consistent, no matter how many people were working at it, or how ordered the thing in itself was. We do have it add up to a big kind of order. Naturally, a Japanese architect did not have to worry about a landscape architect coming in on his job, or a painter, or any object that went into the house, or even the way the food was served, or the way the people lived in the house. It was all part of an order and the architect was guaranteed that. He had it made, right there, because if he obeyed his feeling for order it was naturally going to work with other artists' feelings of order. Everyone's feeling of order, whether they were artists or not, was the same. Their feeling for religion and everything was part of this order. But now it is difficult, because we have so many kinds of order that it is hard to know that someone will be able to participate in the given thing with the same feelings for order that you have, or vice versa. That's one reason I think they say too many cooks spoil the broth. You often have too many kinds of order of conflicting interests at work. I think that is one reason that we have difficulty working as teams or groups.

Question: Isn't it true that when you have order in a group made up of different individuals that there must be some overall discipline or regimentation before order can take place?

Goff: Yes, in order to realize it, there has to be. It is just like on a construction job. If you let the heating-man come in with his sense of order, and the electrician with his sense of order, and someone else with theirs, you would have what we have here [pointing to the room in the architectural school remodeled under the stadium at the University of Oklahoma]. In fact, on some jobs you wouldn't be able to get in and use the place. Because there wouldn't be an overall kind of order—a common denominator of order.

I tried that on a job not long ago, where I had the case of the need for a mural in a church. I had approached the church trying to work out something for them that I thought was within their means. Not only financially but every other way, trying to respect them as a group and trying to recognize their sincerity, and their real faith, which was stronger than many religious groups that I have dealt with. I respected it a great deal; it was a little homespun, but very very sincere. I felt that I should approach the problem very, very sincerely, too. And I did, even though I am not of their faith. I still put on my suit that would allow me to do that kind of thing and tried to accomplish it honestly for them. Then the problem came up that it had to be a mural for this solution, because they wanted an obvious symbol over their baptism tank they could recognize. I felt, well, now here is a good chance to collaborate with an artist, which I still think should be done, even after this experience. I wish there was a common denominator which would enable artists and architects to work closely together and other people, too.

I approached one artist with the idea of doing the mural for this building and he assigned it to one of his students as a project. The student was from back East, which is not meant to be a slam, and was a little bit critical of these plain folks, and had a rather superior attitude toward them. Besides, he knew the work of Paul Klee and they didn't. They had never even heard of Paul Klee. I doubt if they had even heard of Maxfield Parrish, either. They had seen art on calendars, and so on, but you couldn't expect them to know much more about it. It's not their fault and I am not trying to deride them in our favor. It's their upbringing. Anyway, this artist decided to work up a sketch for this mural, and he brought it up to show it to me. The scene that the church people wanted expressed in this mural was the river Jordan, which meant something to them. The artist took a rather cynical view of the whole thing and decided to satirize it. He did a very dreadfully clever interpretation of the river Jordan with a great deal of sophistication. It was just too cute for words. It had a little angel that was knock-kneed. The poor little thing had a warped halo over its head and has holding a little jug and pouring water out of it, symbolizing the river Jordan. It was done with a few sort of Paul Klee shapes and it was very obvious where he had got his idea. I think that Paul Klee is pretty good, too, but I didn't think he was quite the man for this job. This was an approach with a spirit of irreverence and cynicism and sophistication which hardly was in the order of this building and the need for this particular thing. I tried to tell him that, and he immediately assumed that I was unsympathetic. I tried to get him to understand that these people deserved better. Naturally, he couldn't understand it because he didn't have that kind of order within him. He insisted on going up and showing it to the preacher. He asked me if I cared if he showed it to the preacher. I knew what would happen if he did. When he showed it to the reverend, he got this question: "Are you a Christian?" Naturally, one would wonder. Supposing that had been all right, which of course it wasn't, it wasn't in the order of the thing in the first place. It wasn't even in the order of the building. There was nothing in it to relate the mural design in any way, shape, or form, to the forms, or colors, or textures, or scale of the building. It was just an easel painting stuck in there, just the same as he would have put it there or somewhere else.

It had no particular reason to be in that building, even if you overlooked the other part, just the aesthetic direction of it was totally foreign to the feeling that was in the building. So another artist tried it, and he vowed, too, that he would not have a tree or a river Jordan. He, too, failed. And now they have the tree and the river Jordan [yet another work—one that was finally chosen]. But is it art? No, it's horrible, and it has ruined the building. But it doesn't do it any more than those others would have done, you see. At least it is part of their order, of the way they feel and think about religion, which the others weren't. It has nothing to do with the building. It's corny and emphasizes the worst things about the idea of the mural.

But the earlier artists in their approach to this problem immediately assumed that the problem was wrong. That is the first thing you always assume when you have a problem, and it's wrong. You try and figure out how to try and beat the rap. If you are pretty clever, you might. In this case, the artists couldn't take the idea of the symbolism that these people wanted, the river Jordan and the tree. That was thought of as corny. I think that Gustav Klimt could have done something with that theme, and I think he could had made it fit the building. I think a good artist could. He could have given them something they would have known was a tree, and something they would have known was the river Jordan. Have you ever seen the screen by Korin of the beautiful stream and trees? It is one of the great works of art. As corny as that, just a tree and a stream, but it looks awful good. Why was it below his dignity to paint just a tree and a stream and make it so beautiful? That doesn't mean that the modern artist would paint it the same way; of course he wouldn't. But that doesn't mean, just because that was the problem, that he should be so snooty

about it either, unless he could offer something better. I
think he should have at least recognized that part of the
problem.

Well, this is a long-winded story, but it naturally makes
an architect mistrust working with fellow artists. That
brought home very forcibly to me this idea that it is so
hard for us as individuals to think together on something.
It wasn't so hard in older days in Japan, the Gothic days,
the Greek days, or the Egyptian days. You could be pretty
sure that the different kinds of artists could get together
and produce something harmonious. Now it is such a free-
for-all that you have to be awfully careful who you pick.
It naturally makes architects very wary of artists, and the
other way around. It is too bad; we should be able to work
together. We won't be able to until we have enough of a
common denominator of culture, or civilization in the big
sense of order, to enable us to be our part of that order. It
is awfully hard to find someone of like mind.

The Japanese have a poem, "Somewhere gazing at the
morning moon, is one of like mind with me, but I have
no way to find him out." That may be the way it is today.
There may be plenty of people who have like mind, who
have the same feeling for order, but you have no way of
finding it out. Very rarely can you find this kind person, or
persons, who can feel and think about things the way you
can. Eric Mendelsohn, the architect, told me that he had a
terrifically difficult time finding people who could pick up
where he left off in his synagogues, in the matter of decoration and so on. He couldn't find people who would be
able to go on with the feeling that he had, and to heighten
it, and make it even more beautiful in specific instances as
art beyond architecture, or apart from architecture, or part
of architecture, whichever way you look at it. He couldn't

find people like that. The result of all of this is that the architects are just building the buildings and the painters are hanging up the paintings. We don't know what we're going to get in that respect. You might strike it lucky and you might not. Odds are that we won't. You will find a modern building with antique furniture in it and you will find an old building with modern furniture in it, you see.

That situation carries through so much of our work. I think it is very difficult to have teamwork unless there is a dominant force in the design that can set the order and the others are willing to work within that kind of order. That's why it's better to work for yourself than someone else, because you can control that order better than you can where you are part of another kind of order than your own. But all this individual feeling for order is chaotic when you try to work together, usually. That is why I think it is very bad in school to have teamwork problems, because usually they end up with one person doing the work and several other people getting credit for it. I have seen it in other schools, and noticed it very carefully, because we have been criticized for not having teamwork problems. Naturally, we have to learn to adjust to other kinds of order than our own. I think you are going to have enough of that to do. That is something you can very well learn when you get out of school. I think it is more important to learn the kind of order you have within yourself while you are in school, because it is the only time you will ever have the time to take an inventory of your sense of order, and get a sense of direction that's based on that kind of order that you find within yourself. After you get out of school, you will have to adjust that to "the hard cruel world," of course—the kind of order that is in your environment. In the meantime, you have to know what you are, before you can adjust what you are to something else. Many of us don't have any idea of what we are. Do you stop to wonder?

Order in a personal way is subjective, but it is objective in an impersonal way, too. Both of those qualities exist in a real work of art, objective and subjective. You have the way you feel about it, but you also have to approach it objectively enough so that other people can feel about it, too, and not necessarily just the way you feel about it. If it is really a great work of art, I think you will find that it always has those two qualities. If it is just subjective, it might not mean anything to anyone but yourself, and if it just objective it could mean something to someone else.

Question: The people who seem to have accomplished a sense of order with their work, like Frank Lloyd Wright, Albert Einstein, yourself, don't seem to be that different.

Goff: The greatest compliment I ever got was when someone met me for the first time and said, "You are not anything like I thought you would be—you're just like anybody." I think that it is true that we don't breathe any different kind of air, or paint our toenails gold, or anything like that. We are only human. But someone who is trying to do something, if he is willing to pay the price, and willing to make it his main aim, his main goal, is going to have to work very consciously for certain things. It doesn't mean he is any smarter than anyone else, or any better. I don't think that I have any more talent than anybody in this room. That is not being overly modest, and it's not boasting. I really don't think that I have any more talent than anybody. I do have a healthy curiosity that a lot of people don't have. That has led me into curious paths, and it has made me realize certain values that have caused me to do certain things in my work. I am sure that anyone who does creative work will do things that they feel have to be done. The fact that

Mr. Wright has accomplished this sense of order, over and above the order of physical things, I think is to his credit. I don't think it means he is any more superior, as a human being, than anybody—that is not the point. He does see certain things and respond to certain things because of his own nature, which distinguishes him from someone else, but it doesn't mean he is any better. He is responding to things because of his makeup that no one else can, and someone else can respond to things that he can't, you see. No one can respond to everything, I guess. We have our own kind of food we like; we have our own things that we feel of like mind with. Naturally, we will try to develop those. The kind of order that comes out of those developments is personal and impersonal at the same time. Subjective and objective. Because Mr. Wright is a human being, he is more than just Mr. Wright, as any other person is more than just themselves, in that sense. They are working for a lot more than themselves.

Question: What has happened to many of the students who have studied with you? For you have shown me photographs of former students who no longer practice architecture. The casualty rate seems to be awfully high. Why?

Goff: The rate is tremendous. Naturally, you wonder why. There are lots of reasons. One thing, sometimes people get afraid. They get afraid of what they are themselves; they get afraid of where they are going, and they begin to suspect they are headed in a certain direction. Some of them can't pay the price of being noticed, of having the spotlight thrown on them. Some of them feel very conspicuous if what they do is noticed. Some of them haven't the stamina or the strength to fight it out. They might have the ability to produce things, and some of them aren't willing to pay the price to fight it out. Some of them don't want to sacrifice what they need to sometimes do that. The reasons would be enough to fill a whole book, I am sure, if you dug into individual cases. It is too bad. Just as there are more good buildings designed than are every built, there are many, many good artists who are never realized. The casualty rate is very high in artists and in their works. So many things happen. Sometimes they are tied down with obligations that force them to do things to make a living, not just for themselves but for someone else; or maybe they are tied up, involved in things in ways they can't help. In one of these cases, for instance, the man in the restaurant, is potentially a great artist I am sure, but in his case it is either give it up or give up his wife. Because he has children, he thinks he better keep his wife. That is the kind of value that he feels. Certainly we have to respect that; whether we think he should give up his wife or not, we have to admire him for taking a stand one way or the other. If he feels it is more humane and important to sacrifice what he could be as an artist, in that case because his wife has told him right out that if he stays in architecture she will divorce him, that's his business, of course. There are many many reasons for that and I wouldn't even try to go into all of them now. It is good to analyze them and it is good to think about them.

Question: What do you feel about the artist being in the right place at the right time?

Goff: Sometimes an artist is lucky to be born at a certain time when something had to happen and he is it. That is true, but the fatalists would all say, "What will be, will be, and this is preordained, and predestined, and all that." Who is to say? I don't know. There is an awful lot about being in the right spot at the right time. But we all are really, in the right spot at the right time if we only can take advantage of the situation. As I told the students in the forty-one class today, the thing Carlyle said, "The ideal is within yourself, your condition is but the stuff that you are to shape that same ideal out of." These conditions, no matter how unfavorable or difficult or detrimental they are to your progress as a creative individual, can be used as excuses for not doing something. Or they can be used as the conditions that you will shape that same ideal out of, if you are given enough room to handle it. That is a big order. Too often we have excuses. Mr. Wright said, "If a man must eat at the expense of his ideals let the oaf eat." Groucho Marx said, "I wish you wouldn't look at me when you say that." It is true; we usually feel that we are quick to justify our selling out, or giving up, on the grounds of something we have to do. People who do that are always trying to run you down if you don't. In a meeting of architects in Tulsa the word got around that it was no wonder I could do the crazy stuff I do because I never had to work for a living—that I was born with a silver spoon in my mouth—that my father was a rich architect. All of which was untrue. My father wasn't even an architect, let alone a rich one.

Three

The New and Different in Architecture

The subject that we hear a lot about around here, and I think we should talk about it and I hope you will do some of the talking, too, is, "What is New and Different?"

We believe that here in this school we are very different, and I guess we are. In fact we might even be called "odditects" at times. We do seek to do something that is creative in architecture—at least, we are branded for that. We are condemned or praised accordingly. Not all of us are guilty. But we do, I think, try to do something creative in our own work. That's a very laudable thing in my book, providing that you keep your eyes open for cliches, mannerisms, and habits that are so easy to form when you are trying to be different. In other words, it can be the same old usual unusual stuff, which I think we are in danger of some times. That is why I wanted to talk about this tonight.

It is no longer fresh to do some of the things that have been done now since 1900, even though they still may be very different to most people. We should not avoid something just because it has been done, if there is a good reason for doing it. If our problem calls for a cantilever, I don't see any reason why we should not use a cantilever, just because someone else has. On the other hand, I don't think

Goff was interested in what was meant by the words new *and* different *in architecture. People had expressed concern that the school was just striving for effect, and in this lecture (given on October 28, 1953, to the School of Architecture in Norman) Goff develops the concept in a clear, lucid manner to demonstrate that the new and different in design is a very natural process, of great importance to any designer who wishes to continue to grow.*

we should think just in terms of the cantilever, or any other structure that we already know. In other words, we could approach each problem with an open mind, not the kind that's open where things keep going through all the time, like bats or something—but the kind that is open enough so that new ideas can come into it—and then some of these ideas retained for our creative work where a position can be established in regards to something we are doing, some principle at stake . . . can come through the work. I think this is part of having an open mind, part of growing, and I think that first of all we have to keep growing if we are going to produce anything vital or real. Naturally, growth entails change—change for us as individuals and change for the good old ways of doing things.

If you have ever read the story "The Devil in the Belfry," by Edgar Allan Poe, you can see he pointed out a moral, which I will recap very briefly. The city of Vondervotteimittiss in Holland was a very orderly place; everything was going along fine, everyone knew what to expect, nothing disturbed the good ways of doing. The city was laid out so that the streets all radiated from the center of the city, which was the city hall. Every house was just alike and they all had a garden and each garden had twelve rows of twelve cabbages. Clocks were everywhere and they all kept perfect time and the time was synchronized with the big clock in the village steeple. When the clock would ring one, all the Dutchmen, sitting on their front porches, all smoking their pipes, would all say, "One." Then it would ring two and they would say, "Two," and so on. When the clock stopped striking, they would close their watches with a very satisfied feeling that everything was in order, and put their watches back in their pockets and wait for the next time for the clock to strike. Everything was very orderly and very peaceful, until one day a stranger appeared from over the hill. He was an unusual stranger because he didn't walk like other people, but he sort of capered around. There was something odd about his appearance and his wild look. He had a big bass fiddle that he was cutting all kinds of capers with as he came down the hill into the little town of Vondervotteimittiss. About that time, all the big clocks started to strike twelve, so no one could worry too much about this stranger; they started to look at their watches as usual and count the time out. Everything was going according to Hoyle on the time, but they hadn't noticed that this stranger had gone into the village hall and up into the clock tower. Finally, when the clock struck twelve everyone was satisfied that everything was in order and put their watches back in their pockets. Then the clock struck thirteen. Things were in an awful mess. The clock kept striking all sorts of hours. There were strange sounds coming out of the tower, too, because there was a mad bull fiddle playing up there along with these bells striking all kinds of hours. Everything went into a disorderly mess. All the clocks in town started going around in all directions and telling all sorts of times. The cats were running all over the place and climbing up the walls, and everyone was upset. This little thing, the clock striking thirteen, had disorganized the entire community, which had been so well oiled before. Summing it up, Poe said, "The moral to the story was, never change the good old course of things."

Well, that I think is the safest thing to do. If you want to get along without straining, "never change the good old course of things." You can do that here just as you can anywhere. You can do the same old unusual stuff here, and while it might be very strange and odd some place else, if it's the same old thing here, then no one is going to worry very much about it. But what I would like to see is the clock striking thirteen around here. I would like to see something strange, and new, and different. I don't mean that it should be done just to be different. That is not the point. It is easy to be different if you want to be different. It is also easy to create some kind of a sensation if that is all you are interested in, but what I mean is that I would like to see some fresh approaches to the problems. More than we have. We are inclined to remain in ruts. Sometimes we are interested more in just drawing beautiful drawings. Sometimes we are interested in only one thing. I think the current craze around here is intersecting geometry. Even the freshman are talking about it now. I don't say there is anything wrong with intersecting geometry, but it shouldn't become a fetish any more than any other thing should. I think that we have to keep an open and inquiring mind as to possibilities of form. We have to keep reevaluating the principles, the materials, the things we use. I don't know if we are going to come up with any new and different principles basically. I hope we can, but after all, they have been going on for thousands of years and they are pretty well mulled over by now. I would like to see someone come up with new principles if they could. But if they can't, then let's try and reevaluate them in a way that we don't already know so well. To be curious and to explore the things we don't know. It is true when you get out in "the hard cruel world," as many people say, and I think with reason, that it is hard enough to get the usual unusual stuff done.

I believe that one reason that many so-called modern architects have difficulty with their clients is that they don't go far enough. They still have one foot in the grave. They are trying, on one hand, to be new and different, and, on the other hand, they are trying to hold on to something tried and true to the point of watering down the fresh idea that might give their design real vitality.

When we look back over history, the people who interest us the most are the ones who had ideas, and the freshest ideas. There were other composers during the time of many of our so-called classical masters, but why do we just hear of certain ones the most? Usually because they were the ones that broke the path and who opened up new horizons for their art. I don't think that any of them went too far, although almost all of them were accused of it, of course. They always will be accused of it, just as you will be if you try to go beyond what is known today.

I am not assuming that change always means progress; that is something I want to get square right now. Just because we change doesn't mean that it is any better. It is only through change that we can keep growing ourselves, and we can keep our art alive. You find then that immediately the leaders in art, of all sorts, will fall into two general classifications: the ones who lead, who break the path, or the trail, who find some big idea that will open up the whole horizon for others—these are the leaders; then you will find the followers who come along and so a very good job applying what someone else has already found out. For instance, we can't say that Mr. Elmslie was anywhere near the leader in architecture that Mr. Wright is, although that doesn't mean he is not a good architect. He is a very fine architect. When the history of architecture is written, the man who counts the most is the man with the ideas to start with, and who puts them into practice, and accomplishes something with them. Just having the idea is not enough. It is necessary to realize it through one's art for the people. That is the job that our great men like Sullivan and Wright, and all those who try to think things out for themselves, accomplish. We are not trying to follow, or be disciples, but we are trying to find our own way. Not with the idea of building onto where someone else left off, but with the idea of applying principles, old or new. If they are good principles, they are ever new; no matter whether the Babylonians used them or whether we use them, they will still be principles that are useful. We should be able to think of those in a fresh way, just as well as we should be able to use brick, a material that is thousands of years old, in a fresh way, too.

In working out new ways, new possibilities, I think we have to realize first of all that no matter how fine things are that have been done, and are now being done, they are not concerning us directly when we try to solve a problem—only indirectly. We shouldn't be trying to remember. If we try to remember, then, we are diluting our problem, right away, with hangovers from other solutions other people or ourselves have made to other problems. I think that there is a difference in consciously trying to remember and in knowledge that we have for ourselves—knowledge being something that we have assimilated from experiences in considering work, or principles, as worked out by other people, or in nature, or in any other way. We are not trying to deny in any way the great work that has been done or that is being done. We are not trying to set ourselves up as superior in any sense. I think we should try to assimilate our experiences to the point that we do not have to consciously seek to remember them when we go to work. They should be just as much a part of us as the fact that we can move our arms to write without having to worry about how we are moving them, or how someone else moves them. We don't worry about that, do we? We shouldn't have to worry about it in the field of ideas either. We should have already been inspired, influenced, and, as Mr. Wright says, "enriched," refreshed, whatever you want to call it, through your experiences.

We will assume then that that process has already taken place. I hope it has. I don't think that anyone is suffi-cient unto themselves without a great deal of absorption, of knowing what is going on, and what principles have been in back of what is going on. It helps us a great deal to have the authority, when we design something of our own, to know our background—to be a part of our present fore-ground and to know the background—to look forward as much as we can. I would say then that in not trying to re-member, we want to realize that that doesn't mean we are ignorant of what has gone on and what is going on. We must realize that that doesn't concern us directly in a par-ticular problem so much as indirectly. We have to be fit for battle when we go into a design problem unharassed by a lot of hangovers. We have to be able to approach it as freshly as we can without any idea of what "they" are doing, or what "they" have done, or what is acceptable to commercial success, or what isn't.

What is the thing that we need to do? We will feel a need to do something if we listen to that feeling and try to carry it out. I think we are on pretty safe grounds because the good things that happen, and have happened, have almost all come about from need. There was a reason why some-one felt the way they did about something. Maybe they are not always aware of it. Maybe Stravinsky wasn't aware that the *Rite of Spring* had to be composed, and that he was the one who had to do it. I don't know whether he was or not. As Schoenberg said one time, "Someone had to be Schoen-berg, and I am it." Not everyone realizes that they have to be someone and that they have to do things because of some need, either within themselves, or within our society, or within our art, or all together. We do feel the need to do certain things, and I think we have to feel that need in order to make it genuine. This striving for freshness. I think that in avoiding cliches, we have to consciously try to do that sometimes, because we are so surrounded with cliches that it is easy to drift into those things just out of habit.

For instance, when I first came here and did the Ledbetter house over on Brooks and Chatauqua, here in Norman, Oklahoma, there was a rash of things suspended, and broken stone walls, by the students copying from my design of the house. Maybe there was a need to do it, but I don't think there was. I felt a need to do it, and that is why I did it. I don't think many of the people in school who did it felt the need, except they thought it would be acceptable and maybe help their grades. They soon found out that didn't work. They didn't have reasons for doing those things, and I think I had reasons.

During this time we had epidemics of all sorts of things. Someone in the school discovered the ridged bent, and we had a whole rash of ridged bents showing up in architectural design problems even where they are not used structurally at all, but for the ridged-bent effect. Now that is as stale as yesterday's toast. It has no meaning at all unless it needs to be in your problem. I am not saying you shouldn't use a ridged bent, don't get me wrong. Only use it if you need it. If you feel the need for it and it is doing something, fine, use it, but it isn't enough to use it because it looks tricky, or modernistic, or something like that.

We have, in general, two rather opposite feelings about design, I think. One group are the students who are really trying to do something new and different, not the ones who follow along blindly, but the ones who are seeking. We find one camp devoted to geometry and another devoted to free form. We have had some royal battles on the subject out in the halls. I hear repercussions of it occasionally. That is good, I am glad you do: it shows you are alive. I hope there will be lots more blood shed on these subjects before you are out of school. That's a good thing, for you have to learn to defend your ideas. Someone said once, "The only thing accomplished in an argument is that you convince yourself more." That's quite a lot. If you can do that, then it's worth arguing about. If you can see things one way or the other, what's the difference? There is plenty of room in geometry yet. One time I asked Mr. Wright why he never tried free form and he said, "I still found plenty of room in the square, the circle, and the triangle to express what I have to say." He said, "I will leave the rest to you." It was a very beneficent gesture.

Then there are other people who look at Gaudí's work and they say he is the apostle of free form. Actually probably not so much an apostle of free form as one who has given geometry a laxative. Gotten it moving a little bit. Anyway, geometry is still hidden in there, somewhere. Probably the greatest field open for unexplored conquest would be in free form as far as mankind is concerned. Gaudí himself said, "The straight line was man's and the curved line was God's." He felt that something free in form was the next step I am sure. He was working toward it more and more. Probably he represents the transition into that way of thinking. I don't think we have any examples of free-form architecture yet anywhere, except in nature. Now by free form I mean forms that are not imitations of geometric forms. Some things that appear to be free are only approximate geometric forms. Maybe they are curved a little, but still basically geometric in concept. We are assuming, right now, just talking about it like this, that those are the two kinds of form, geometric and free. By free form we mean things that are not geometric. Well, that covers a lot of unknown territory right there. Just like in the old days there was Europe, and then there was the New World. No one knew what the New World consisted of then, except it was just a big formless blob on the other side of the globe. No one knew the shape of it, or what was in it, or anything, but it was just called the New World. When we think of free form, are we thinking of livers, and kidneys, and wiggly lines that don't mean anything, or are we thinking of forms that are not restricted geometrically with geometry as the basis? If we are thinking of that, would there be any other kind of form that would be possible that we haven't even thought of at all, not to even call it a name. Would it be possible?

For instance some scientists claim that there are three fields of color and that we see one field of color ranging from infrared to ultraviolet rays. I wonder what the other two are like? Can you imagine any colors you have never seen? They exist somewhere, theoretically. I don't know whether we will ever be able to see them; maybe we will invent something someday so that we could see them. It is interesting to speculate on that. It may not be very practical if we can't see them, or we can't use them. Maybe they won't do us much good on our next design problem, but isn't it interesting to know that there are at least two other fields of color, whether we can know them or not? I think so—I am glad it isn't all settled like yesterday's hash. We have something to look forward to, to try to understand.

It is interesting to me to think of everything as potentially possible. Maybe we won't be able to realize structures lighter than air in our lifetime, but it is interesting to think about it. Someday, maybe we will accomplish it. I am sure that long before people knew how to fly there were plenty of people who felt the need to fly. It took a great deal of technology, and work, to accomplish the feat, didn't it? I think it is going to take a lot of technology and work to accomplish some of the feats we are able to think of as ideas, and still not able to put into practice today.

What is the good of thinking of things you can't do? I think for one thing it makes you realize that what you are doing is in a very primitive stage. This is not a healthy feeling if we think of it as a handicap. If we can think of it as a sign that we are young and growing, not at the end of an epoch, but at the beginning of one, then I think it is exciting. If we think of ourselves as ending an epoch then it is dismal. Mr. Wright thinks of himself pretty much as ending and he says "Architecture is headed for the gutter and it is on the brink." I think it is in many ways. But suppose it goes over the brink, where is it going then? Maybe some place better. Just because the water goes over a waterfall doesn't mean that it is finished, does it? Maybe it has to take a drop to go some place else, and maybe the drop isn't inferior.

I think there is a great deal of hope in knowing that it is possible to do right now potentially almost anything that we can think of. When Jules Verne was thinking of submarines and Leonardo da Vinci was thinking of submarines, they couldn't actually do them, but it gave them a great deal of hope that someday they could. I think it loosens up your mental processes, keeps you from getting in ruts and feeling that you have arrived, that this is the latest thing out, that this is it, when in fact you haven't even scratched the surface. Suppose we do have the tricks that we have now? What do they amount to except a way to express our feelings, our real aesthetic values, and other functional values? Just as grammar and just as language they do not mean much unless we can say something with

them, do they? I think principles don't mean very much
either unless we can say something with them, no matter
how good they are. They don't have real meaning for us until we see them realized through something that someone
does. Still these same principles we have been wrestling
with for thousands of years are so broad and so big that
they allow for all sorts of solutions.

It isn't enough just to be different, it has to say something
that we have to say. On the other hand I think it isn't bad
to try or to seek something different providing we have a
good reason. How many of us are interested in hearing the
same thing over and over. If someone rushes in the door
here right away and says, "Hold everything! I have just discovered a steam engine." What would we say? I don't think
we would be very thrilled. If he could say, "I discovered a
steam engine that runs without any fuel," we might lift our
ears a little bit. We would be mildly interested, wouldn't
we, even though it was an old-fashioned steam engine? I
think that we have to keep striving to design something interesting, and to be interesting we have to have change. It
needs to have the quality of surprise.

Surprise, of course, isn't enough if it doesn't have mystery to sustain interest along with it. I think we can get to
a point where we are depending on the same old surprises
too much. I would like to see a lot more experimenting and
a lot more attempts at finding something that isn't already
a dime a dozen.

It is getting so now that practically anyone can design
something passable. We have all kinds of books on good
taste. They not only publish them, but now they focus in
on what we are supposed to think about them. We have in
the new *House Beautiful* magazine a whole issue devoted to
a house. To give it authority, right under the title picture is a

statement by Mr. Wright, which I am sure doesn't express a wholehearted acclamation for this particular job. But it says it is an attempt, and maybe it is. But so what, there are lots of attempts, that doesn't necessarily mean anything. You can say it is sincere; maybe it is, but sincerity isn't enough. Why do the editors of the magazine have to tell us what we should think about the house. The trouble is that in all the editorial policies that go along with magazines, books and other publications, we are in danger of falling into certain cliches in thinking, or in working, because there is so much information around us. We do it automatically. The thing is that everybody and his brother can learn to be a good designer if he does it that way. He can read that a certain place is where you get your ideas. Then he can go to that place and get his ideas and he knows he is safe.

We have besides the geometric and the free-form approach, the nature boy and the popular mechanics approach. One tribe thinks that everything must be inspired by nature, and another tribe thinks that everything must be inspired by mechanical gadgets, or the looks of mechanical things. Why? Why must it be all one or the other? Why can't you enjoy it, or be inspired, or refreshed, or whatever you want to call it, with more than one kind of idea? Today, Phil Welch told me, after his famous quiz, several people had listed me as being basically influenced by nature. He asked me if that were true? I had a hard time answering him, because I don't know whether it is true. If I am, it sort of slipped in on me somehow. It is true that I have a great love for nature, and I have been refreshed, if you want to put it that way, by nature, and I still am. I enjoy it tremendously, and I enjoy the wonderful things that have been done with nature as inspiration. The music of Debussy and great Japanese art, and Mr. Wright's thinking about organic architecture, and so on. I can see all of that pretty well and I can go along with it. I don't rebel against it or think it is wrong or right, or anything. It seems perfectly logical and fine. Whether it's basic with me or not I don't know. Maybe it is. Still, I can go see the pseudotechnical movies like the *War of the Worlds* and all that sort of thing, and I can get a bang out of such things. I can enjoy all that, too. I can see a great deal of beauty in cross sections of motors and in power booster stations, insulators, ventilators, and all kinds of things like that. I can enjoy them, too. I can't see why if I can enjoy one I can't the other. On the other hand, why should I be satisfied, or content, with just trying to understand those two seemingly opposite ideas.

Why not keep looking for some other ideas, too? There, I think, is the only way we can have something to offer as individuals instead of a reevaluation, or reinterpretation, of something already very familiar. We can reevaluate the same old principles, and we can do a lot that is new and different that way. But if we can find some new principles, some new ideas to work for, some new inspirations that are not cliche, or not timeworn, you might say, then I think we are ready to make a very big step. Maybe too big a step to make all at once. Maybe we have to slip up on it gradually. In making a big step of that sort I don't think it means that we renounce, in any way, what we already know, or what is good in what has been done, or what is being done. I don't think it invalidates that at all. Seems to me that just because we like roast beef is no reason to say ham is no good. Why couldn't we find some new kind of food that we have never tasted. Wouldn't that be interesting? Something new.

In thinking of principles, we usually dedicate our lives to one or two basic ones. We can say that the organic principle is the only principle worth working with, or we can say, as Mies does, that the inorganic principle is the one. We can take either side, can't we? Or we can say they are both right, if the two opposite ideas exist in the same thing. What is synthetic and what is inorganic is right along with what is organic. We can understand them as part of the same thing, which would be one way of looking at it, or reevaluating those two ideas. Or we could say are those the only two principles that we can create with, or are there others? Are there others that maybe already exist that are different from those two approaches? Are those the only two approaches? Can we find, in what we already know as principles, any other way? I think we should try, and if we can't find another way, maybe we can invent one.

I don't think there is very much invention going on. Most people working in art are content to follow the leader and to work within the framework of inventions already established. Of course, you could say why keep striving for something different? Why not try to perfect what we already have? Why keep straining at the leash and seeking something that is only ephemeral, or a shadow, or maybe not even that? Why do we want something else? Well, I think we have to feel a need for change. In order to change, you have to need to change. You can't change by keeping on doing the same things or thinking the same ways.

I find myself, even with this desire ever present, always apt to drift into accepting things that I like very much as art. I like oriental art tremendously, and I like to have it around me, but I don't think I should. I would prefer to have it where I could look at it and be refreshed by it, but I don't think that I should be living in an oriental art museum. I think that I need art around me that is as forward-looking and as far-seeking as I want my own work to be. I think that I should strive to live that way myself. I find it a real battle, because so much of what I like is something that is already established.

In music, I admire Debussy tremendously, as you know. Still I keep wanting to hear new things, hoping that somewhere, someone is finding something as new for now, as Debussy did for his time. That doesn't mean that Debussy is no longer valid. It doesn't mean that what the Egyptians did is no longer valid. Everything that has been done that has real authority is still valid, but not in the same way as when it was created. The original meaning, the reason for it is gone, but something exists, something has filtered down through us, through time, which represents more than maybe what the artist intended, what he realized he was doing. We begin to read other things into it, and meanings change. The reasons seem to change for why we like it. The feeling of mystery we get out of an Egyptian sculpture is not, I am sure, the feeling the sculptor had when he did it. I think he had quite a different feeling about the mystery in it. Our reaction is colored through maybe ignorance, or glamorized because it is remote from us in time, or other factors that enter into it, or because of things that we have learned since then. We keep reevaluating the past through history. We try to understand it in our own way always. That is why our notion of any culture of the past is different, I am sure, from the notion held a hundred years ago, even though they had the same facts at their disposal. Their attitude toward it would be quite different from ours, because we are looking for something different in history now. I think that this new sensation that we are after, this new experience, this new change, is necessarily related with all the new changes that have gone on in the past.

The feeling of the need for change has always existed; we would be back in the caves if someone hadn't felt the need for change. Maybe we would have been better off, I don't know; I can't argue that point because I have never lived in a cave. I think that we do maintain a tradition, probably one of the greatest traditions, in our desire for change. That is what keeps things from stagnating and growing stale. It's what keeps art alive. The minute that it ceases to change it gets overripe, decadent, ingrown, looses its vitality. Someone has to come along and upset the applecart all over again so we can have a fresh breath of air in art. That doesn't mean we can't enjoy what has been done, of course. But "what has been done" is ever changing, too, through time, because of our attitude toward it. We are recreating the past in the light of the present, always. When we listen to old music, we are not hearing it as they did. We are hearing it as we hear it, and that is quite different. So we are recreating the old music when we hear it. We are recreating the old buildings when we look at them. We are recreating the old literature when we read it. A lot of what was in it originally, the core of it, is still there in substance, of course. Our understanding of it is changing, is what I mean to say. It is always changing.

Are we going to be content with just understanding what has been done and what is being done? Or are we looking for this new sensation? If you know the story by Pierre Louis called "The New Sensation," and I hope if you haven't read it you will, you will remember the author was feeling rather despondent, sitting alone in his room one evening, when suddenly he heard a noise in back of him and he turned around. Here was an Egyptian lady, a very beautiful Egyptian queen who appeared out of the past, quite impossibly. They got to talking and she was deriding our time in comparison with her time. He felt the necessity to defend our time. They got into an argument. Everything he would point out as a sign of progress, or change, or something better than the Egyptians had, she was able to counteract it with something else that showed they had something even more superior than whatever we think is so great. Finally he decided he had a trump card, that there was one thing we certainly knew more about than the Egyptians, and that was love. But she convinced him that that was wrong. Then he admitted his defeat and decided the only recourse was to light up a cigarette, just as we usually do. He lit up his cigarette, and she said, "What is that?" He told her it was a cigarette. She asked, "What is a cigarette?" He gave her a drag on it and she lit up and said, "Ah, this is indeed a new sensation." That makes you wonder, is that all our time has to offer?

Not long ago I was given a Japanese print rolled up in a tube; some of you have seen it in my office. It was a nice looking tube, obviously Japanese in design, and I pulled the lid off of it and looked inside and it said Blatz Beer. It was made from an old G.I. beer can, I imagine, although they had transformed it. Is that what our civilization is? Is that our change? Someday we may have museums with collections of different beer cans showing the different varieties, or something like that. Seriously, I am convinced we have a lot more than the design of our beer cans to offer.

I think that we have not even started yet in architecture, because I don't think we have ever had an architect. I know that is sacrilege, but with all due respect to the living and the dead, I don't believe we have ever had an architect, yet. The reason I say that is because to me an architect would be a person who would have full command of all his resources, meaning everything he needs to exercise his art. The architect should not have to depend on someone else to orchestrate his idea. A composer who is a great composer doesn't have to hire someone to do orchestration, does he—

unless he is Irving Berlin. If he is a really great composer, he would know how to orchestrate his music. He would know how to invent new kinds of approaches to sound and would be reevaluating ideas of the old instruments, thinking up new ways to make sound, and new possibilities out of the means that we have today or that we can develop. He would not depend on someone else to do those things. He would know how himself. He would know how to get the job done. He would know how to write it down in some way that other people could understand it, and he would know how to see it executed, or get it done, and he would know what it would be like when it was done. He would have complete control of the operation all the way through.

Now architecture is such a vast field that we are inclined, we of the older generation, including most of the young people, to say it is too much for one person to master. We can consider architecture as a big idea, as a great big circle, or sphere, if you want to get three dimensional about this, and we are in the middle of it. Within this sphere is a field that has to do with structure to make things stand up. There is a field that has to do with aesthetics and design, and a field here with specifications and working drawings, and all the other gore that goes along with architecture. We would say, how could anyone be a master of all of this. It is too much; we have to specialize. In this day and age we do specialize a great deal in principles, and we specialize in practically everything. We are specialists indeed. I think to be a complete architect we would have to have command of all these resources. Whether we actually had the time to execute all of it or not is another matter. Probably, if we didn't try so much, and tried to do what we did do better, we would have a little more time to do it. Eventually, we could develop enough architects so that no one of us would have to do so many things, but could concentrate on doing a few things well. I hope that day will come sometime. As it is, there isn't time to move at the pace we have to move, and to do all the things that we should do in a building, even if we could. The point is that we should be able to do all these things. If we were a great architect I think we can be even greater, because we would be able to do all these things. You can say it isn't necessary to know how to figure structure, but you can have a feeling for structure. That's true; nowadays that is probably true. You can say it isn't necessary to know all the details we go through in the Architecture 273 design course to know how to design something, that you use your feelings, and you will automatically come out with something pretty good, even if you don't know what overlapping counterpoint is, or something like that. Your feeling is the safest thing to rely on, and I think it is the one quality that we have that is really our own, and that can be our own if it is our own feeling, of course. If we are not borrowing our feeling, too. In realizing this feeling, in putting it into practice, we go through the mechanics, or the physical means to give it real substance.

I think that the more we can know about the science of design, or the science of structure, or the science of anything or the technology of it, or the ways we can realize it, the better, although we shouldn't let that be an end in itself, but consider it a means to an end. There is the danger, of course, that a technician can be just a technician if he doesn't know what to do with what he knows. If he considers that particular speciality as an end in itself, he is sunk, whether he is a designer of aesthetic matters, or a designer of some other kind of matters. He can't let it stay just that way. If this idea were applied to all the great architects we have known in the past, I don't think any of them could qualify. They could be very highly rated in certain fields and in other fields they would be weak. Even in the fields they are not great in, maybe through feeling or intuition, they can create situations which can be analyzed and proven later somehow. It seems to me that the great architects would be even greater in their work if they were thoroughly conscious of the means and if they were aware of the possibilities—not the possibilities as they . . . they have been accomplished, but the possibilities that haven't been accomplished: the unknowns. I think that the more we would know about any technology, if we use it as a means to an end, the more it would awaken within us, as creative artists, the ways and means to express this new technology through our work. That's why I think we must always be seeking even if we don't know the answers. If we don't know enough about how things can be done, the next best thing is our intuition. I would rather have both intuition and really know, too. For many years I have been working with design: you might say I have been specializing in design. Someone once gave me a great compliment, or he thought he did, when he said, "You have design by the tail." I don't know if that was a great compliment, but I don't feel that way. I don't think I know all there is to know about design; I don't think that anyone does. In fact, I can go along with what many other people say, "The more you know about something, the more you know you don't know." The more you realize what there is to know, the more hopeful it becomes that someday you will discover, or invent, some of the things that need to be done, as potential, or possibilities, which will be probabilities or actualities through our efforts.

I do know that for many years I worked with design intuitively. I have a strong intuition so I stumbled onto a few things; I lucked onto a few things, but I still believe in intuition, too. I know through my own experience that I can save lots of time, lots of lost motion, lots of unfortunate mistakes; I may be making others, but at least I can avoid a lot of what is called trial and error the more I know about design and the way it works. The more scientifically I can regard design as the ways and means of doing something the more it saves me from resorting to trial and error as a result of just intuition. I think the same thing can be said about what you know about structure or anything else. It is much better to know than it is to guess, or to feel your way along without knowing. I think feeling is of prime importance. In understanding and attempting to understand the science of design, I would say that that is just as worthless as understanding the science of structure, or anything else, if it isn't used as a manifestation of your feeling. That is always necessary; that is the driving force that will make it come about.

In thinking again about something new and different, if we feel the need for change, I think we should change. If we don't feel the need for change, I don't see any reason why we should. I think that some of us will naturally be content to work along with what is already known. Just like Mr. Elmslie worked along with what was already known by Wright, Sullivan, and other people—and he did a very fine job within those limits. I am not trying to belittle Mr. Elmslies. I think there is a place for Mr. Elmslies in any kind of work. I also think that those of us who feel the need for doing something new and different should really do something new and different and not just be satisfied with what was new and different. It is amazing to me how much stuff we think is new and different now is really old hat. Every once in a while, when students are looking through old magazines, or old books, and they see something in the way of a painting, or a building, or something done thirty years ago, it surprises them a great deal how much it is like some of our students' designs here in the School of Architecture. It would be better to say how much our stuff is like the work in the old magazines and books.

We are considered an art nouveau school by many people. How many of you know what art nouveau is? I think some of you have been through it a little bit; you have had it some in different ways. I think there is such a thing as arriving at similar results because of needs. Two Englishmen were here not long ago and they wanted to write an article for a magazine in England on this school as an art nouveau school. They thought that that was our guiding principle here. I wouldn't say it, but I think they are going to say it anyway. I am sure that they are sold on the idea and they are stuck with it. Well, if they call something [that is] New and Different, art nouveau, we are guilty, of course. And we are guilty of not being New and Different, too, in many ways.

When we look at things, what is there really new about them? What is fresh? What is it that stays fresh over hundreds of years? I think it is only the great works of art that had freshness in them to start with, that retain their freshness. Just as Mr. Wright, who has always been young, is still young. The reason he is young is because he has always been young and he has never grown up in one sense; he has stayed a boy hasn't he? That is wonderful. He is still fresh as a person, he is still interesting. I think in art it is the same way. The great art of the past and the great art of the present does have the quality of freshness. The reason it is fresh is because it is not warmed over. It is something that has something to say that hasn't already been said. That doesn't mean what we are going to say is any better, or any worse, than what has been said. I don't think we need to regard it that way, we can regard it as our own statement and it can have whatever values, or principles, we have, or should have, or seek. It certainly isn't going to be fresh unless we try and make it fresh. It is going to have to be a conscious effort because more now than ever people are too wise—there is too much knowledge floating about. It is too easy to find out things. It used to be more natural for people to be fresh and different because they didn't know what was going on some place else. I doubt very much if the American Indian, when he evolved the tepee, had any idea of what was going on in Greece, or some other place. He probably wasn't even concerned about that; he was trying to work out something himself. Now it would be awfully hard for an Indian to design a tepee because he would know too many other things, too many other ways to do it. He would probably be very confused and he probably would not be able to design a tepee, you see.

We can look upon the spreading of knowledge as a great thing, and I think it is. It also carries along with it a by-product of obscuring our vision and reason by confronting us with so many principles and so many realizations of principles. And it is complicated by time factors, such as past, present, and future . . . so that we are apt to be thoroughly confused and not speaking our own language. Well, you could say, should we speak our own language, or should we be seeking an Esperanto in design. Should we give up all this idea of trying to be New and Different as individuals and just swim along with this big current of universal knowledge that is being compiled. It seems to me we have the two opposite ways of doing, which may be the same thing in one sense, too. We can drift along with the tide and try to find something in all this confusion. Or we can take stands as individuals and try to establish ideas, or invent ideas, that are so strong that they will change all of this tide, just the same as they have in the past in the same way. Think how little has been done really in architecture, anywhere, when you consider how much building is going on. Still, the little bit that has been done, that has become architecture, has changed many things because of its great influence and great power. If we do take a stand in our way, as Wright calls it, "Truth against the world," just as he took a stand, or Sullivan took one, or anyone took one, we are going to have to have something to offer. We can't do it just by waving the same flag. We are going to have to really have the goods. Maybe our little pebble isn't much of a pebble, but if it is really a pebble it will cause a big series of repercussions all through the world, just the same as they always have. But it takes more to do it all the time. And it takes a lot better sense of balance and orientation on our part as artists all the time in order to not be bewildered, or befuddled, or confused with all the tremendous amount of knowledge that is floating around. That doesn't mean we should remain ignorant of it. I think it is all the more necessary that we know it, and that we know who our enemies are, that we know who our friends are, that we know the principles that we can consider beneficial to us in any kind of thing. I am not complaining about the universality of knowledge; in fact, I welcome it and I am hoping it will lead to an enlightened age, instead of one of confusion. I believe that the only way it can be beneficial will be for us to attempt to assimilate it more and more within ourselves. It isn't enough for the scientists to get off in a little place by themselves and say, "Everything is Science," and it isn't enough for the artists to get off in a little place by themselves and say, "Everything is Art." I think the scientists need to know something about art and the artists need to know something about science. We still need to keep our head above water, and keep our bearings, and our sense of direction, and to remember that feeling, after all, is the paramount thing that we need to make it valid.

The artist, and the architect, is going to have to be a bigger person than has ever existed, because he is dealing with a subject that is bigger than it ever has been in the past. It keeps increasing in scope all the time. The architect is going to have to keep increasing in scope, too, in order to handle this problem, this art, and to know why he is doing what he is doing. He can't consider any part of it as a separate thing, or something that is a speciality. None of it is a speciality in the completed work, is it? It shouldn't be anyway. The structure shouldn't be the speciality, or the design shouldn't be the speciality. No part of it should be apart from the rest or it would be lopsided. So this superman who is going to do all this is—the architect that we all have to try to become. Some of us can become that architect more easily than others. Maybe no one will ever become such a superman, I don't know, for it is an awfully big order. Particularly for those of us who have been working with it. Those of you who are just starting have that opportunity, and probably you will be able to do more with it—it is potentially possible.

Not very long ago, I was severely criticized by another architect because he said that I always looked on each design problem as an opportunity, and he thought an architect should look upon each design problem as an obligation. Where could you draw the line? I regard it as an obligation, too—obligation to architecture, as an idea. A big abstract idea that is out there apart from any of us. Architecture is no one's property. The idea that architecture is something bigger than anyone who has ever lived—something that is completely impersonal until we make it personal. The same with the idea of music, or the idea of literature. We are only very small fry, even the biggest, in regard to that idea. That idea is only small fry in regard to larger ideas that encompass those.

Why shouldn't we regard opportunity and obligation together instead of separately? Of course I regard it as an opportunity. I think even a hot-dog stand is an opportunity. Anything that we do is an opportunity. Any kind of problem. And an obligation, too. In order for it to be an opportunity, don't we have to consider it as something new, and fresh, and different in our approach to make it valid. Are we going to be satisfied with doing something that is already done? We could say we could do it about like something already done, only try and do it better. That is alright for the people who can't do any more. But those of you who could do more, why settle for less? We have people here in school who can do more than that, I don't say all of you can. Maybe in the whole school of two hundred and fifty there would be twelve who could do more. That is a high percentage. Maybe you are one of them. If you are not, don't feel bad because there is plenty of room for the person who can do something better than is already done. That is nothing small either. That's a big field right there. I think there is no disgrace is doing that; in fact maybe that is what constitutes the bulk of our civilization, or culture, as Mr. Wright would call it.

If you have a time that is really cultured, you will have many people, many artists, trying to do things better that are already known. You will always have the advanced artist seeking to kick over all traces and to stretch the limits further. There are always exceptions and always a minority, and probably always will be. I hate to think that there would ever be a time when we wouldn't have such people.

Wouldn't it be awful if the world could be just the way we want it? If it could stay that way; if everyone liked what we liked and no one would ever change it; wouldn't that be terrible? Have you ever stopped to think how awful that would be? We keep working all the time, hoping for some kind of nirvana that would produce an ideal world where everyone would think and feel as we do. Actually it would be deadly. The fact that we can always know there is an escape valve in any civilization, or culture, that it does not stop any place, and it continues, there is no beginning, and no ending. There is always a constant, ever changing flow, the "continuous present," as Gertrude Stein says. Something always happening, something always able to happen. I think that is very encouraging, very inspiring, and I don't mean, as I said before, to belittle in any way what has been done or what is being done. It is all very important as part of this. The thing that interests us the most is discovering something new, something that has freshness. I think for that reason we are going to have to try to develop a very self-conscious attitude towards habits, mannerisms, and cliches. Check our work all the time for that. That doesn't mean that because someone is using a dome they can't use it because domes have already been used. That's foolish. Are we using the dome in any way that is our own, or are we just trying to imitate someone else's dome. That is the important thing. Can we come up with a dome that is our own, like Bucky Fuller has? Whether it is his own or not I don't know, but at least he is getting credit for having his own private little dome. I think if any of you can come up with a dome that is not like his, or anything seen on land, or sea, why not, if you want a dome. If you want what a dome will do, do your own dome if you can. Why be stuck with doing a dome, unless that is the only reasonable way you feel about your design. Why accept it so easily that that's the thing to do just because it is easy to take your compass and run a ring on paper.

Aren't we pretty much slaves of our means, just as the artists of the immediate past have been? Don't the buildings that we design here in school look pretty much like a drawing, pretty often? Or a model, pretty often? How do you design? Do you design with elevations, a perspective, or models? Or do you design through the quality of drawing? All of those can lead to cliches, too. They all have their own private dangers, too. For instance, some people find it much easier to design with elevations, but they are apt to fall into the peril of designing two-dimensionally. Some think you should design with floor plans, and extrude them. That has a danger of designing two-dimensionally, also. Some say we should design with perspective, that shows the thing three-dimensionally. True, but only from one point of view at a time. Are we really thinking about how it looks from other points of view? Some say the only safe thing to do is to design with models, because only through models can you see it as a whole. There is a big danger there in the problem of scale, and you can fool yourself very easily. We have buildings now that have modelitis and moduleitis, just the same as we used to have elevationitis and planitis, you see. Those are only ways of putting in a tangible form what we have in mind, so that someone else can understand it. Another way they can be regarded is as a way to test what we have in mind, to verify it, or to see what we are doing. Of course, we are apt to change what we are doing in the course of that because maybe possibilities will crop up that we hadn't anticipated. Sometimes bad and sometimes good.

The thing that I wanted to say is, in using T squares and triangles and compasses, think how that still affects us a great deal. How easy it is to hook a line across the page with a T square or slide a vertical up on a triangle. Or, if we want something going around this way we use a compass. Is it what we really want, or is it just an approximate, easy-to-get way to do something, you see? Do we really want a circle, or do we want something that isn't a circle at all? It might have a form that isn't a square, or rectangle, or triangle, maybe not a circle, either, but maybe circle is the easiest thing to hit upon. So we do a circle. I think we sell ourselves down the river, all the way along the line, when we go to use our tools to work with. I am not saying we shouldn't use circles, triangles, squares. Any of those are perfectly good and legitimate means, and always will be. There is lots to be discovered in them yet. But are you always trying to accept what they will do as the only way in trying to think of something New and Different. Are you going to depend on the means all the time? The means will have to be considered, naturally, as part of it. But what does architecture have to do really, this big idea of architecture that is impersonal, with squares, triangles, circles, T squares, compasses, and tracing paper, and all that. Those are only little bits of means to work with. It isn't the matter of free form, it isn't the matter of geometry, it isn't the matter of whether you draw it free hand, or whether you draw it with instruments, or whether you make models. What is it? It is the matter of idea, isn't it? An awful lot can be done without any idea at all, as you know. It is easy. Especially if you put good matte on it. That does wonders.

When you see problems displayed out here in the architectural school's display area, ask yourself what is the idea of it? What are they trying to do? What are you trying to do besides just solve the problem? How are you trying to solve it and what idea are you using? What are you striving for in solving the problem? What is this thing that is the generating force of what you are doing? I think that is where almost all of us fall down on doing something fresh and New and Different. Lots of time the ideas are hand-me-down. We can dress it up in a different face; we can put a different kind of clothing on; we can use a circle instead of a square, or something like that; or we can put a wiggly line around it and call it a free form. But lots of times it's the same old thing inside, or maybe nothing's inside. Lots of time we are just going though the motions when we compose things. Maybe we are experts; we can do a very creditable job of putting together things that are not doing anything at all. I know lots of art that you can almost respect because it has been so skillfully put together. Many symphonies are very beautifully constructed, but often without any real idea. Debussy said, "Most symphonies are made of themes one heard as a child, and when we knock on the door we find nobody home." I think there is an awful lot of lost motion going on in art all the time. Too many people painting in the manner of, too many people doing buildings in the manner of, too many people trying to remember what has been done or what is being done. I don't think we are one bit ahead of the eclectics of the past who used to try to do a good crib on Greece or Rome or Gothic or some other place. If we ourselves are casting about for an anchor somewhere, something that we already know that has been pretty good stuff, something we accept, as a place to tie our wagon to, aren't we doing the same thing, even if it does have a new look? If it doesn't have a genuine idea, that is a real idea of our own, it still has no authority or validity, really. It is an also-ran. Even in the best examples.

I hope we are not too easily satisfied. I hope we can really live up to our reputation here for doing something strange and New and Different. Not to be strange, just as a name,

because that will never work. What you do if you do something that we are talking about here, having an idea of your
own, will naturally seem strange. That will be a natural
by-product of it.

At least at first.

Four

Honesty in Architecture

Tonight I want to talk about something I think concerns us all a great deal and gives many of us added pain to our growing pains. It has to do with honesty—honesty as applied to architecture particularly. We don't want to think of honesty too self-consciously, but to know it and to feel it automatically or intuitively or as a part of what we do, rather than as a self-conscious effort.

To start with, then, we say that honesty in architecture has to do with truth, doesn't it? As near as we can understand truth. What truth is may be questionable, too, because there is a great deal of argument about what is true and what isn't. Different people would naturally come up with different ideas about that. As a general center line, or as something to guide us and help us along the way, we will say we wish to be truthful in architectural design all the way through the design.

This lecture was the first in a series of two major presentations made to the School of Architecture in October 1953 in an effort to encourage creative individual design. In this first presentation (October 7) Goff developed the concept of honesty in architectural design: honesty in principles, in structure, in circulation, in materials, in the way the design fits into the community, and in the way we ourselves feel. Goff's direct, individual approach is as important today as it was in his own time.

Truthful in structure, truthful in circulation, truthful in the use of materials, the way we apply principles, and the way we feel about it ourselves, the way it fits into our community, and other people's way of living. That is a big order, isn't it?

Truth and honesty, I guess, go right along together. Of course, you could be honest about something that wasn't true, too. Usually we like to think we are being honest about the truth. I think the big mistake we make is when we say "the Truth" because there seems to be more than one, which confuses the issue considerably.

I think in design particularly we need to approach our problem from many ways. To think about it quite a lot, to draw quite a lot toward the solution. Debussy said, "How much we must first discover and then reject to arrive at the naked truth of inspiration." First of all, that implies that we need to discover many things first, doesn't it? We can't just sit around and wait for this naked truth of inspiration, but we are going to have to think and act many ways to find it. In design particularly we need to approach our problem from many ways. I think there is a tendency in our school to feel each line is solid gold and we must not waste it. We must hold back till we've got this naked truth right in our head and then do it. It seems to me that is something that you learn by doing.

Stravinsky for instance has said, "I work a little every day, and it isn't always gold, or truth, or honesty." He works a little every day, keeps his technique up, and every once in awhile when he does have a flash it comes out well, because his technical ability is able to cope with it with his experience and practice. Also, by actually doing, sometimes we find truth in doing something, providing we have approached it honestly in our effort. When we approach a problem then with the idea of trying ideas, don't be afraid to discard ideas and don't be afraid to give them up. I know it is hard sometimes, especially if you like some feature about the design. You should be able to sit down and draw hundreds of solutions to any problem you have and not remember a single one of them, but be able to start all over and approach the problem honestly each time and come out with a different answer. I think you can, if you don't try to remember.

In this process of trying things and discarding we eliminate a great deal that is dishonest or untruthful. We begin to separate the wheat from the chaff and then we begin to realize that a truth is beginning to come out of this solution. If you want to approach the problem honestly, to arrive at a truth in design, you could say, "Well, I want the orientation to be honest. I want it to be facing the right way for the view or the sun," or whatever is around it with respect to physical conditions. That would be an honest approach for access, for arriving at this place. How would you normally arrive? Or you could say let's design this plan all the way through to arrive at some effect. I think that would be dishonest, providing you forced it to the point where it was unreasonable. Now I don't mean to assume a holy attitude with a halo and say that we must never force a design or that we must never tell a little white lie. The truth is a desirable principle in everyday living. I think we all agree that truth is something we should strive for and we should desire, but sometimes truth hurts constructively or destructively. Sometimes the worst thing you can do is to tell the truth no matter how right the principle is in real life. Sometimes it would be an inhumane act to tell the truth. Sometimes a white lie is much more constructive and closer to the truth in the end. I am not recommending we all turn out to be liars either. I am saying that there is a matter of adjustment and common sense, horse sense, or whatever you want to call it: a reason that tempers this thing we call truth and honesty. We have to take that into account when we are dealing with this subject.

It may be very true that a design someone makes is pretty bad, but if your saying that is going to discourage

the student to the point where he would never be able to
do anything else and give him an inferiority complex and
make him feel absolutely useless, then it would be a very
cruel thing to say. I think that we can deal with the subject and get the student to realize what is not so good, and
still extend some hope without coming right out and ly-
ing about it or without glossing it over either. In the matter
of dealing with materials, structure, or any of these things
in a building, there are times when you have to rob Peter
to pay Paul. Sometimes, because there are so many factors
that have to get along with each other, we have to give the
right-of-way to some things, give preference to some things
rather than others. That is where our judgment has to come
into play; where we draw the line and it is pretty much
where we wish to draw it, too, whether we are going to say
that circulation takes precedence over regular construction
or something like that. If we allowed everything in a building to be done in the way that each person connected to the
building would feel it was the truth, we probably wouldn't
be able to get into it, because there would be no one deciding where the truth should be used and just how much of
the truth should be used, and just how honest each phase
of the building should be.

I think we have to be the policeman, in a way. The architect is sort of the policeman to all of this. He has to decide
when he is going to let a little white lie come into his building and when he is going to demand absolute honesty and
truth. We say for instance we want to be truthful with materials. We want a brick to be a brick and a board to be a
board and a cement block to be a block and all that stuff.
Sure we do, but that isn't enough. It has to be a lot more
than that if it is going to be architecture, because we would
expect that in just a good building. That would be part of

being a good building, but the truth would be more than that, wouldn't it? The honest use of the material might stop with that: you could use brick honestly, or you could force it to a way that it wouldn't be an honest use of brick. To arrive at truth through honesty, then, I think you would have to have a little more than that. You would have to have something that would transcend the nature of the materials. It would have to have the nature of the material, but it would have to go way beyond it as it does in the finest architecture. We are not so concerned after all with honesty in the final result. It is a good yardstick to measure things with, but we don't think of that at first, usually, when we are looking at a fine piece of architecture. We are not so conscious of this as a brick or that as a board. It is taken for granted. It should be taken for granted that that's part of it, that's part of the whole thing. We expect more than that, just as we expect more than that in a person. It isn't enough that someone is an honest person. We hope they are, but we want them to be more than just that, don't we? A person can be very honest and still be very dull, very uninteresting. Sometimes a crook is a lot more interesting. Sometimes a person who is honest through the use of a material or a structural system or anything can honestly apply his talent where the truth of all this transcends the physical limitation of honesty, we might say. Then we arrive at something that is closer to architecture with a capital *A*.

You could argue, for instance, that architecture is impure because it is solving so many problems, physical problems, utilitarian problems; that it is handicapped by being alloyed with so many extraneous and extracurricular ideas that as an art it's impure no matter how honestly all of this is used. If you compared it with music, say, music can be directly expressive without having to represent anything or without having to serve a utilitarian purpose. It is easier for a composer of music to arrive at something that transcends the fact that this is being played by a tuba or a French horn or a flute. Who cares when we hear the *Prelude to the Afternoon of a Faun* whether it is a flute playing, the first cello, or whether it is a clarinet? That doesn't matter. To the musicians it would, of course, but to those of us who listen to enjoy it, we are satisfied, we have the feeling that the instruments are used truthfully, honestly, and that they are directed by feeling. We are not so worried about whether it is honest or truthful in expressing the nature of the flute so much as we are at our capacity to feel along with the music and to react to this thing that transcends the fact that it is played on instruments by people and that it is written down with little black notes on a piece of paper.

I think that you could have in architecture the idea that architecture would be a pure art, you might say, where it existed primarily for architecture. Not to solve problems. Not to symbolize the struggle between crude and refined oil or the fallen dead of some war. Not to glorify anyone, even the architect. Not to serve any purpose except to let people understand architecture in the sense that it would not be tied to any kind of utilitarianism. Then you could argue: Is that Architecture, or would it be sculpture? Of course there is a fine line to draw there. I am not saying we should all forget solving problems now, that we should all rush out and try to build beautiful things that do not serve any purpose except for the enjoyment we get out of them. I am saying that architecture, as we understand it today, is using all these other things and depending on them, even honestly. It could be argued that it is not being quite truthful to the art in the sense that painting, music and some other arts might be. At present we work within these practical limits and accept the limits in order to work. I think that some day we will have architects who can create great architecture without having to represent anything with it or having to use it, but create it just for the enjoyment of being around it, and in it, and with it, and so on. The pleasure that we would receive from this experience is very much the same feeling we can get from music.

Today we need to solve problems honestly with what we have to work with. I think that many times we bend over backwards trying to be honest, as we say, trying to limit ourselves to things we feel are honest without realizing honesty in a bigger sense. We may be very honest with a board as a board, but are we honest with the board as something else? Does our honesty stop being honest with the board, or does it use that as a means to an end? Does it become a part of something that is so much more important that it transcends it and you don't even have to think of that—you would take for granted that it is.

I think that most of our architecture of recent years is dishonest basically because it doesn't start from any genuine impulse. Too much of it arrives from copying things or trying to get into the swing of things, whether you get it out of a magazine or whether you imitate something here in the school. No matter where you lift it, if you are just doing something to be fashionable, something to please someone who doesn't know anything about it, then I think you are pretty apt to be dishonest about it, or at least not as honest as you could be. I think that one reason for a lot of this dishonesty is a lack of knowledge on the part of the architect, the lack of having any faith or feeling of security in himself because he doesn't know enough about structure, or about materials, or about aesthetics to feel safe. He has to rely on other people's feelings and ideas in order to hide his ignorance, and that means lifting something that others have done. I am not blaming him, because that is the way most people have been brought up and I doubt if they think of it as anything dishonest. We think of eclecticism here in this school pretty much as something dishonest, but eclecticism to many people is a virtue rather than a vice. They think of it as a way of showing your good taste—knowing what to select from what has been done. They wouldn't feel dishonest about it at all. In fact, they would argue with you that it is better to use someone else's good taste than their own bad taste. But, of course, that would be assuming that they wouldn't be able to have good taste.

As an example, let us look back at the first skyscraper in this country. Here the architects were forced to deal with a problem they hadn't before: a tall building for commercial purposes that couldn't symbolize anything religious and couldn't be a government building with big important flights of steps. It was right on the ground, usually, and they had to give this idea architectural expression.

Well, of course, you know what happened. The architects had to clothe this frame that the engineers had evolved; the architects had not evolved it. The plumbers had to invent ways to get plumbing up, and the heat up, and all of this. The architects were caught literally with their culture down; they didn't know what to do. The only thing they could do was to look into the past and see if there wasn't something they could borrow to put on this thing, this big ugly frame that was going up like a grid. The grid was just a series of post-and-lintel constructions out of steel or concrete, after they got away from the wall-bearing system. It seemed ugly to the people who were high in aesthetic places. They had no aesthetic to comprehend this sort of thing. They had to cover it up very quickly. The only way they knew to cover it up was to adapt things that had already been done.

As you know, the first examples were layers of different Greek Orders, one above the other, more or less like a club sandwich. If it was a three-story building, you could have an order at the bottom, maybe Doric, and then an Ionic Order, and then a Corinthian Order at the top. There were only five so-called Greek Orders, so they couldn't go more than five stories that way. Then someone hit on the brilliant idea of making each Order more than one story and that was good for about three or four stories. Then they could work that awhile and have a real club sandwich out of the thing. They could put a cornice on top and finish it all off in good style, and punch holes in between the columns. It seems utterly ridiculous to us, but there they are staring us in the face in many big cities.

Now, after awhile, even those people began to realize how junky it looked, and it cost too much besides, because these were for commercial purposes. Then someone had a real brainstorm and took out all the Orders in between the top one and the bottom one and had a brick wall punched full of holes. They had an Order down at the bottom where everyone could see it, and they had one up at the top that stuck up above the other buildings. It never got around the corner hardly ever, but at least from some view you could see it. This capped it all off; this idea of the three parts— the base, the superstructure, and the entablature—came through again in that way. There was hardly any recognition of the frame or where the bones in the building happened to be or that it even had any. It was just a facade, just a fa- cial, and pretty bad. The architects were actually ashamed of the height of the buildings; they seemed awkward to them. They had no way to cope with this problem aesthetically.

Till Sullivan came along, and he said that all this rising up, this tremendous growth that was going on in Chicago and the Midwest, was the expression of democracy in building, and that the architects should recognize this honestly and be more truthful by trying to accentuate this growth, this rising spirit that was showing literally through the design of the building, by trying to get the feeling of growth in the design. Instead of being ashamed of the height of the building, they should accentuate it by putting great emphasis on the vertical aspect of the design. Sullivan did this in the Wainwright Building, which you know—the first example of a building to stress the verticality of the tall building in its design.

He didn't do that quite honestly in the building if you want to be actually truthful about this thing, because he didn't follow the structure of the building quite as frankly as he might have. For one thing he had this regular rhythm set up of piers and mullions alternating. Every other pier is a mullion. Still, they were expressed the same in the design of the main shaft, the same width and the same depth. The base was more truthful, more expressive of where the frame was within, of the bones within. When he got up into the shaft of the building, he was more concerned with the soaring effect and the regular rhythm of it than he was whether this was a column and this a mullion, you see.

Then, of course, there is still a sense of base, superstructure, and entablature in the design from the classical models of form. There was also the big heavy corner to stop the march of verticals that were going around on the sides and to terminate the side elevations. So we still have part of something old there; it isn't nearly so revolutionary to us now as it was then. The floors of the building are minimized in expression by setting the spandrels back of the piers and by ornamenting them very heavily so that they cast deep shadows which give a dark effect that will correspond to the dark effect of the windows. This accentuates the vertical piers. So that isn't quite so truthful either, is it? In other words instead of showing us where the floors are, there is more the sense that it is all one big thing there. If we wanted to, we could be very puritanical about this and say that every floor level and every column should be expressed through the design. But there was something that transcended these flaws, if we think of these as flaws in our argument about honesty, and something that makes you forget those little white lies because it adds up to something a whole lot more than that. Even looking at the building today, with that in mind, you can't help but be moved by it as architecture. It is still the most beautiful building in St. Louis, even if some of the new buildings do show where the columns and the floor slabs are. It takes a little more than just being true.

Sullivan himself felt that he wasn't saying what was true and he kept searching and kept trying ideas and discarding them to arrive at the naked truth of inspiration. He tried all sorts of things. He tried in the Condict Building in New York, for example, to show the piers, or the structural vertical members, by emphasizing them in width and making the mullions for the windows smaller, while still setting the spandrels back between the windows, and minimizing the floor heights again in order to accentuate the vertical effect of the design. He was a little closer to showing what actually goes on there, but he wasn't satisfied even with that. He still was trying ideas and discarding them.

Sullivan tried again in the Carson Pirie Scott Building in Chicago, where he finally came to grips with the real problem of the cage. The vertical elements are clearly expressed through the architecture and so are the beams. The horizontal elements are also expressed through that. He looked the problem right square in the eyes there and he solved it very beautifully. In fact, it was so well done that it is hard for anyone designing a cage now to think of it in any other way. While he was beginning to find that out, other architects, who had been borrowing from the Greeks and the Romans, even the Egyptians sometimes, decided that verticality was the thing. We had a rash of Gothic office buildings, like the Woolworth Building in New York which started that trend. They didn't see why you had to go off the deep end as Sullivan did to get a vertical building: you could get one simply by using vertical piers and mullions and still set the spandrels back to get dark shadows as Sullivan had. You could make it go up and have pinnacles all around the top and just stress the heck out of it up and down and still be within the sanction of a style that was respectable and recognized and in perfect good taste. That was fine until the terra-cotta started falling off, and one thing and another. One school of architects found out you could do this other thing, have the fancy bottom and the fancy top and the plain in between, that you could stretch up or down no matter how high the building was. That was the easy way; that was for the architect who didn't care very much what he was doing.

The ones who were still going at it for art as a capital *A*, in the old beaux arts sense, were going Gothic. When the Chicago Tribune Building had its famous competition, you know what won the prize, a *Gothic skyscraper*. They had some solutions submitted, with all the trash they got, which were closer to the truth and were certainly more honest expressions of the structure of the building. If any of you have not seen the book on the Chicago Tribune competition in the library, I urge you all to look at it; you will get a good laugh or two out of it, if nothing else. It's hard for us to realize now that architects in their right minds could have done some of the things that are in there. I think it is a good thing that we can realize that. Many people at that time could have looked through that book and not seen anything funny about any of the designs. So I guess the fact that we can see there is something funny about them shows a little progress.

What had happened then was the Gothic stuff was too expensive. Sullivan had shown a way to handle the grid in the Carson Pirie Scott Building, but even that was too expensive as he had a fancy cast-iron base around the bottom of it and he had elaborate terra-cotta work at the top. It had to be cheaper still. So the big-shot architects started trying to get the vertical emphasis by leaving out the ornaments and the fancy materials except at the street level and simplifying the whole business by taking alternate pier, window pier, window pier, and window. The large News Building by Howell and Hood in New York is an example of that. The building has a vertical set of stripes of brick, and windows, and dark spandrels and brick, windows, and dark spandrels, with the same rhythm marching all around the building and never stopping any place. It goes up and up—it could be fifty stories high or twenty-five stories high or thirty stories high. It wouldn't make any difference, because you just brought it all up to where you had to stop and then lopped it off. That was the way they felt they should solve this problem. That was when everything was vertical. Democracy in those days was vertical.

Now democracy has become horizontal. We spread out now instead of going up. It was very easy then to take this building of stripes that went up this way and turn it on its side. So we have examples of modern building from three stories up to as high as you wanted to go where it is a series of layers but horizontal now, with ribbon windows. Some of the architects have bothered to set the frame back a little bit, maybe a few inches, so that the windows can honestly go by. Others have fudged by putting dark brick spandrels horizontally instead of vertically in between the windows to make them look like one continuous band. There are lots of ways to fudge that. Some of them aren't sure which way they should go and they have some running up and down and some sticking out like the Philadelphia Savings Fund Society Building by Howe and Lescaze—they had it either way: no matter which way you turned you were sure to get it one way or the other. If you wanted horizontal stuff you looked at the front; if you wanted vertical stuff you looked at the sides.

In Mr. Wright's solution to the problem, he cantilevered the floors, as in the St. Mark's Building, from either the central core, or in the National Insurance Building he designed for Chicago, from columns down the corridors; the exteriors were sort of fabric of glass and copper screens that hung over the whole thing without any particular recognition of floor levels. A very beautiful all-over kind of pattern and texture to the whole thing, maybe not quite honest when it comes to showing floors, but creating, nevertheless, a very beautiful building. More than just being honest, too.

We do have an example of Wright's from his very early days—his design for the Luxfer Prism Building, where he had a grid, even before Sullivan used it, where the vertical and the horizontal members of the structure were honestly expressed in the design and the glass panels filled in between. Although it never was built, this was a very early example in 1895, probably one of the earliest, to recognize in design this honest approach toward the recognition of this form of structure.

Now we have the other side of the camp that is bending

over backwards saying we must be honest about it all and show every rivet and every beam and every H column. So the bones must all be expressed, clearly visible, even if they are in the way. They must stick outside of everything, or inside of everything, in a way that shows they are clearly divorced from what is going on and free from it. That is their idea of honesty.

Of course if you examine what it amounts to, like Mies's apartment house of steel columns, you can see that he started with a steel column. He had to fireproof it with concrete because of the building and fire codes. So you could say he lost the feeling of the steel when he put the concrete around it, so the concrete made it dishonest. Or, you could say the concrete made it honest because it protected the steel from the fire and it couldn't have been as small a column as it was if it hadn't had the steel in it, perhaps. I don't know. But Mendel Glickman could tell you that better than I can, but I would guess that. Maybe you would know, if you knew about structure that it was that small even though it looked like concrete because it had a steel column inside of it. Mies said, "No that isn't it, we must put a steel plate on the outside to make it honest, to show that it is a steel column." Now there is a question whether that is fudging or not because it isn't that kind of a steel column to start with. It is an H column and not a box column and it isn't that big as a steel column. The steel is a plate that is put on, which I think is just as dishonest as a Renaissance pilaster. Now if you want to justify it from the standpoint of design, that is another matter; but if you try to say that is truth and it is perfectly honest, then I think it is a question. Not only is this plate that is put on the column not quite true of what is going on inside the column, but, also, it requires a tremendous amount of upkeep. It is painted black so is it honest to paint the steel black? Well, you could say you paint the steel black, or you paint the steel, whether it is black or not. It's white nowadays, I understand. But if you paint it at all is that honest? If it is painted to protect the steel then I suppose that is honest; just as covering the steel with concrete to fireproof it may be honest. It seems that we are covering up an awful lot; we are trying awfully hard to be truthful on the one hand, and to be honest, and then we create conditions which make us dishonest again, like the steel that has to be painted. After all, what we see is the paint, isn't it, and the shape of the column? We don't see the steel as steel. We don't see the concrete as concrete that was used as fireproofing. Nor do we see the original H beam that is inside. It all ends up, after all, as something that isn't very true or honest. I wouldn't object to that, even with all those little white lies, providing it added up to something where it all transcended all of this and made it worthwhile. We could forgive the faults if the virtues were worth it. Whether they are or not will be a matter of individual opinion, I think, for a while, anyway, until we become clear on it.

Here we have then a very honest striving for honesty that has miscarried and gotten bogged down with lots of things that aren't quite true. We can say a flat slab is simple and looks true but it is covering up all of the reinforcing steel it takes to make it that way, and should it be the same thickness all the way through if we are perfectly honest? I doubt it. Of course you could say that to form it to make it that way would cost so much that it wouldn't be feasible; but that is another consideration—economics. Should a column be the same width all the way up just because it is more feasible to form it that way? Those are things I hope you will discuss in one of these sessions on structure. I don't want to get into that part of it now because

I don't know enough about it. I do think there is a lot to investigate in structural honesty. We feel pretty bad that something deflects, but isn't it more honest to show that it does? Aren't we stretching the truth a little bit if we try to kid people into thinking a material wouldn't deflect? But still we would be horrified if we saw any noticeable deflection on anything. That is something you might think about in this connection, structurally, along with aesthetics.

To get back to this truth in Mies's apartment house, we do have an accentuation of where the columns are, the floors though are still minimized, in the old principles that Sullivan went through and discarded, as setting the spandrels back from the verticals. We have a rather begrudging recognition of the vertical columns in the design because he has attempted to set up the rhythm of the steel H sections all around the building which progress regardless of where the columns are. We are conscious of the columns down at the bottom, but you were conscious of them in the Wainwright Building at the bottom, too. I don't think there is anything gained aesthetically in Mies's building, in the sense of having a regular rhythm, regardless of the vertical columns. The columns are marching along together in a regular rhythm. This isn't quite kosher either for you can see the width is there but it isn't gained honestly, after all, if you want to be very puritanical again. By stressing all of this and running it back to the floor slabs and the beams and so on, I think it is still not telling much truth because they are minimized at the expense of the vertical rhythm that marches around the building. This is the same problem in steel that Sullivan was working on in the beginning in brick and terra-cotta. But Sullivan was smart enough to get away from that. Architects now are still trying to do with steel what he did with brick, not realizing what he had discarded to get at the solution he finally arrived at for this problem.

This gets down to another matter I would like to mention, and that is that we somehow or other never profit from each other's experience very much. While Sullivan had to go through all of this gore of discovering and rejecting to arrive at what he thought was the naked truth and inspiration, who can go on from there further. Instead of taking up where he left off, why don't we go back to principles again and try to find our own way? I think we should. I don't think that any of us can pick up where Mr. Wright leaves off, for instance. I don't think that we should even try. I think we should try to understand what made Mr. Wright tick and what makes anything tick and then we should try to see how we can use the principles that made them tick and make ourselves tick. That isn't a matter of grafting ourselves on someone else or hitching your wagon to a star. We are still going to have to go through this process of discovering and rejecting ourselves to arrive at any honest expression of our own.

But to get back to Mies's apartment building, if he feels he has to cover the columns this way, and he feels he has to cover the beams this way to arrive at an aesthetic that is truthful to him, I will go along with him one hundred percent, even if he is telling some white lies along the way— providing that some disciple doesn't try to force down my throat the idea that that is truth all the way through; that it is truth in structure; that it is truthful expression of structure.

Mies did a building in reinforced concrete, and it is a little more true than the steel apartment building as far as expressing the structure inside. It doesn't look so good, but it does show the columns and the beams, if you want to show them, but it shows them so much that it shows you they are not very good looking. The thing that was pointed out to me by one of his disciples was that this was a big step in architecture because columns were set back as they go up, and as the building diminished in weight, the columns are set back to express that. This was supposed to be a very big step, an honest expression of structure in design. When I asked him why it was that the weight diminished every three stories, because that was the way the columns were diminishing—they would go up a few stories and set back and then up a few more and set back—he thought I was being very unfair and critical. But I said, "Suppose that we say that at least the intention was good to express the diminishing weight of the building as it went up. Why is it in the same kind of problem in the apartment house in the same town by the same architect that it isn't important to do that on the next job? Why cast all of this to the winds and say, to hell with it, we are going to run them straight up this time? The weight is diminishing on the steel building just as it is on the concrete building, and why is it so honest in one case and so unnecessary in the other?" It seems to me that that isn't quite honest, somewhere along the line, if something is honest one time it ought to carry through as a principle if it is worth anything. Maybe he figured it wasn't worth it after he got it up and saw how it looked. Maybe he decided that honesty didn't pay in that sense. I wouldn't criticize him for that either.

I don't mind a few white lies if the result comes out architecture, anymore than I would mind a person telling a few white lies if he is basically honest and sincere and his aim is something good. It seems to me that when we consider this matter of honesty, we need to use some judgment along with it, to temper it, to see if we are bending over too far backwards, or falling flat on our face. As Thurber said, "It's just as bad to bend too far backwards as it is to fall flat on your face." It's true with honesty, too, you can be so damn honest that nothing comes out except honesty, or you can tell lies galore and still have it add up to something pretty keen. It isn't because you are telling lies that it is coming out keen: it is because there was something more important involved.

I think one of the things we need to develop is the sense of when to tell the truth and when not to be so honest. That is, to the point where it hurts. I suppose that if we looked at buildings in the past, such as the Gothic cathedrals, they are honest expressions of structure; they show all the places that carry the weight and show the pinnacles, which were used to hold the flying buttresses down, and show the ribs that make higher vaults. You might say why didn't they show the vaults on the outside? Why did they put a gabled roof on top? Was that honest? Maybe we would rather see the vault showing outside. Probably they felt it was more honest to keep the ridgeline straight than it was to show the vaults exposed to the outside.

We change our minds a lot about what is true and what is honest, just like Sullivan, who felt the vertical accent was honest for democracy, and Wright, who felt the horizontal was honest for democracy. Both, I think, were perfectly honest in their attitude. Why should it be either one way or the other, necessarily? I would say that, in being honest, we should try to be truthful and honest, as a principle, as much as we can. But I think that we have to look at it in a larger sense than in a matter of small individual physical matters. We have to think of it in terms of what it all adds up to, as to purpose and meaning and truth. We could discard a lot of these things and arrive at it that way, too. We could discard a lot of little white lies along the way if the whole thing added up to the naked truth of inspiration.

It seems to me that we need to try to understand the nature of our materials and express that. We need to understand the structural principles we are working with and to have the feeling that the bones are inside even if we don't see them. We need to know that the plumbing, heating, wiring, the veins of the building are doing their job without actually seeing them tacked all over the place. I know of some cases where architects have painted the plumbing red, yellow, blue, and so on, and left it all exposed to show it has plumbing. Well I think we should take for granted that it has. When we go around looking at each other, we don't check to see how our digestive apparatus is working or any such thing. We take for granted that it's all under control. In buildings, I think we should be able to assume that those things are doing their job. I don't mean to minimize the importance of those things, don't get me wrong, because it is necessary to have good heating and ventilating and plumbing and all that. It is certainly part of the design of the building. It should keep its proper place and not become a fetish. That is what I mean.

It seems that our job as architects is to be sort of a policeman to discipline all of this into a kind of order that will add up to something that transcends the nature of the materials. The kind of structure it is, the kind of function it has—all that adds up to something more, that we call architecture. If we can look at it that way, I think, we will realize that the closer we can some to honesty in the handling of all these parts the better. At least we are more apt to arrive at a truthful solution through honesty than we are through a lot of lies. I don't mean to imply by what I said that we should not care what we do so long as it adds up to art. That is not the meaning of this at all. I think we have to learn to discipline and to order all of these things first and to realize what is the most important in architecture over just good building. I wouldn't worry too much about whether the reinforcing steel is showing through the slab, or something like that. We should be able to design a slab, or any structural member, where you would feel that because of the way it is in the design and in the building that it does have such things in it, and it couldn't exist in the forms we see if it didn't have them. Then I think that is honest enough. I don't think you need to have transparent concrete to show that the reinforcing steel is inside.

There is a matter of reason that we have to put into practice in order to balance all of this. We have to strive for truth through honesty, but we have to keep flexible on this. We have to try to realize that there is more than one kind of truth and more than one kind of honesty. Principles are fine, but we can't be too rigid in their application, because we have too many elements to juggle, too many unrelated things to relate to make it all come out without something getting hurt. Something is going to have to give all the way through, but you want to make sure that what gives is not so important. Make the important things win. I think that in doing that you have to discover many things. You have to try lots of things; you have to experiment. School is the place to experiment. You have to reject a lot of these things you have discovered to arrive at something you feel is true. We should be willing to pay that price.

There is another thing I would like to mention very briefly in this connection and with the idea of order that we spoke of the last time. [See #2: Goff had spoken about order the previous month.] Achieving order in a design requires the application of discipline, of certain restrictions, of certain eliminations, or discarding certain things in favor of other things, surely. That doesn't mean putting architecture in a straitjacket just because it is ordered. It doesn't mean that you should freeze up and be afraid to move just because you would be afraid something would get out of order. It means that you should be able to judge and decide whether what you are doing belongs in the same order all the way through the building or is it an acceptable order to the rest of the building, in order to arrive at something that is architecture, and not just a whim, or something you wanted to do at a certain time, at a certain place. Don't look on that as a restriction so far as your imagination is concerned. Don't let it tie you up in knots because you are afraid to move for fear you will have disorder. If you do, you are chickening out on it. What you have to do is to work with all these elements, all these parts, and try to achieve order. But you have to keep your mind wide open so that you can reject anything that you think of in order to achieve what you are after. You can't do that if you are frozen in a straitjacket where you are afraid to move for fear you will do something that is disorderly. You have to try things. If you are not sure—try things. Don't be afraid to try things. Be curious; wonder how it would be some other way. A good thing to always remember is that you will never arrive at *the one* solution to anything, because there is not *the one*, but many many solutions to any problem. You could make many solutions and so could everyone else. When you multiply that together you find there is not just one solution, so why be so timid and afraid? Why not dive in and see what you can find out, and then how you can order together the things you find out that make sense in an overall idea of truth, as you understand it, for that particular solution that you are going to work out. It doesn't mean it is the only true solution, of course. I mention that because I heard after the last talk on order that some got the impression that it was something that would limit them. I don't think it limits you at all: you should be flexible enough to accept and reject all of these different things you need to do in order to find a sense of order, or sense of truth. That's a part of being honest.

I would like to turn now to some discussion. How about some reactions now? Anyone want to say something?

Question: How should honesty be handled when you are striving for a certain effect in your design and the direction you want seems to be dishonest. Is it wrong to try for that certain effect?

Goff: I would say striving for effect is not dishonest in principle. In fact, I would say that it would be a necessity in architecture to strive for effect. If you didn't have effect, you certainly wouldn't be apt to have architecture, because architecture depends upon effect, among other things. You should feel yourself, first of all, that the effect you want is worth it and isn't dishonest. I think if you start feeling that it is dishonest, even though you are striving for it, that you ought to have a kind of guilty conscience. If you don't feel it's honest or worth doing, then who will? You have to believe it more than anyone, because there will be plenty of people who won't think so, no matter how honest you are about it. It has to survive criticism. The hardest part of a building is not to have it withstand the weather, or erosion, or anything like that, so much as it is criticism. That is something we can't calculate. There are no handbooks on it that will give us any real clue. We have to believe it's honest to start with, what we are doing, that our effects are worth achieving, worth striving for.

That doesn't mean that everyone else will think we are honest, especially at first. Debussy once said, "Every beautiful idea has within it something in embryo which seems absurd to fools." That is so true. A beautiful idea would naturally be truthful, we would say in this case. There is something that will seem absurd, ridiculous, and dishonest to other people sometimes. We have to be sure ourselves that it isn't. We have to be sure of that, and of our aim and our goal, or our integrity, or our sincerity (of course sincerity is not enough). We have to believe in what we are doing. We have to have conviction about it. Then these effects we strive for will be honestly worth striving for to us. Now if the effects are honest in more than just our own personal attitude, if they can be honest with other people after they have taken the trouble to find out what we are doing, then I think it stands a chance of getting to be architecture, when it becomes more than just the personal opinion of the man who did it. You'd certainly have to go into the project with an honest mind in the first place, wouldn't you? I don't think that you go at it as a deception very well. It has been done. Kurt Atterberg, the Swedish engineer who composes music on the side, entered the competition sponsored by the Columbia Phonograph Company back before World War II to commemorate Schubert's death. The jury was announced and included very well-known names. Mr. Atterberg, who had been unrecognized pretty much outside of Sweden, musically, decided to enter the competition. He submitted a symphony which won the prize of $50,000. After he got the prize, he came out with an article and told the musical world that it was all a big hoax, that there wasn't an original bar in the music. He said he had stolen every bit of it from well-known pieces by Rimsky-Korsakov, Tchaikovsky, Beethoven, and Brahms and made a big hash of it all. He quoted all the themes that even the critics hadn't been able to recognize. In spite of all that, he did a very wonderful symphony, tongue in cheek. Just as Mr. Wright did a wonderful house, in a playful mood, with the Old English theme in Oak Park. It certainly wasn't honest, was it? He had a good time with it, but we can't rank it as one of Mr. Wright's major achievements in architecture. It's a clever thing and a hoax and was designed deliberately to deceive people—to pull their legs. If that is what you are after, you can do it, of course, but I don't think that falls within the province of art with a capital A.

Question (Mendel Glickman): Wouldn't you say that part of the architect's job, when he is designing a building, is to think of the effect and the means of achieving it at the same time. One isn't subordinate to the other: that you think of both of them and you know you want a certain effect, but you also should bear in mind that the means by which you achieve it is just as important. The architect has to decide whether to obtain the effect with honesty or not to have the effect.

Goff: Yes, I think that is right; in other words, he has to earn his effects and he has to arrive at them through all of these other things we have been talking about. I don't think that they should be the major consideration, just like when Mr. Wright wanted the effect he has in the Johnson Wax column. That was striving for an effect, wasn't it? He arrived at it through reason, through materials, and all that he had to deal with and the way they had to be used and many other considerations. It wasn't just a whim to make the column that shape. It couldn't be realized honestly through some structural means or principle or through the nature of the materials. Certainly we should have a means to help earn our effect; absolutely, it should be part of it.

Question: Speaking about this idea of experimenting, it

is very vital to experiment, but isn't it a matter of degree to a certain extent to experiment?

Goff: That is hard to answer directly. As an example, let's look at the French cathedral at Beauvais. They had to build it three times before they could get it to stand up. They were striving for effect, but they didn't know how light they could make the stone work to get the effect they wanted. The effect they were after was to have something so soaring, even though it was made of stone, so free from the effect of gravity, physically so light and airy that it would transcend the feeling of the weight of the stone, you see. There was no way that they knew to figure out how, so they built it as light as they thought they could and have it still stand up, but after they got it up a ways, it all fell down. Then they realized they hadn't made it quite heavy enough, so the next time, at great expense to the community and the cost of some lives even, they made it a little bit heavier and got up a little higher. It fell down again. The third time they got it up where they wanted it by making it just a little bit heavier. Now they were striving for effect. I suppose if we were moralists, we could say that it wasn't worth it. Why kill these people, why endanger their lives by having this thing fall down, and why try and make it so light anyway? Why not put in a little extra and be sure? Still, today, we are glad they did that, and it was a good thing in general that they did it because it showed how far the material can be used. It had its good effect as well as its bad effect, didn't it? Now we are richer because we know how little we can go in that direction because of their experiment. I think that's an extreme example, but it points out one thing, and that is that sometimes in experiments you earn something at great expense.

Now, of course, it's a question whether you can afford

this expense and whether you should. This is where your judgment comes into play again. If you are doing a house for someone who can't afford to experiment with the materials, then I think you should stick to safer ground or more known ground, or at least you should be pretty sure how it will come out. If you have a client who says they would like you to experiment, then why not?

I don't see anything wrong with building an experiment for the Guggenheims, for instance. They have plenty of money and they were willing to afford it. Mrs. Barnsdall didn't need the palace Mr. Wright built for her, either, but she could afford it. His design probably cost her about three times more than she figured it would, but, anyway, there has been a lot of good come out of it. Still, I think if we just solve the problem and no more, we are selling our client short, too. We have to stretch things to the limit all the time, it seems to me, in order to give people things that they will be happy with and satisfied with. Almost always the problem that is just barely satisfied, without any imagination and without any experiment, without any change or daring or surprise, is pretty apt to be selling your client short, too. There is the same old business of leaning over too far backwards and falling flat on you face again, because I don't believe we should saddle our clients with things they can't afford or shouldn't afford or anything of the sort. On the other hand, I don't think we should just barely meet their requirements. The client should go along with this part way, too. They will feel much better about it even if it hurts a little at first. They will feel much better about it later in almost all cases. I don't think that you could always say though that if a man tells you he wants to spend so much money, you ignore that and try to give him something that you think is a great architectural masterpiece regardless of what it cost, no. On the other hand I don't see anything wrong with experimenting and trying to give him a house for that much money that is still not just that run-of-the-mill design proposition, too. Maybe by experimenting you can get him a better house for that amount of money than you could by following the accepted routines. Of course, you would still have many physical problems to lick if you did because of the FHA and so on.

If you have a client who can only afford a very low-cost house, this is actually where you would have to do a great deal of experimentation to find what could be built. There would be more than the usual way of arriving at the solution and giving the client more for it, but the way loans and all are set up makes it very difficult for us to experiment. When we do experiment we should make certain that it is a good experiment. Mr. Wright experimented on Mrs. Millard when he built his first concrete-block house, and it cost more than she had to spend. He felt obligated to dig down in his own pocket to help her out with it. It came to about $6,500, I think. Well, why not? He probably didn't have the money, but he probably felt it was worth getting the money to do that, and I think it was. Mrs. Millard was certainly happy with the house, as you know. So even though the roof leaked and the water washed the mud over the floors (I think I told you that story about the many things wrong with it, because of this experimentation), she was still happy with it. She was glad she had this house by Frank Lloyd Wright. Of course, not all your clients would be that well mannered about it, that's for sure.

Question: Suppose you are called upon to design a house, some sort of a building, whose function you disapprove of. For example, the Rosicrucian Society building, or the Institute for Dianetic Research, or a prison for juvenile delinquents.

Goff: Of course, you wouldn't have to take the job. That is one way out. Of course, I think the architect is in the unfortunate position of having to take on all comers, you might say, whether you believe in what their purpose is or not. Actually, we might not do any work at all if we questioned that too much. For instance, we might know a man and a woman who are married and think they shouldn't be and be called on to do a house for them. Then we could say, I don't want to do this house for you because I don't believe in your having a house. I don't think we could do that because if we didn't want to do it, we shouldn't do it in the first place if it is against our grain and our fiber. As an example, I might hate fish and not want to eat fish. Still, if I had a chance to design a seafood restaurant, I think I would do it. I believe I could design a good seafood restaurant even if I didn't go in it to eat fish. The same with a church, perhaps, or something else. I think we have to be very broadminded about that so long as our business depends on getting the job.

I heard one architect, not so long ago, give a speech about architecture and he said the most important thing is to get the job. That's the usual commercial attitude. Many people claim having originated that saying, but I don't think it is anything to be proud of, myself. Someone is supposed to have said the main thing is "get the job, get the job, get the job." I don't think it's that bad. We have a choice, after all, on this sort of thing, about what we are going to do. If someone asks us to do a house on a fifty-foot lot and we don't think the house should be on a fifty-foot lot, we don't have to do it. Of course, you can argue that someone else would. Well, so they would, but your conscience would be clear if you felt that very strongly. I would have a difficult time doing something for the Rosicrucians, probably because I don't believe as they do, but I think I could do something for them anyway. I could put on my Rosicrucian suit and try to go along with them, just the same as I would any other religion or philosophy. I feel my duty, as an architect, is to interpret these problems for people. I should be able to be flexible enough to interpret their needs through my work. If the client wanted me to make a stairway that was two feet wide, then I wouldn't do it, even though maybe it would suit them perfectly.

I did something like that one time, much to my sorrow. We were doing a house and I was just a kid in the office. The client was supposed to be intelligent. At least he was the superintendent of public schools, so you would think he would be. But at the last minute he wanted a den tacked on the back of his house. The house was already planned. We tried putting the den so it would not block out the light of the breakfast area or the living room by straddling the two, so you could get into the den from either one of those rooms and still have some outside light at the end of the house. He insisted on it being outside of the breakfast room, because that is the way he first thought of it. He couldn't go along with the idea of straddling so that you could get windows in both rooms. Much against our better judgment, we listened to him. After all, it was his house and his money and that was the way he wanted it. And we did it the way he wanted it. We put the den back of the breakfast room, which meant that even with two so-called French doors, opening from the breakfast room into the den, it was still dark as a closet in there unless you turned the light on. It suited him all right until his friends started coming in and saying, "My gosh, what kind of an architect did you have? You don't have any windows in your breakfast room and here it is on the east side of the house." He just said it was the crazy architects, you know how that is, they don't have any sense about these things. So he ended by saying it was our idea all the way along. That taught me a very good lesson not to do things that I knew to be wrong, because if you do, you are going to get blamed for them even if you are trying to satisfy your client, and do, at least until their friends come along. I wouldn't do something like that now. I won't do things that I know won't work.

So far as to the kind of job it is, if I didn't believe in what they were doing enough to go along with them on it, then I just wouldn't take the job.

Question: You bring up this point that you should work as honestly as you can. A little bit later on you bring up the point that eventually as more people come to understand your architecture, it is possible that your viewpoint will be found valid. There is a paradox here, that sincerity is not quite enough. We have a yardstick, so to speak, but without any markings on it.

Goff: Well, I wish I could give you a formula for a yardstick with the markings on it. Actually, it is a matter of principle. Sullivan once said he was looking for a principle so broad as to admit of no exceptions. That is what you want, too. I think that the principle was right under his nose, and that is there is no principle. There will always be exceptions and there should be exceptions. You can make rules and regulations and formulas and establish laws, and all of this, and still when it comes right down to it, it is a matter of judgment, isn't it, of balance, of deciding what is equitable in relation to something else? When you do that, you're not always going to be equally honest with everything, are you? I mean, it's the same thing as "give and take" or "robbing Peter to pay Paul" again. You have to try to be sure no matter how much of that goes on that your basic principle is honest and that you are striving for truth and in the long run that you will have more truth than dishonesty. I wish I could tell just how to do that, but I can't. I think it is something you aim for more than you can say there is a way to do it. What I am saying is you should strive to find a balance always in what is true and honest, and what you can afford to call expendable in that direction. I don't think you will ever arrive at it by having everything as true as you know how to make it. There will have to be some alloy in the design that may not be quite that true. Maybe that is necessary; maybe you need some of that negative in order to make the positive seem more possible, I don't know.

Question: To reach an honest solution, you have to be realistic, or see things as they are, yet different people have different ideas on what is realistic.

Goff: Realistic is usually tied up with that nasty word *practical*, isn't it? That gets down to another big subject which we should try again sometime: What is practical? Being realistic I think doesn't necessarily mean accepting everything that is as the way it should be, or even could be. We can be realistic about what is around us and resign ourselves to that, or we can be even more realistic and say, well we know that this is it, but, as Carlyle said, the ideal is within yourself, your condition is but the stuff you are to shape that same ideal out of, you see. Now if you practice that, then you can say, well, being realistic about this I can accept that as a limitation, can't you? Or you could say that is the stuff you are going to shape your ideal out of. I think it depends on how you recognize these so-called realistic requirements or the demands that are put upon you, whether you accept it as limitation or as means. If you accept it as means then you stand a good chance of bringing something more out of the problem. If people say you should be realistic about the cost, that you should keep it within ten thousand dollars and that is all the money they have, sure you should if that is all they have. But on the other hand, accepting that doesn't mean you have to sell out and do them something inferior just because they just have ten thousand dollars, does it? In being realistic about that you could say, well they have ten thousand dollars, let's see how much we can do with ten thousand dollars for them. Not as a handicap, but as a means, you see.

Honesty is a principle you can profit with in many ways. You could say it's honest to do a certain thing because we are taught that that is honest, and maybe a person in some other part of the world would not think it was honest at all. I believe, though, that in spite of geographical boundaries and time boundaries and all that, that we do have basic ideas of what is honest as a principle. The way we apply it, though, would be quite varied, I am sure. I think it should be. I think we should be flexible about it and I think it is a virtue that we should strive for. But I don't think we can define it so exactly that we could say that it's a principle that admits of no exception. In other words, like the Indian who believed that a circle shouldn't be completed because the evil spirits couldn't get out, you see, and leaving an imperfection in a basket for the same reason, it is a good idea to have an escape valve. That shouldn't diminish the idea that it is a good principle to work for.

We can be awfully prudish about this at our own expense, of course. I know people who are very prudish about things, for instance, about stealing. They would think it is a great crime to steal. They would never be caught stealing anything in the way of physical things from someone else, such as stealing money, or food, or belongings, things like that. Still, they wouldn't hesitate to steal someone else's ideas, would they? Where do you draw the line? I know people who say they will always tell the truth and nothing but the truth, so help me God. Is that sensible if in telling the truth you are going to hurt someone? I don't think so. I believe it is wrong to steal and I go along with that as a principle. But if I know a man who can't eat unless he steals, and that is the only way he can eat, I won't hold it against him. I would say all right this time, wouldn't you? But I know fanatics who would say he should be put in prison. They feel he should die before he should steal. If they want to believe it, they can, but I wouldn't believe that. In other words, I have a sliding scale of values that I try to adjust to suit the occasion. I will admit you can't slide all over the place; you have to keep within limits and you have to try to maintain a center of gravity there. Still you have to make exceptions.

In design, when it comes to the question of whether you are going to emphasize the structure this time or whether you are going to do something else, you have to make a choice, don't you? No matter what you choose you are going to sacrifice something in the design no doubt. The trick is to lose as little as you can in the transaction.

Question: How can you be truthful in the design of a small-house problem with all the limitations involved?

Goff: To be truthful in the solution of a small-house problem with all the conditions that are tied to it would be very difficult, wouldn't it? To satisfy zoning requirements, loan requirements, and many other physical requirements and still produce a good small house is almost a magician's feat. In the first place, all of these things that are applied to that, all these limitations we are speaking of, or handicaps, or hurdles, are not put there for the reason of making it better architecture. They are there for financial and other reasons.

I suppose if you are going to be honest in solving those problems, you will have to recognize them as existing, but then the trick is to see how you can eliminate some of them as hurdles and handicaps and how you can use them to your advantage. Even then, there are bound to be times when it won't work because reason is not the basis of it. You can take the FHA handbook and comply with the letter of the law all the way through, and still, as you probably know, you can design a solution that will follow those requirements, still be a good building, and still they won't accept it. Because it isn't what they had in mind, is it? The reason it isn't what they had in mind is because they don't have a mind to start with. If they do have it, it isn't capable of working in that direction. It is a little bit like a Balinese trying to talk to an Eskimo. No matter how right each one may feel, there is no common ground for them to get together on. In dealing with FHA, then, you are up against a pretty tough nut, I will admit. The only way I can see out of that dilemma is either to try to improve FHA or try to talk your clients into getting the money some other way, if they can. If they can't, and nothing else can be done, then the most you can do is to try to solve, as honestly as you can, the design within all the limitations you have. It may end up in a mess even so—it is pretty apt to—but at least your own conscience would be clear, and it won't be any worse than they would have had anyway. That would be slicing it pretty thin sometimes.

I think that is one of our big jobs, as architects, to keep battling away on that very thing. That is why I tackle small houses, because, Lord knows, there is no money in them. I do feel it is our obligation to ourselves and to people who are hard up, to see what we can do in that direction. Little by little it helps, even though it is very discouraging when you just begin to win over one regime in FHA, as we found here in our local city, just as we had begun to loosen them up and get them to go along with us, they changed management and you have to do it all over again. I was able to get things by FHA in Chicago, which I couldn't do if I were in Chicago now. I had worked on them a long time to soften them up, but the trouble is there are always more where those came from. About the time you get one bunch where they can see the way you do your designs, they change the staff and you have to do it all over again. The main trouble is that you are not getting at the real source of the trouble, which is the boss of the boss, you see. We are up against a problem there of trying to educate the people who really have charge of FHA, not the local distributors, because they are only following orders. They are the ones that don't dare do anything on their own, unless it is in the book. They go strictly by what they see in the book to a certain point and then when they can't do that anymore, they go on prejudice. We have to loosen it up, and that is part of our job, and we have to keep working on that and keep trying. It is discouraging lots of times and you feel you are not making any headway.

Just think, here is Mr. Wright (I hate to keep talking about him all the time, but he is a good illustration of this point), who has done over six hundred and some buildings that are actually built. It is peanuts when compared to the amount of buildings that are done in the United States, isn't it? Not even a drop of water in the ocean so far as volume is concerned. Well you can say, was it worth it? How much good has actually been achieved except in individual instances by all of this? All the sweat, blood, and tears that he has gone through. Has it been worth it, just for six hundred and some little jobs? Well, it is a lot like a pebble dropped in a quiet pool where nothing has disturbed it. Nothing is going to happen to the surface of this water until something disturbs it. Mr. Wright has disturbed the surface of the water, and we are feeling the outer rings of it now, you see, way out from the starting point. He has dropped six hundred and some pebbles in the water, you might say. Even though each one is small compared to the Empire State Building and the Pentagon, and so on. They would make a bigger splash, no doubt, that way. And, still, why is it that something so small as the Morris Store in San Francisco can mean so much as compared to some big enterprise like the new Prudential Building in Chicago, you see? It isn't size, is it? It isn't cost? It is something more important. It is worth doing so long as that idea can survive all of this, and mean something to all of us who are trying to do something; gives us faith and encouragement and inspiration. It is worth it, no matter how much trouble or how discouraging it was.

It isn't easy, I know. No one is going to welcome you because you are a genius, that's for sure, but they are going to put every obstacle they can in your way in most cases. Still, it is worth it in the overall picture. You have to do it anyway; it is something you feel the need of; it is something that has to be accomplished. You have to be as fanatic about that as a missionary is. You have to really believe in what you are doing. You have to work within your limits always. Mr. Wright says, "Limitations are your best friends." Sometimes you will question that, I know, particularly with the FHA. It is awfully hard to believe that and work with them, but you still have to keep trying to do something in that respect.

Architecture has to serve our people in the broadest sense, and it can't do it unless it is taking care of low-cost houses, too. That is something we are trying to ignore by burying our heads in the sand, and something we have to face squarely or else we are never going to have the respect of people, in general, toward architecture. Architecture is losing face rapidly because of that.

It won't be very long until you won't even have an architect; you will have somebody who is employed by engineering firms or commercial firms. The day of the artist architect will be gone. The businessman-architect is certain to be gone, very rapidly. I mean by that the man who is just in architecture to make money. The big companies can do it better, make more money, and quicker. They all have the formulas now; they take the professional magazines and see how to produce the ribbon windows, the blank walls, and the flat slabs and throw in an angle or curve. They have got that formula and they can hire anybody to do it that way. How can an individual enterprise compete with that on a money basis? You can't. But one way you can still compete with them is that you can have ideas, if you have the guts to have them. You can produce something they can't, which is architecture. They can produce good buildings, but you will have it within your power to produce good architecture, and you are the only ones who can have it within your power. I am not saying that you all will, but you can. If you have it, then you have no competition, or very little. That is why I think it is so important for us to be architects in the real sense of the word, rather than commercial expedients. The commercially expedient architect is fast disappearing into another business that isn't architecture; it is building, just building. We have to face that. The reason we have to face it is because the architects have dropped the ball. We won't pick it up again until we have proven to the people that architecture means more than just building. It is up to us to do it. Who else can, and who else will? Who is willing to pay the price to do it? Only the fanatics like some of us, you see. That is the only thing that can save the idea

of architecture from going into the gutter, as Mr. Wright
says. We have to take a stand on that. Why is it that these
architects are suddenly becoming concerned with aesthetics when heretofore all they have been talking about are
fees and ethics and so on. Why is it they are so worried
about aesthetics all of sudden? It is pretty sudden, too, believe me. There is a reason—because they are beginning to
realize that is the only thing you can't buy at the corner
drugstore. It is the only thing they have within their domain, you might say, that the other people don't have. Of
course, just having them thinking it's their domain doesn't
mean anything unless they have it themselves. It isn't something you get overnight either. You have to work a little for
it; you have to earn it just like anything else. That is the
only salvation for architecture that is over and above good
building.

We have plan factories now. There is an agency in
Chicago, for instance, where even Mies van der Rohe takes
his sketches in and feeds them into the machine and they
go through this tremendous office with hundreds of draftsmen. They have mechanical engineers, they have structural
engineers, and they have everything all regimented. Things
go through just like a big machine and out come working drawings, specifications, everything all wrapped up in
a bundle. Mies doesn't have to have an office; all he has
to do is feed in an idea, you see, and it all goes through
there. The trouble is that anyone else can, too. What comes
out for Mies may be much better than what comes out for
Mr. Joe Dokes, who sends in a pretty sorry idea to start
with. The result is that this machinery is set up, but it can
be misused as well as used. The only way I know to do really good work in architecture, if you are the architect, is to
see it through yourselves regardless of how good your ma-

chinery is. To produce it, you have to keep your eye on it all the way through, or it is going to fall short somewhere.

You find these machines even in towns like Oklahoma City, now. One of the first signs of this machine office coming is that architects swap draftsmen now. When I was starting in, that was unheard of. In almost any office, they would either keep you through famine and feast or they would fire you when they didn't have any more work. Most offices that saw any possibility of work coming up at all would keep you when there were stretches of very little to do, because they realized it was more important to keep a force together that knew how to work together, than to use just anyone who happened to come along. Nowadays, architects will use you so long as they have something to do and then if you do good work they won't let you go. But they will farm you out to some other architect who happens to have a job on the condition that he will not keep you but allow them to call you back when they want you. In that way, they argue, you get the benefit of the experience in different offices. It is all an indication of the plan sweatshop that is coming. That is just what it is going to be. Of course, there will be draftsman unions—I don't know, maybe they have them now, or designers' unions, or detailers' unions, or fire escape detailers' unions. Probably highly specialized, but that isn't the way that architecture is going to be done. That is what we have to face in the immediate future when it comes to turning out buildings. No doubt they will have a very efficient way worked out to turn out a good building. Maybe better than an architect would.

Today there are a lot of builders who can do better than a lot of architects, I am sorry to say. Just because a man has a license doesn't mean he is an architect. There are lots of good architects who don't have a license and never will.

Having a license is not a sign that you are a good architect. I think that the only hold we have on this thing is in our purpose and our integrity in what we are trying to do to be architects. If we ever lose that we will have sunk clear down to the bottom, because that is the only thing that is going to keep us afloat and is going to keep architecture as a live art. It is something you are all going to have to face pretty soon. Architects are getting pretty jittery. Some of them welcome the idea of a plan sweatshop where they can feed the designs in and it comes out readymade. But on the other hand, the ones who are striving to maintain that kind of business on their own will naturally fall flat on their face like the independent groceries do with our chain-store system. It won't be very long until the plan sweatshops will be chain-plan sweatshops and they will be thoroughly unionized. I think it is only a question of time until license laws will be junked, too. I think that in time, because of the abuse and misuse in many places of license laws, that the same thing will happen that happened in Colorado recently, where, because of improper use of the law, it was thrown out entirely. Whether that is a good thing or not I can't say, but I do know that the big engineering companies, the mass-production boys, are not going to want to fool around with license laws, and they won't have to, because they will have money back of them that will buy about anything except architecture. It seems to me that we have to work hard to maintain any semblance of a profession that we once had. It used to be that you would meet an architect you disagreed with—maybe he was an old eclectic architect who stuck columns all over a railway station or something—but even so he had something in him that made you feel he was trying to do something better than just a shed or a minimum deal of some kind; he was working for something. You might not believe in

what he was working for, but you would have to admit
that he was working for a heck of a lot more than some of
the boys now who are only after the money. I respect the
other fellow more even if I don't agree with him. I respect
a man like Bertram Goodhue, who did Gothic churches—
they were very well done within those limits—much more
than I do some modern shyster who knows how to put a
ribbon-band window around a building just because it sells
and has no convictions about anything. At least Goodhue
had some convictions. Whether they were right or wrong,
he had them. But who has any convictions now?

I bet anything if the magazines would start a new fad to-
morrow to make all of the buildings Burmese in style that
they could swing it. I really believe they could, and I bet
you that the schools would start turning out students who
could design in Burmese style. Seems ridiculous, doesn't it?
But that is what is happening. It is what is happening now.
Not through any conviction, real conviction, but through
expediency, because they realize they have to get on the
bandwagon. When I go to architectural conventions and I
hear someone get up and say, "After all we are working for
the same thing: the creative individual and organic architecture," it just makes me sick, because it just makes me
realize that these architects are saying these words just to
get on the bandwagon, but they have no convictions. They
are just going through the motions and saying the same
words that you think are so sacred and still sound false.
It is getting so now that you can't say anything without
sounding pretty sorry, because all these words like beauty,
honesty, integrity, ideal, organic, all of these words have
become minimized to the point where they mean so many
things that they mean nothing. You have heard them misused so much without any convictions or anything back

of them, that they are empty. Still it doesn't mean that they don't mean anything; it means that they have been misused too much. You are going to hear an awful lot of people talk about the same things that you talk about and they don't believe them at all, but they will say the same words.

Question: I have a question on form. We find in the work of good architecture a form that can be recognized as a circle or square or a rectangle, and yet in the study of circulation as the true form of the building develops, is it truthful to take this form into our own hands and guide the movement of the occupants when, if we were to follow natural human movements, more than likely we would develop a free form?

Goff: In the first place, I don't think you should start with a square or a circle or a triangle or a free form as a beginning. You would arrive at that because of the way the design is going to work, partly—or you should, anyway, I think. If the way it is going to work resolves itself pretty much into a square or a circle, then I think that in using that geometric shape you would be justified in working it out in that direction. If you worked it out because of that reason, the chances are that the movements of the clients within would be compatible with that, and vice versa. If you started with any kind of form and squeezed the works inside, and the clients inside of that, then naturally that wouldn't do the job, would it? I don't think that we should do that as architects, either.

There is a great deal of argument about whether architecture should be geometric or free form. I do believe you have answered your own question. If you have arrived at the geometry of the building, or the free form of the building, because of the way it works, then naturally you are not squeezing your clients into it. If you started with that as the consideration first of all and then tried to squeeze the clients into it, I don't think that is very good. If you have something that demands a circular circulation and you put it in a square building then something is going to have to give, or vice versa. If you put something that demands square circulation into a circular building then something has to give. You could do it, and you might reconcile the design somehow, but still it would be an approximation, wouldn't it? I believe you answered your own question by saying that by approaching the problem from inside out, that you would arrive at something that would be compatible anyway. I want to go into this question more fully later, and discuss the merits of geometry and free form.

Five

The Idea in Architecture

This recording, made with only Goff and me on the third floor of the School of Architecture, Norman, Oklahoma, was taped January 17, 1954. I asked him to discuss how the design idea develops in architecture. In an exposition ranging over the work of many artists and architects and an extensive period of history, Goff demonstrated that the "idea" behind any worthy design must be recognized, followed, and allowed to expand as the design grows.

Very often we wonder where our ideas come from. If we are going to have an idea in a building, a sense of order in a building, design, or a piece of music, or anything, we want to know, lots of times, where these ideas come from. I think that is a rather mysterious subject. First of all because our talent I think is inherited—what we call talent or aptitude in a certain direction. We might say it is handed down to us, just as our physical characteristics are. Of course, when we consider that we are descended from our mothers and fathers, and they from their mothers and fathers, it doesn't take many generations to get a very complex background. It has come down through all of these people and was inherited by us as individuals. Naturally, the physical characteristics are quite obvious many times; the racial characteristics certainly are. The more obscure things, such as feelings and talents, are much more mysterious, more personal with each of us. Still they have come to us from all of this background. We hardly know just how.

We can go a long way on our talent. If we happen to get into music, or painting, or architecture, or any art, we can produce a lot from what is within us without taking anything in to fertilize these talents, or to make them richer in any way. Some people have so much within them they can put out all their lives without bothering to absorb anything else to develop their talents. I think, generally speaking, that is a rather dangerous proceeding, even for people with lots of talent, because it tends to get them too much in a rut, too one-track in their direction. Just as we need to take in outside things physically, such as to breathe, drink water, to exercise, eat, and all that, to keep ourselves going physically, in order to keep our minds from petrifying in certain directions, we have to keep absorbing and enriching ourselves in our experiences. It seems to me that our being sensitive through our sense is a very important thing to enrich our natural talents. We can, and we should, be aware of all our senses, particularly if we are creative artists, because a sense of sight, hearing, smell, touch, and all of these are so directly concerned with what we do. We see things but we usually don't see them, and we hear things and not really hear them. People eat food without tasting it. I think by not using the senses we miss a great deal that we should experience in order to live fully. This living fully through our senses is important in developing and enriching what talent we may have to start with.

A person who has inherited a great talent may be in much the same position as someone who has inherited a large sum of money. He can proceed to write checks on that fund in the form of drawing ideas from it for some time. But unless he knows how to invest it and compound the interest, or keeps making deposits to add to the capital, he is pretty apt to be writing hot checks before long. I think that many artists, who started out with a great deal of promise, did end up writing hot checks on their talent. They were just repeating over and over something that they had already established. The fear of changing from that was so great because there was nothing going in to enrich what was already there. I think it is very necessary for an artist to be curious and to keep adding to this store. In adding to this store, we may be taking experiences from almost any place. Something we see or hear or touch or smell can have preferably an indirect reaction through our work.

I think that if we consider the way painters would go about painting a poppy, for instance, we might get a little closer to this idea. The realistic painter would see a poppy in the field and would be moved by it to paint it pretty much as he sees it. If he is a good technical painter, he may end up with something as "good" as a Kodachrome slide of it—maybe so real that bees would come to it. That would be a photographic sort of likeness of the subject. Very little of the artist has gone into it. It is just seeing the poppy and recording it pretty much as is without any feeling about it particularly. Then we could have the painter who would look at the poppy and understand it as something that he has some feelings about. Maybe it is the color of it that particularly interests him and the way the sun happens to be shining on it. Maybe he thinks the form of it isn't so important as this brilliant color. If he were an Impressionist, he might try to paint something that would have the effect of light that this poppy would give off and not be so interested in the form of it, perhaps. If he were an Expressionist, he might try to present it in a way that would give something of his reaction to it psychologically. If he were a Cubist, he might try to show it from many different positions. If he were a Futurist, he might try to show it blowing in the wind to show the motion of it. If he were an Abstractionist, he might look at it and try to use it as a point of departure to make a composition from it. He may be particularly interested in any one phase of it and still go on and develop it into a composition. Perhaps the poppy would have been lost long ago in the process of doing this to the point where you wouldn't recognize the poppy at all, and still, that was the generating point that the composition came from.

If you were a Surrealist you might look at the poppy as a thing that you could have some other associations with which were not particularly related, apparently, and the friction of the two or more ideas would create a strange kind of atmosphere. You would paint it very realistically all the same so that you might say that you associate poppies with lemons and fried eggs, or something. You could combine those into a composition where they may set up this friction which would make something else out of all three subjects.

If you were an Oriental artist, you would go about this quite differently. Rather than rushing in to paint a portrait of the poppy, or trying to put down your emotional or psychological reaction one way or the other about it, you would study the poppy first and try to become conscious of its order and the particular characteristics that make this poppy different from any other kind of flower. It may be different from any other poppy. You would understand the architecture of this poppy. You would not rush in to paint, but after observing and digesting this experience, you would consider the poppy much more important than yourself and you would realize that your personal reaction to it is a minor thing really, that the poppy is the important thing. So you would humble yourself, probably, in your attitude much more than a Western artist usually would, rather than trying to interpret it. You would try to understand it to the point where you could, from memory, draw the essential things about the poppy, not as your interpretation of it, but of the real essence of the thing itself. This is one of the big differences between Oriental and Occidental art in that approach where the artist subordinates himself to nature or to his idea, rather than using it as a means of expression, as we do. Naturally, even so, the Oriental artists vary as individuals. Hokusai would produce a different kind of poppy, even from the same flower, than Hiroshige, or Okio, or Jakuchū Itō, or someone else, because their individual characteristics would come through their composition and their brush strokes, and all that. Essentially, their attitude toward it would be much the same, whereas in Western art the artist would approach the subject as something to be handled through him as the medium primarily.

In understanding the poppy, then, the Oriental artist would try to record the essence of it through beautiful composition, and all of that, of course, but it wouldn't be so much an expression of personal feeling as the goal. Now there would be another way that you could experience this, too. That would be to not paint it at all, but to observe it, and to understand it in any of these ways that we could, and to put that experience away in our bank. To have digested and assimilated such an experience, whether you actually painted the poppy or not, wouldn't be so important as to have really felt and understood this experience. These impressions and feelings that come from such actions are stored up within us. It is very difficult to say how they might come out or whether they would ever come out in visible or tangible form. We know that they enrich our understanding, our sense of color and our sense of texture and all of that. Having exercised all those capacities, we are much freer to use them in our own works. We may not be at all conscious of where they come from. In fact I think it is better if we are not, because then we are closer to the essence of the thing rather than the outward form. These impressions and experiences that we go through are stored within us, and when we design something or com-

pose a piece of music, or whatever we are doing, we are
drawing from this store. This has enriched our own talent,
our own understanding of things, and comes out in our
work. It would be very difficult to trace just where these
sources are. I think the experience of understanding such
things helps us to understand the order that exists in anything and in everything. It helps us to realize that what we
do must have order and unity and purpose and so on.

Of course, the architect is in a somewhat different position from other creative artists because the composer or
the painter, or almost any other artist, can record pretty directly what he feels in his work without having the same
obligation toward it later that the architect has. We architects are more or less obligated to our clients and to other
people when we build something, because it is there all the
time. If people don't like a piece of music, they can ignore
it and not play it, but a building is there, of course, and it
represents an investment that our clients have had to make
at a sacrifice usually to them. It has to have some kind of
idea or something that makes it worthwhile to distinguish
it from just an ordinary building. This idea we are talking
about is what gives it unity and order and strength. It is not
a matter of just one idea, but it can be working several ideas
together. I think too many times our works lack the counterpoint and the interest that can be gotten through using
ideas together. We too often settle for one good idea, where
perhaps the idea could be enriched or made more interesting by using it with other ideas. No matter how many ideas
we use together, or how simple or complex it appears, there
should be the same sense of order that carries through the
design. You would know that in this particular composition it has a life of its own and is not obligated in any way
to any other composition that you have done, or that any-

one else has. In this sense, each work that we do would add up to the whole thing—that would be independent. It would certainly be related to other things, because nothing would happen without some roots or some relationships with other things. I think that we need to work for each individual thing we do having its own life and being an entity in itself.

Too many times, artists are more concerned about a trademark. When they have an idea that comes off well and is successful there is always the temptation to want to repeat that success, to do something that will identify the new work with them, so that anyone who looks at this composition can say that's a so-and-so, by so-and-so, that makes it a good marketable commodity. I think that many times artists are satisfied with that sort of thing. They feel they have to establish themselves through some formula or pattern. It may be a very good one. Then they are sort of stuck with it and they want to keep repeating it over and over so that everyone will know that it is theirs. Debussy once said, "The struggle to surpass others is never really great if dissociated from the noble ideal of surpassing one's self, though this involves the sacrifice of one's cherished personality." Now this cherished personality is the thing that most people hesitate to risk when they are composing or doing something with an idea. Too often they try to remember what they have done, or what someone else has done. They work it out so that anyone would recognize immediately that that's off the same bolt of goods as their other work. Artists who do not work this way are usually criticized, by their contemporaries at least, as being irrational and without direction, jumping off every which way, not having any real purpose in their overall effect.

I think in architecture, and any other art, so long as we

solve problems individually and try to give each work that we do a life of its own and find its order through what we do, that we can't possibly end up with this trademark idea because everything we do would be different from anything else we have done, or that anyone else has done. We do have to keep changing and we should never be afraid to change. There is always more where that came from and the more we change the more we grow. If we stop changing, then naturally we have stopped growing and we stay at a certain place.

In the finest art, first of all there has to be an impetus that makes it a necessity for being. We can manufacture art, just as we can manufacture anything else. If we have what is called taste and good background, we can concoct all sorts of things in art, but dealing with inspiration that comes through working out problems for specific reasons and because of inner necessity, we can't help but arrive at individual solutions for individual problems. I think that they are much more valid and authoritative than the sort of thing that is just manufactured, no matter how skillfully that may be. We do need to recognize this in order to keep growing; otherwise we will end up doing the same thing over and over no matter how well we may be doing it.

Many artists have started out rather bravely, taking stands, and doing individual works, and then eventually working themselves into a formula where they keep repeating things in a more polished manner. Of course, this other method I am speaking of is usually attacked or criticized on the grounds that it doesn't allow you to perfect an idea, that you are supposed to work an idea over and over all the time, until you refine it and perfect it. This process may end up with a slicker finished object, but many times it has worked all the life out of it, too. I think, in most cases, rather than perfecting the idea, it is more the notion of variations on a theme. I believe it is much more important for us to strive for perfection in each thing we do; rather to consider it merely a stepping stone to something later. If we feel that each thing we do has to stand or fall on its own merits, not in relation to the rest of our work or other people's work, then I think we are more apt to come out with something than if we feel it is just a little bit of the whole pattern.

Each work that a great artists does, a really great artist, is an individual thing, and it has its own life. You wouldn't have to know any other work by that artist or anyone else to recognize that. In the case of great artists like Debussy, Korin, Hokusai, and Mr. Wright you can sense that each one has its own life, and no matter how many times we experience these particular works, we can never quite add up the whole picture. For instance, we may understand the *Prelude to the Afternoon of a Faun*, which is certainly a composition which has its own order and own life. We can also understand the piano prelude, *The Girl with the Flaxen Hair*, which is a very simple little sketch and still with its own feeling and own atmosphere. We can understand *La Mer* or *Le Martyre de Saint Sebastian* or any of these pieces as individual efforts that have their own life and are independent of each other. After becoming well acquainted with all of Debussy's work we can understand more about Debussy. There is no time when we can comprehend it as a whole in a larger sense, as we find in nature, where we may break down each item in nature. We find a snow crystal and we can analyze that, we can analyze a certain tree, or a certain mineral, a drop of water, or something else, but it is impossible for us to think of it all together, except in a very general and abstract kind of way. The same is true, on a lesser scale of course, in the work that a person does.

When we look at Mr. Wright's work, we can sense that Unity Temple has it own kind of order, certainly related to the order that we find in the Larkin Building, but quite different because even using the square and flat plane idea that he used in both of these works, in one he comes out with a religious atmosphere and in the other he comes out with a business administration atmosphere. There is quite a subtle difference there in the way he has achieved it. It is very mysterious. We can think of the kind of order that is in the Coonley House and the kind that is in the Johnson Wax Building and the kind that is in any of his great works. We can understand them individually as separate things in themselves, and we can understand them collectively as part of Mr. Wright. I don't think that any one of them is Mr. Wright completely; nor do I think that any one thing in nature is nature completely. It seems to me that it's all part of this same thing. Part of the mystery is the fact that we can't understand it all no matter how much we analyze any part of it.

An artist who does seek change, who is curious, and wants to find out how to extend the horizons of his art, who is able to make each composition an entity in itself, with its own life and its own idea, is usually blamed for experimenting, or shopping around you might say, and not staying put. There is a certain feeling of security that some people have when they can pigeonhole an artist—when they feel they know what he would do. They can say this is obviously a Matisse or this is obviously a somebody else. It worries them a great deal when they can't put all of, say, Max Ernst's work in one category. He is apt to pull a rabbit out of the hat every so often and throw them all off base.

Usually the critics are very disturbed by artists who change this way because they have already made up their minds what this artist is and what he should be doing according to what he has already done. If he does something they are not expecting, then their attitude is it couldn't be good because it isn't what they had in mind. What could they have in mind anyway of what this artist can grow into and what he can do? Maybe this artist himself doesn't have it in mind. Maybe he has to find it and discover it as he goes along. Sometimes the artist will have a general sense of direction, or the feeling of need, the necessity to do something, for certain reasons. How he is going to do it may surprise himself when he comes to actually solving it and finding the order that will do that. Such artists are usually accused of going too far because they won't stay put.

All we have to do to answer that is to examine the past and ask ourselves who in the past ever went too far. It seems ridiculous looking backwards, although at the time almost any great artist was blamed by his contemporaries for that very thing. Even Beethoven in his last string quartets was accused of going too far, or writing music that sounded awful because he couldn't hear; he was deaf. People argued that if he could actually hear it, he wouldn't have written it because it sounded so bad and that he had gone too far. Now we consider those last works his best. Wagner was accused of going too far. People decided it was dangerous to listen to Wagner—that it would undermine your morals, and so on; that it would weaken you to go along with Wagner in music. Now it is pretty staple fare.

Debussy, of course, was considered as one who went too far, and Stravinsky, and Schoenberg. Practically anyone who has done anything has been accused of going too far. Still, after they have accomplished what they could in their lifespan and have been dead long enough so we can begin to get a little perspective on what they have done, we realize that worse things are happening now than what they did. Then we are apt to settle back and say they weren't so bad after all. Instead of feeling they went too far, we are apt to say, why didn't they go further? An artist who worries about going too far is like someone who wants to get their foot in the water and not get wet. The furthest we can go is very little, because we are limited very much by all the factors that enter into the production of any kind of art.

Architects particularly have a tougher time working with their limitations than any other artist, because they get into physical and monetary matters very rapidly, much more than any other art. That is why we don't have to worry about anyone going too far. The idea that can be built is certainly not going too far. It may stretch some materials and some methods, be it to the breaking point to what we have right now, but it is usually something that has to be done sooner or later and we might as well do it. When Schoenberg was accused of writing such horrible music and someone asked him why it sounded so bad he said, "Someone had to be Schoenberg and I am it." It is true in any kind of work that someone has to do it, someone has to make the changes and have the courage to stand by it and to fight for it if necessary so that the order can keep changing in our work and not have it all off the same bolt of goods.

Every civilization that has produced a culture has always done this very thing. After it is all dead and gone and we look back upon it, we don't know the names of the individuals who contributed to all of this, so we lump it all together as Egyptian or pre-Columbian, or Japanese, or something. Still those works of art were done by individuals, too, just as ours are. They had the advantage of having a more solidified culture than we have in religion and general ideas of race, climate, materials, and all, being much more restricted. Whereas here we have everything under the sun, all kinds of races, religions, landscapes, and materials. There is no material that is strictly indigenous anymore, because we use materials that have to be brought in from other places. Transportation makes it easy to have almost any material from most any place. Our condition has changed a great deal and that allows us much more freedom and flexibility. Still, within all this physical freedom and flexibility, physically and in ideas in our complex modern life, we have to establish a discipline. Discipline must be sought in freedom and it has to be free and it has to be disciplined. Just being free, of course, isn't enough, but in disciplining freedom one way we do it is by finding the order in a given composition, understanding the real reason and the necessity for its being, and working it out through this order and letting the feeling of order—or ideas, we call it sometimes—discipline the entire composition. That means we would reject certain things that might not fit within that kind of order. Of course the thing that would distinguish an authoritative work of art from an amateurish one would be largely that. Many times, when we are beginning, we want to put all our eggs in one basket, we want to try every idea we ever had and throw it all into the pot and make a hash out of it, whereas the older an artist becomes, and the more experienced he is, the more able he is to make ideas go further and to use fewer of them to get his sense of order. We sometimes blame him for his lack of spontaneity and youthful enthusiasm that maybe he has lost in the process of disciplining his work. If he is a great artist, I don't think that he has really lost that. He has probably learned to control it better. He wouldn't be the artist that [French composer]

Rameau said, when he was talking about himself, "Day by day his taste was improving but he was losing his genius." The greatest artist would be able to stay young all his life because no matter how old he was he would be working with ideas each time that were fresh and changing. At the same time, he would have the benefit of experience of simplification, weeding out unessentials, and making the order count for more, with less. This wouldn't necessarily need to be a matter of sterility; in fact, it wouldn't be if the artist had enough within him to keep absorbing and understanding, so that the more we do discipline our work, we will still have plenty to choose from in the way of experience to keep us from ending up in a very sterile abstraction.

Mr. Wright once said that architecture came from three places within us: from the head, the hand, and the heart—usually only from the hand, a little from the head, and hardly any from the heart. By heart I think he meant feeling or being sensitive to our senses and our experiences we get from them. It seems to me that most work does stop short of that; that quite often it is intellectual; quite often it is well done by the hand, but very little of it carries feeling to any nth power. I think that is why we don't get the thrill or the real satisfaction out of a lot of art that is good, but not really super. It seems that we are satisfied when we get something good and are afraid to take the chance to risk everything to make it really good. Cocteau said, "A real artist is one who, after he had finished a work of art, took the necessary steps to risk all in order to really complete it." Very few of us will take that risk because it means taking a chance. Most of us like the security of something that is good and acceptable, rather than running the risk of doing something that might lose everything in the process, or might gain everything. Still, the thing that makes an art work thrilling, and really authoritative and vital, and that gives it real life, is taking that chance over and above the call of duty. We must really feel the need to raise it to the nth power and not being merely nice or pleasant, but making it vital and really alive. We are too apt to stop along the way and we don't profit from the experience. For example, the experience that Hokusai had when he was asked how it felt to be such a great artist at seventy-five. He said when he was six he had shown an aptitude for drawing; when he was sixteen he had been admitted as an apprentice to a master; when he was forty-five he was able to please his friends— he could have stopped then; when he was seventy-five he felt that anything he had done before then was worthless because only then was he beginning to understand nature. If he could have ten years more he might be able to understand nature enough to give it real expression through his work. But if he could have ten years more beyond that, he could hope to make every line and dot live with life. By this, I think, he meant life not only of nature, but life of its own. In other words he would have assimilated nature to the point where it would have been second nature with him, and the expression of it through his work would exist in its own right, too, with a life of its own. That is where very few of us understand nature, because we are too content to see it and to interpret it and to try to record our feeling about it as individuals. Hardly ever are we able to carry it to the point to where our understanding of it has been assimilated so much that what we do has its own life, aside from nature or anything else, although nature has certainly been the guiding inspiration through it.

This attempt to solve problems and to assimilate influences and inspirations through imitation or emulation or digested experiences seems to me to add up to something

more than all of that so far as our individual works are concerned. The finished product has to have a life of its own,
independent of all of this, even though it came about because of it. It isn't going to have a life of its own unless it
has come about because of it, and it isn't going to have that
unless the artist is able to find, out of all these influences
and ingredients that have gone into it, an order that will
allow it to have that.

If we look at the work in the past—take an Egyptian
sculpture—we do not have to worry about who the god is
that is portrayed; we don't have to have a deep understanding of Egyptian religion, nor do we have to understand the
nature of the granite it's carved in, understand the life of
the man who did it, or anything like that. We know that
has all gone into it. We can only partially understand all
that as the person did who did the sculpture. Still, what he
achieved was an order that was independent of all of that,
and timeless, and one that we can tune in on if we are receptive to many of the ingredients that went into making it.
By retracing some of those steps, or experiencing some of
those ways, we can learn to understand the order that does
exist in that sculpture. We will probably never understand
it in the same way, because our experience will never be exactly the same. We will be able to go along with it enough
to understand something of the order that exists within it.
That is above any person—even the person who created it,
or the time, or the religion, or the material, or anything else
that went into making it. It has its own life, and its own order. I think that after all is said and done, no matter what
we achieve, that is the thing that gives our work its greatest authority. We do have to solve our problems; we have
to meet all the physical requirements. We have to solve
them with our talent which has been enriched through our

senses and experiences. We have to work through the nature of our materials so that they have a life of their own, even in the finished work, and haven't lost their identity so that we can reevaluate their identity through what has been done. Over and above all of that, we find the solution that we make has to be, in the end, not only personal but also impersonal; not only timely, but also timeless. In that way, only, can I understand a work of art as having real authority.

Bruce Goff at his Price Tower studio,
Bartlesville, Oklahoma, 1958. "For four
months the two of us sat there while he
told his stories . . ." (Welch, Preface)

Bruce Goff with Japanese paper lantern.

Philip Welch took this photograph of Bruce Goff working on his second mural in the 1962 Vernon Rudd House in San Mateo County, California, January 1964.

School of Architecture, corridor in
Building 604, North Campus, Univer-
sity of Oklahoma, circa 1950. Herb
Greene's drawings are on display.

Model of Crystal Chapel project, University of Oklahoma, Norman, 1949.

Hopewell Baptist Church, near Edmond, Oklahoma, 1948.

Hopewell Baptist Church. Interior view
of sanctuary skylight and chandelier
of pie pans and plastic ornaments.
A "wonderful interplay of curves and
domelike volumes . . ." (Welch,
Introduction)

Ruth Ford House, Aurora, Illinois, 1947–50.

Ruth Ford House. Detail of one of the
bedroom domes.

Eugene Bavinger House, Norman, Oklahoma, 1950. View from north.

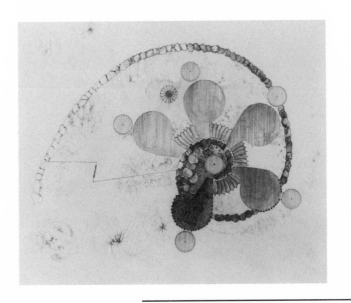

Eugene Bavinger House. Rendering of
floor plan, showing upper levels, by
Herb Greene.

Eugene Bavinger House. View from
southeast.

John Garvey House project, Urbana Illinois, 1952. Rendering of perspective, first design, by Herb Greene. ". . . a continuous space which is ever changing." (Goff, #10)

John Garvey House project. Rendering
of interior perspective, first design, by
Herb Greene. "Going around this circular ramp, we are going around an
interior garden . . . that will be comfortable in winter and summer." (Goff,
#10)

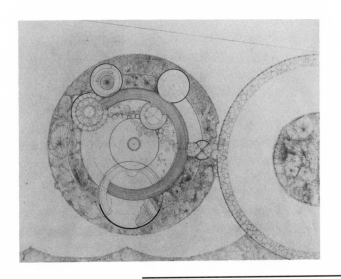

John Garvey House project. Rendering of floor plan, first design, by Herb Greene. "This circular motion established by the driveway and the revolving door seemed to indicate a circular feeling that might be carried through as an idea." (Goff, #10)

Bruce Goff composition, "Squircle,"
1952. "A 'squircle' is a square circle. . . .
It moves with a little more of [a] jerk
than a circle . . ." (Goff, #10)

Six

The Continuous Present in Architecture

I got into architecture at a very early age without my wish, or consent, or knowledge. It was purely accidental and according to the laws of chance. So I was into it as part of the continuous present, you might say, right from the beginning, since I had no choice in the matter. After I got into it, I liked it so much I didn't think anything about getting out of it. One time Debussy said he had to be a musician because he hadn't been taught anything else. That was about the fix I found myself in.

So architecture has been my passion for so long that it seems to be sort of a religion or something that I am dedicated to. No matter how many buildings you have built, if you think of each one as a new experience, and new solutions for new problems, which is always the case, and don't try to remember what you did before, or what someone else did before, but try to approach each problem as freshly as possible, you find that you are always doing something strange and new and different. Sometimes you look at it and wonder, did that come out of me? I can tell you now that I have never done a house that I would want myself.

This event was recorded at the University of Santa Clara (where I was chairman of the School of Art and Architecture) on April 3, 1967. Goff was our invited architect-in-residence. The talk was the conclusion of his two-week visit, and a large exhibit of his work was on display. Goff, sitting on a stool in front of a large screen on which we simultaneously projected two pictures of his work (not in linear order), was unable to see the images. We wanted to create a "continuous present" environment, and Goff presented an outstanding example of the process.

This probably strikes you as funny, but it is true, because I haven't built a house for myself yet. I am scared to death to try it. I can assure you it wouldn't be a house; it would have to be more like a warehouse, I think. Anyway people often think that if you do these peculiar looking things that you must be doing what you want in a house or building, rather than what the client wants. So these things are said about you and people get the idea that you are forcing your clients to live in strange and unusual affairs.

I remember one time Alfonso Iannelli gave a talk at the University of Oklahoma. The Bavinger House had just been constructed there and one of the people, who hated this house more than anyone at the talk, asked Mr. Iannelli, after his talk, if he thought an architect was justified in making a client live in a spiral. That was a loaded question, of course, and it was obvious what was meant. Mr. Iannelli said, "Well I suppose you are referring to the Bavinger House, and I see Bruce out in the audience there, so how would you answer that, Bruce?" I said that I could answer, but I wished Mr. Bavinger was here to answer it because I thought anything I would say might sound like an excuse or an apology or alibi or something. Much to my amazement, Mr. Bavinger was in the audience at the back of the room, and he spoke up and said, "I am here Bruce and I would like to answer that question." He then proceeded to do it in a way I could never have done. He answered as the client, as the consumer. He said, "You know, I resent the question, because it implies that my wife and I are a couple of stupes that had no idea of what we were getting into, and that we were forced into this design by someone. It is true we never dreamed we would live in a spiral, never thought of it. We told him what we wanted, what we liked, what we didn't like, and it ended up with a spiral, and we are damned glad it did. I really don't think it's anybody else's business."

The Bavinger House was built out in the country on a dirt road without any fanfare and without any money. They couldn't get a loan on it, of course, and to make matters worse the man was an art professor, and you know they never have any money. He was very good at hard work; he was more like a truck driver in his build, and he liked to get out and dig and move large rocks and that sort of thing. His hobby was growing plants indoors and he was a very sensitive painter. After he got the house started with the help of some students, who had volunteered their labor in exchange for paintings, he tired of people coming around to see it. One day he decided to stop this by charging them a dollar apiece. This really encouraged it, because many people who would hesitate to come and ask to see the place felt perfectly at ease if they could pay a buck. After they saw it, they couldn't believe it; they would go back and try to describe it to their friends, and their friends couldn't believe it, and they would come and spend another dollar. So this process started making money. Then tax problems came up, of course, and they had to get a smart lawyer to show them how to get out of paying what legally is called an amusement tax. This went on until they had taken in over fifty thousand dollars, and it was getting so they couldn't eat, or sleep, or take a bath, without people coming to see the house. They finally decided it was time to stop all of this foolishness and live in it. So they stopped it.

One day, a big white Cadillac drove up after they had stopped. It had steer horns out in front of it, and it was obviously from Texas. There was a large gentleman at the wheel who had on a ten-gallon hat with a passenger who was a very flashy blonde. He drove up to where Bavinger

was working out in the yard, moving rocks. Mr. Bavinger
was all sweaty, dirty, needed a shave, and was wearing his
army fatigues. The fellow stopped and thought he was
one of the hired help, and asked where he could find Mr.
Bavinger. He said, "I am Bavinger, what can I do for you?"
The man said, "Are you Bavinger?" Bavinger said, "What
do you want?" The man said, "My wife and I just drove
up from Dallas and we want to see your house." Bavinger
said, "That's too bad because we are not showing it anymore." The man said, "You can't do that." Bavinger said, "I
can't do what?" The man said, "When you have a work of
art you must share with people—you shouldn't keep it all
to yourself. We really want to see it." Bavinger said, "Well,
I am an artist and I appreciate your point of view, but do
you really mean it?" The man said, "What do you mean, do
I really mean it?" Bavinger said, "Well, do you believe you
should share a work of art with others." The man said, "Of
course." Bavinger asked, "Is that your wife?" So you see,
all sorts of things happen. Anyway the man and his wife
didn't get to see the house.

I could tell you all sorts of stories all evening, but I would
rather talk about architecture in relation to the continuous
present. This is a subject that has fascinated me for some
time, and it is something that is making itself apparent in
many arts, music, literature, painting, and others. That is
the way we regard a work of art, whether we think of it as
a hermetically sealed design that has a beginning, a development, and an ending, which I think is the old classical
concept that most works of art seem to have as a basis. But
though their effect is often longer than this, or extends beyond it, their influence, their results, their inspiration, and
all that, the overtones, you might say, go beyond the composition itself. We have more and more the feeling that each

thing we do, each work of art we do, whatever it is, is not really something that has a beginning or an ending. It is something that is continuing. We are beginning to understand more and more that change is necessary, always. As one of my students said, "Stop moving and you are dead." You have to keep changing. Change does not necessarily mean progress, as we often like to think. Change is a necessary thing to keep happening, to keep things vital and alive. So if we stop to think about it, even if we start a composition, or building, or piece of music, or whatever we are doing, you might say, we are tuning in instead of starting, because it has taken us all our lives, and many other people's lives before us, to be part of a continuing thing, before we are able to continue through into this composition. So we really don't start it when we start the composition; we don't really begin then, we begin again and again, as Gertrude Stein says. We have to think of it as something continuous and something growing; something becoming, always becoming. The composer Boulez once said, "I like to think of music as something that is constantly changing, continuing, and that each composition is a burrow where I store my ideas. And after a while these ideas are discovered, and found out, then I need another burrow to store some more ideas." It is rather a curious notion of why he composes, you see.

I think if you examine the way a building is done, in the old beaux arts sense, based on classical models, mostly Greek and Roman, you will find that there is a need felt for a beginning, a grand entrance, foyer, vestibule, a grand hall as something to go into, and then you proceed through the building in a very prescribed route, and you end up with the main hall, or the climax of the building, the rotunda, or some effect that is supposed to knock you out, and this is the climax. This is all according to a prescribed route. It involves a sense of time, like, I have been here, and I am here, and I am going there. This is a sense of having a beginning and an ending. Most compositions used to have this. Music usually had an introduction, then there was the development section, then it ended up with a climax (or anticlimax) and it was supposed to return to its original key or original idea and have sort of a cornice at the end, so you would know when to applaud. There was always this sense that it had to end, somewhere, and you had to be prepared for the ending. This has happened in architecture with the three-part form, where you have the base, the superstructure, and the entablature. This is a very old notion that has come from way back in Greek times. You will notice that even in Frank Lloyd Wright's early work, for example the Larkin Building, that had a base, much simpler than the Greek base, it had a blocky kind of base, then a superstructure, and then a cap or something at the top to finish it off. Later, Mr. Wright abandoned all of this and did away with the base, and the top, you see. Artists have been going through this process in painting. We no longer feel we have to enter a painting at a certain place and follow around somebody's arms and legs and draperies and tables and things to arrive back where we started, you see. That used to be considered a good composition. Now we can enter a painting any place we please, can't we? And we can find our way through it anyway we want to. The same is true of sculpture; the same is true of many other art forms. In the individual work of art, whether it is a painting, a building, or a piece of music, we no longer demand that the form be a sandwich of an ABA; or a base, superstructure, and entablature; or a beginning, development, and a climax.

We can approach this from all sorts of ways. We can think

of this more easily perhaps if we were to visualize it as a park. Say there is a beautiful woods out here with streams, maybe a waterfall, and some nice trees and rocks and so on. Before anything is done about this, while in its natural state, before any road or path or anything is in place, you could wander into this area if it isn't even fenced in. You would be able to walk around in it, and it wouldn't have any beginning, would it? And it wouldn't have any development, or any climax. You could go through it many different ways, couldn't you? In nature, there is no beginning and no ending; you know it is a continuing thing. You could go through all of this in many different ways, and it would seem quite different, according to the season, or the time of day, or the way you felt, or all sorts of things. It would always be an ever new experience. You would never be traveling the same route twice.

Now supposing some city planner, or park planner, or someone comes in and prescribes a route. He says I want you to go by this particular place to get a view from here, I want you to see this group of trees, I want you to come over to the water at this point, I want to put some restrooms here, and I want a place over here where you end up and really knock you out, for this will be the grand climax, maybe a plaque or something. Then you go through it according to someone's idea of what a composition is, you see. This I think is rather a crude illustration, but I believe you get the idea. On the one hand, you have a very free kind of composition that you can enter and go through in many ways, and on the other, you have a very prescribed route, where whoever is doing the design calls the shots and builds you up, or lets you down, or lets you rest, or catch your breath, or whatever you need to do, and rings out of you every bit of emotion that he can.

This type of planned composition is often true of music, as you know. Then there is the other kind of music like
Debussy's *La Mer* in which you have a feeling of great organization, not in the old classical sense of form, but a very
orderly kind of discipline, and still it has considerable depth
always and much of interest is happening. No matter how
many times you hear it, there is always some fresh relationship you can sense in the parts. I can vouch for this because
I have heard it hundreds of times, and always like to hear
it, because I get something different out of the arrangement
of it every time. It isn't one of those pieces that you play
by chance, as some of the composers are doing now, where
they have parts that can be interchanged or played at will,
and all sorts of things, according to the laws of chance, as
they say. There is the law of chance composition, and then
there is the type where you prescribe generally what is happening, and then there is a certain amount of chance in how
you happen to hear it, or see it. I think this looking into
a composition, giving it depth, is another dimension that
has a great deal of meaning. Instead of looking at a building
or a painting, you look into it, as you do nature. You don't
look at nature. If you look at the sky you are not looking at
a flat plane, but are looking into clouds or through trees or
into water or the depths of shadows. In buildings, if you are
looking at a building, it is not a very good building usually
because it is two dimensional. If it has a flat facade it photographs beautifully, and a good photographer can make a
fine presentation out of just about anything, if he knows
how. The more two dimensional it is, the more apt it is to be
a good photograph. On the other hand, many things that
have depth and mystery are not easily photographed. Many
times our buildings suffer from reproductions and pictures.
Sometimes they gain considerably. I have seen buildings

in pictures I thought were quite handsome; I have gone to see the building and tried to figure our where in the world the picture was taken from, because they don't have this presence in the real building that was in the photograph. Sometimes I found the photographer was on his stomach in the grass with a few blades of grass in front of him, or something like that. It's a good trick.

Looking into things is as important as looking out, or beyond. We often think of infinity as something way out there, somewhere in outer space, don't we? We also know that infinity is within and we have never reached infinity within, or without. I don't believe we can even grasp it. We can say things about it; we can think about it; but I don't think we can really know where the end is, or the beginning is, in anything. We can split things down into atoms, molecules, particles, and all sorts of units so we can think about them, but we still haven't found the mystery in this way, and I doubt if we will find it in the other direction, out to infinity. We keep exploring, we keep wanting to know, and I think the more we explore, and the more we find out, the more mysterious all of this becomes. This is very rewarding. Mystery is a quality that all great art has, and I think all great people have. Nature certainly has it—animals have it. It is a very fine quality. In art, we often are content to surprise someone with shock, and we say, "That sure knocked them off their feet." If that is all it did, and there is no mystery to back it up, it is apt to be pretty shallow and meaningless, no matter how big a noise it makes. Someone could shoot off a gun in this room and make everybody jump, but then what after we jump? You'd have to have some feeling of why did he shoot the gun off, of what is going to happen next, or something like that. Otherwise, you are just startled and you would get over it, or maybe you could even get used to it if you heard guns going off all the time; in a shooting gallery, you might get to where it didn't bother you at all. I think we do develop this kind of immunity in our environment. We look around us and we see the same monotony of nothingness everywhere we look, and the same drabness, the same lifelessness, the same fadisms, of old times and new times. We get a sort of immunity to this commonness, this ugliness, and we don't question it. I think we should question it, if we ever get to where it doesn't bother us. It is too bad, I think, if we get used to piped-in music around us where we can't stand it if it goes off. There is something wrong, because we are not really listening to it while it is going on, but if it is gone we feel there is something wrong because we are by ourselves again. I do think we need to keep alert and alive to all our senses and our environments and try to improve them as much as we can.

Now this quality of mystery, after something has surprised us, mystery is what holds our attention. The more we know some things the more mysterious they seem. Right now, as artists, we have more at our command in the way of things to take in—all the art of the world, old and new. We have access to music of the entire world, old and new. We have access to reproductions, models, and almost everything that's known that has been accomplished. We have all the literature in our libraries, and we are exposed to new developments, technologies, new materials. We have everything to do work with. Wherever you get your inspiration, or your kicks, or whatever you want to call them, there comes a time when you have to do them. You have to do something about them. If we don't do something about them, we are not functioning as we are able to, and we are thwarted and handicapped in this way. I don't think talent is so rare that only very few people have it. But I think what is rare is when anyone does anything about it. This is too bad, because there are too many casualties, and too many people who could do things, but are not doing them.

We have all the resources, and now we need to do more with them. People annoy me who consider architecture a package already wrapped up, or any other art, and say, "Well, we've got it made." I often talk to American Institute of Architects groups, and quite often they come around and say, "Why are you stirring around architecture? We are just getting things under control so we can use it." Meaning they're getting some forms they can crib, you see; they can use forms that are already done by so-called "form givers" and they become "forms takers" and they can use them with immunity, because the magazines pat them on the back for their discipline, and their restraint, in using these things. On the other hand, they knock the guy who doesn't do this—the fellow who is not in the mainstream. The fellows who are in the mainstream of the past are usually the ones who have been loners, who were not in the mainstream at the time, but now we realize that, after all, they were in the mainstream. There are many examples in history to prove this. So what is in the mainstream, and what isn't, is a moot point always. You will usually find at the time the person who is criticized for this is considered avant garde, or very much out of everything, a kind of a freak because he isn't doing what everyone else is doing. The sad thing is that there is always a time when people catch up with him, and they put him in a little pigeonhole and say, "He fits right in here because this is the part of the mainstream he was in."

I don't think this is anything to worry about, particularly, except to realize there are no fads, no conventions of what is good discipline in art, that are really much good. Any rules that are made can be broken and proven false. I think you have to use discipline: there is no such thing as doing a work of art without discipline and order. If it is a work of art it will have these things. Discipline does not mean punishment, or self-denial in this sense; it means a sense of order, and a sense of being together, and belonging together, you see. It isn't a matter of disciplining something according to the way the fashion is today. The fashion keeps changing, and what was the fashion yesterday is not the fashion for today, you see. It is all part of the continuing present again. We are always changing this.

So what is valid, and what does hold true? Is there anything that gives all of this unity and meaning? Mr. Wright once said, "Principle is the safe precedent." I think that is quite true, because there are principles involved in any creative work which are very basic—which were used by the Egyptians, the Greeks, the Chinese, the pre-Columbians, and us or anyone who is attempting to do anything. These principles are subject to various interpretations and changes. For instance, if you are using the principle of balance, it doesn't mean there is a law that says you have to have something here to balance something here. It isn't that simple anymore—you can achieve balance in many ways. You can achieve it in many ways that have never been achieved, too. You do need to consider this as something that is integral and part of what you are doing. Rhythm is the same. I think that most of our contemporary architecture today is sterile, rhythmically. This is curious, because in music our compositions have become much more complex rhythmically, but in architecture we are still in the fence-post and telegraph-pole sense of rhythm, where there is something every so many feet, you see. Regular as clockwork. Once in a while, they might leave out a post, or something, but you feel that it is still there. Most of our popular music is still very stodgy, rhythmically, compared with so-called modern classical music, or whatever you want to call it.

The natives are way up on us with rhythm. One time, Stravinsky heard a composition for five drums, played by five African drummers, each playing a rhythmic pattern in counterpoint with each other. He thought, at first, that this was just a jam session that hadn't been worked out or couldn't be repeated. In recording this several different times, and comparing recordings, they found that it was a fixed composition and it did always come out the same way. Stravinsky, who is no slouch in rhythm and was considered pretty wild when he composed *The Rite of Spring*, said, "I felt like a schoolboy when I listened to these Africans." I think the same can be said about our architecture when we see the great rhythmic patterns set up in Oriental buildings, and many others. We still are in a pretty stodgy state there. The new music, though, is becoming quite free.

You see, whatever these principles are, whether they have to do with color, or texture, or scale, or proportion, or rhythm, or any of the things that make up design, balance, symmetry, and all these things, they are still there whether you are using very new materials, or very old materials, or are doing a doghouse, or a cathedral. One problem the architect faces in doing his work is being part of the continuous present of living. His work is naturally part of the whole continuous present pattern of living, as part of society, and what is needed by society for the environment. He is not free to operate in the sense that most artists are. He has to do things that are commissioned, always. He has to do a job with what he is building, doesn't he? If he is building a house it has to be something someone can live in, usually a very specific family—or a business building, or a church, or a school, or a hot-dog stand, or whatever it is: it's serving a function and a purpose. He has to be able to be sort of a chameleon that can change his ways at a moment's notice and enter into the spirit of the occasion. If he is thinking about doing a magnificent cathedral and someone comes in and wants a bowling alley, what does he do? Say, "Go away I am thinking of cathedrals." No, he quickly puts on his bowling-alley suit and does a bowling alley; even if he doesn't care about bowling he has to suddenly develop an intense interest in it so he can do a good bowling alley, or whatever it is he is doing. He has to become a good friend of his client; he has to enter into the client's way of feeling or living, in the sense of giving them the kind of expression and plan that they need. The client is part of all this.

Now, it is also necessary for us, as architects, to do some absolute architecture, too, where we not only solve problems of a utilitarian nature but where we can build things for architectural expression, that you might call absolute architecture, just as a composer of music, or painters, or sculptors, or dancers, or any other kinds of artists can. This will offer considerable freedom and will require an even more intense discipline. Speaking of discipline, this is one of the things that I am accused of not having. Particularly by many architects. They think that what you do is done "just for effect"—this supposed to be bad because it implies that if you do something just for effect that it can't have very much depth, or meaning, or reason. I plead guilty to working for effect. I think that architecture has to have effect to be more than just building.

All the great architecture that has been accomplished certainly achieves effect, doesn't it? The Greeks didn't have to go to all the trouble they did on the Parthenon just to have a building there. Even with columns around the building, they could have had straight up and down columns without emphasis. They could have had no fluting. They could have skipped all that monkey business about bases, and capitals, and all that. They could have had them straight up and down and all even by spacing instead of getting them closer together as they got out toward the end of the building. Why did they do that? For effect, didn't they? They were trying to correct optical illusions and they were trying to make it seem better to look at. They knew that the platform the building was built on looked like it sagged out on the corners. Who cares whether the floor is level, you see? Then they had the columns closer together as they got out to the end because they seemed to fall apart if they weren't closer. They were smart enough to know that. Why did they have the center lines of all the columns on the Parthenon converge at one point about a mile above the building if it wasn't for effect? Why did Phidias design his sculpture around inside the frieze of the colonnades of the Parthenon so that they would be lighted from below rather than above—because he knew the effect was going to be that way, didn't he? He knew that the sun would never shine on them from above because the roof extended out over them. He did know that the effect of light would come from the sun shining on the platform and bouncing back up to the frieze underneath the overhang. He knew that would be the effect, so he designed his sculpture to take advantage of this effect, you see. These effects were all genuine, thought out, earned, predetermined, and they called their shots and they got their effects.

I think the pitiful thing is when someone tries for effect and doesn't get it. So, I hope that I get it—I work hard enough sometimes. There is more to it than just effect; it is necessary to get effect, to give it character, quality, and additional interest. After this effect, which may be mild or wild, then there has to be more to it. There has to be depth and reason, and it becomes part of much more, which is a part of the continuous present, again, you see. It is not a matter of creating a beginning, a development, and an ending. These are things we learn from history, and as Gertrude Stein says, "Let me recite what history teaches, history teaches," you see. It does. This is nothing new; it is something that has been known for thousands of years. It is new to us as we discover it each time, as we become part of the continuous present, the thing that keeps changing, that keeps adjusting itself to different kinds of life and purposes. One of the exciting things about architecture is that it is something you actually live in, or work in, or worship in, or whatever you do within it; it is part of your life existence, part of your environment, and it becomes a very important part of our lives. It is not like a painting you hang on the wall that you can take down if you don't like it. If it is a building you build, you are stuck with it, aren't you?

Architecture, the way it is now, is entirely too static, too earthbound, and I think it is only a question of time till some of it will be disposable, like picnic plates. The Balinese have a good idea about architecture: they say why should we build buildings for the people to come? Let's build our own buildings and let them build theirs. Part of this is due to the fact that nothing lasts very long there on account of the climate in the way of stone and building material. In a way, that is good because each generation gets to build something themselves. Here we get stuck with hand-me-downs, like this building, and we have to stay with it, even after it is obsolete. Even most of our commercial buildings are obsolete the minute they are built because the purpose changes, always, whether it is a loft building or an apartment building. This all changes according to the changes of the town. What is the fashionable district now, isn't later. Or what is suitable for an office now, may be only a warehouse district later. The buildings are built so much for a specific purpose, so loaded with columns, like this lecture hall, that there is no flexibility. Even as business investments they are poor, because they don't have this flexibility.

Why should we always go into a room and have it the same color? That doesn't mean you would have to paint it every day, but there are ways of changing colors right now, and there will even be new ways of doing this. Why should we always go into the same volume of space? Why should we have to go through doors always? There are all kinds of fascinating possibilities here. Why should our buildings be earthbound, anchored to a little spot of earth? All of this may sound like Buck Rogers stuff or science fiction, but so would many of the things that we accept today as accomplished facts, that have been thought of just a few years ago. The architect is faced with an entirely different problem now than ever before. As schools change, he is going to have to change his designs for schools, isn't he? If it ever comes to where schools are eliminated and education is dispensed via television of some sort, think of what a difference that will make in homes. Think what a difference it will make when people retire and get paid for retiring, to the point where the husband is around the house all the time. Women are complaining about this already. They resent the loss of the freedom they used to have when the old man was working downtown at the office. So the house has to take care of this situation, doesn't it? Most houses have no place for children. About the only concession given to them is to have a little room for a bedroom, and a room called a rumpus room, or a game room, or something like

this, which is usually the living room for the entire family.
Why don't they live in the living room? That is what the
decorator did, and we mustn't mess it up, you see. That is
just for nice times, like the parlor used to be for the Sunday
preacher. All of these conditions keep changing. Whatever
social structures become, or however the people become,
naturally affects what the house has to become to take care
of them. If it becomes necessary to have drive-in churches,
we would have drive-in churches. They would have to be
different from drive-in theaters, wouldn't they? The architect doesn't determine these things in that sense; he has to
go along with the crowd with whatever is happening. He
can remedy some of these situations in various ways, or he
can point out ways that would be better sometimes, but he
is not a prophet. He can't make over the social structure
of his town, but he certainly has to work with it, whatever
it is. The economic structure, too. This is all part of the
continuous present.

If you are doing a house, you are not doing a house for
just one person, usually, you are doing it for a family. All of
the various people involved have certain things they want.
You have to accommodate them. Now the question always
comes up, supposing you did do a house that met the requirements of the family perfectly, and then they had to sell
it. Who else would want it? Fortunately, we still have many
of the same needs—all of us. We all have two ears and two
eyes, a nose, and a mouth, don't we? We have bathrooms
and we have kitchens (even in my houses!)—closets, and
many of the niceties of living are in any kind of house. Air
conditioning, plumbing, heating, wiring, and all this. Who
would buy such a thing if it were ever for sale? Well, it
would be some other nut, it would be some nut that wanted
something that was different. He would want this particu-

lar design, you see. There would not be as large a market for resale as you might have with the usual ranchburgers and Cape Cod fishes and things, but you would have a better market because if he wanted it he would want it bad and would be willing to pay more for it. It becomes more in the category of a work of art which increases in value.

If you go to Oak Park today, where Frank Lloyd Wright did many, many houses back about 1900 to 1910, you will see newspapers advertising some of these houses. Every one of the houses is called a Frank Lloyd Wright masterpiece—even the ones that aren't. Even the imitation ones are called this. There is a premium on them. People want things that have quality and they are willing to pay for them. There are no real fine works of architecture sitting empty and unused anywhere that I know of. They are always sold immediately. The loan companies have recognized this, finally, and it's not anywhere near the problem to get a loan, if your client is stable, as it used to be. This is encouraging.

There are more people that want architecture than ever wanted it before. Especially after Ayn Rand wrote *The Fountainhead*. More people want to become architects than ever before, especially after Ayn Rand wrote *The Fountainhead*. They found out it was a pretty sexy business, especially in the second chapter. Speaking of *The Fountainhead*, I asked Mr. Wright one time if he was considered the model for the hero; he chuckled and said, "Ayn sent me the first two chapters of the book and asked me to read them and tell her what I thought." He didn't read them; he was busy and didn't pay any attention. Finally, she sent him the rest of the manuscript and she said, "I have taken the trouble to write this, and you are the model for the main character, so I think the least you can do is to read it." He said he read it and he thought it was "damn good." Then it be-

came a best-seller and a movie. She wanted him to do the
sets for the movie, but by then he was getting to be a little
alarmed because the book was getting a pretty sensational
response. Everybody was reading it. He finally decided he
better not get identified with this too closely, so he turned
down their offer of $180,000 for designing the sets, which
he needed badly then. But he said no, he couldn't do it unless they let him direct the movie. It is too bad they didn't
take him up on it because that would have been a curious
affair, no doubt. People do get the idea sometimes that architecture is a very glamorous profession, and I suppose it
is in many ways. It is certainly a very interesting one, because you work closely with people and that is part of the
fun of it.

People now want architecture. The need is felt. But there
is very little architecture of real quality being done. This is
nothing new, either. The Greeks didn't always build classic Parthenons; the Gothic builders didn't always turn out
the great cathedrals for other buildings. Architecture has
always been rare, and the people doing great art in architecture, or in painting, or in sculpture, or music, or any other
form, have been in the minority when many people are operating in the field. Very few are trying to do very much
with this field, or trying to extend the boundaries of the
field. It is a rarity and probably always will be, as anything
of quality is. It isn't a matter of snobbism or exclusiveness.
I think that anyone can have a work of architecture, if he
can have a house at all, but he has to go to an architect to get
it. Most architects don't want to fool with houses; they say
you can't make any money doing them. Which is true. It
takes as much time and more effort, more patience, to do a
single house than it would to do a commercial building that
cost four or five times as much and you get that much more

fee, you see. So why fool with houses? Personal houses are
becoming regarded as a luxury item more and more.

The tract builders have houses, and they have gone with
it. They advertise, sometimes, that they aim to individual-
ize their productions. Some of them will give you a choice.
You can have a choice of colonial light fixtures or modern,
or you can choose the color for your wall, or you can even
move a door or window if it isn't too late. This personalizes
it. That is about as far as most people get their buildings
personalized. About the only way they can really personal-
ize it is to do it in the furnishings, and this is sometimes too
late. That is why we have these migrations of furniture that
are always going on, where the furniture doesn't look right,
no matter where it is, you see. I know my mother had this
problem. Every month the furniture had to be changed. It
wasn't any better after it was changed, but at least it got
moved around because there was no good place for it to be.

Most of our houses are started as an outside concern
where we think about how we want them to look. Usually
we start with a rectangle because we are used to rectangular thinking. This is curious, because Lord Raglan, who
is not an architect or an artist but an economist and so-
cialist, made a very intensive study of the housing of man.
He found that the majority of people in all civilizations,
lumped together, have lived in circular houses. If you go out
to these new subdivisions and build a circular house they
will scream their heads off, even now. They will say, "That's
a round house," and this is supposed to be far out. Look
how many round houses have been built by natives. Why
do you think they built them round? Not because they were
trying to be strange and new and different; they were trying
to accomplish the most with the least. It took less material
to go around the same amount of area in a circle than it

did any other way. A square or rectangle would take more. The circle was stronger, too. The Africans with their huts, and the Indians with their tepees, and the Eskimos with their igloos, and the pit houses of Asians, and the homes of many other primitive people, so called, have been circular houses. Still, it is considered a very radical thing to do today.

I remember when I did the Boston Avenue Church in Tulsa, Oklahoma, in 1926, I had a circular auditorium. This was considered very irreligious and downright sinful. I won't say why, but anyway it was. It also had a driveway entrance to the church and this was considered sacrilegious. You were supposed to suffer and walk through the rain from where you parked. You were supposed to sit on hard pews instead of a comfortable seat. All in the name of religion. That's all right for those who want it.

The concept of design keeps changing and we find that there is no form, no color, no texture, no line, or anything that should be taboo; they should all be part of an architect's vernacular, his vocabulary. The architect should be free to operate with any color, any texture and he shouldn't have to apologize for doing a certain design, or have to justify himself. Some people say, how do you justify this or that? It isn't a matter of justifying things or being on trial; it is a matter of having a great many ideas to use and being able to use them to make a whole design that is still part of the continuous present in our society.

We never can consider our work done. When we build a house, we don't just build a house; we build the house with the yard or the site; we consider the community; we consider the elements, the climate, the neighbors—everything we can. We try to anticipate how these things will change. No matter how strange they may seem at the time, people usually get used to them, and eventually they become friends with them. I think that this is a strange thing, because almost always our first impulse, if we see something we don't understand, is to laugh at it, or to ridicule it, or to make fun of it. Debussy said, "There is something in embryo in every beautiful idea, which seems absurd to fools." That is often true. Fortunately, people finally begin to understand this. I will trust the public any day quicker than I will the critics, because the public usually acts according to their feeling and their emotions. Sometimes this reaction is not thought out, but eventually they will see the reason, and understand it better than the man who criticizes the design because it isn't what he had in mind. The public is more apt to understand it, in the long run, than the critics. Sibelius said, "No one ever erected a monument to a critic." Stravinsky said, "Critics don't know five percent of what I know. A work of art is like the nose on your face: it cannot be criticized." People keep trying to criticize it; they keep trying to analyze things, "They keep trying," as Debussy said, "to destroy the mysteries by pulling things to pieces. People regard a work of art as something to analyze, to pull apart, like they used to pull apart their dolls, only to find sawdust inside. They are always trying to slay the mysteries in cold blood." Fortunately, this can't be done. Because there is always more, if there is anything there at all.

Another thing that Debussy said in this regard was that the enthusiasm of the public for an artist made him suspicious of this artist, because he might be too much a part of this same public. I don't think he meant this in a snobbish or high-hat sort of way; I think he meant that many times the public hasn't gotten adjusted to it yet. If it is something that they immediately accept as something very great, it is probably something that is a flash in the pan. He said, "Rather than a first night's success, I would prefer a last night's success." I think that is what he is getting. One time he said about his work, and understanding of it, "On that distant day, I trust it is still very far off, when I am no longer a cause for strife, I will reproach myself bitterly, for that odious hypocrisy which enables one to please all mankind will inevitably have triumphed, even in those last works." He didn't want things to be accepted right away; he was afraid if they were accepted right away there was something wrong. Sometimes it takes a little time.

All of this acceptance is still part of the continuous present. It is still something that is part of the whole picture. After a while, we accept these things and we wonder what all the fuss was about. Someone said once, "Revolution is merely evolution made apparent." Sometimes what seems radical, unusual, and wild at first blush, we soon find out is a matter of evolution or continuous change again. Many times we wonder what in the world scared people about this; it doesn't seem very strange now. It is hard when we hear Beethoven's last quartets to think of them as radical anymore, isn't it, unless we can project ourselves into his time? I remember reading about the Surprise Symphony of Haydn; he was tired of the audience going to sleep in the slow movements, so he put in a chord that was supposed to really jolt them—wake them up at a certain point. I thought that was quite an idea and I would like to hear it. So I got the record and I played it, and I didn't get jolted once, because I had been jolted a lot more by experts. What was supposed to be jolting was perfectly acceptable to me without any surprise. I had to listen to it many times before I would put my finger on the spot where I was supposed to be jolted.

Sometimes you do get used to things so that it is hard to imagine what surprised people before. I don't think that should be our aim. I think that if I wanted to scare people,

I could, but this isn't my aim. I am not trying to shock anyone; I am just trying to work and trying to be part of the
continuous present as I understand my art of architecture.

I am interested in exploring new materials when I can.
Sometimes you can't; sometimes you are forced to use materials that are as old as the hills, because of availability, or
because of costs, or something. Just the same I like to keep
looking ahead, trying to figure out what we can do. I always say the worst is yet to come. Don't be surprised if you
see something happen that is not like anything you have
seen of mine here on these walls. I guarantee that each time
I do anything it is not going to be like any of this. All of
these drawings are water under the bridge and it all stands
for something for specific cases. Sometimes this is hard for
people to understand, because they will see a house you do
some place, and they will say, "We would like you to do our
house, but we always wanted a two-story house." Maybe
they saw a one-story that you did. One comment I had once
was, "We always wanted you to do our house, but we always
wanted a house with a screened porch." Why not? They can
have a screened porch. It is all right with me. In fact, I have a
lot of fun with screened porches. Another person said, "We
would like to have one of your houses but we always wanted
a brick house." Well, why not? I have no bad feelings
against brick. You see you get all of these peculiar notions
that if they see a round house you have done somewhere,
all your houses must be round; if they see a triangular one,
they think they all must be triangular; or a shingle house,
they are all made of shingles. Whatever they see must be
what you do, and they don't want any of that. They can't
seem to realize that you are trying to do what they want.

The hardest client to deal with is the person who won't
tell you what he wants or who doesn't know what he wants.

I had a client come in not long ago who had seen a house I had done out on the prairies of Oklahoma, in the Panhandle. These people liked this house and they asked the owner if she thought I would do them a house. She said she thought I surely would, but don't tell him how to do it. She tried to brainwash them, you see. She said to just go in and tell him what you need and let him figure it out. As a result, I had an awful time finding out what they wanted and what they needed. I said, "What do you need? How many bedrooms for instance?" They said, "That all depends on you." I said, "How do you figure that." They said, "We don't want to cramp your style." I said, "I don't have any style, what do you mean cramp my style?" They said, "We don't want to interfere with your ideas. We want you to do what you feel you should do." I said "You're going to live in it. How many children do you have?" They replied, "Three girls and a boy." I said, "Do you want all the girls to sleep in the same room, or do you want them to have individual rooms? How do you want this?" They said, "Well, we really don't care; whatever you think they should be." This was very difficult because I am not the one that is going to live there, but I have to know how they want to live in it.

One time I had a client who had very little to say: his wife did all the talking, and she knew how many washcloths went on certain shelves and how many cups went into this cupboard. She had it all pretty well in mind as to how the thing should work. I noticed that the husband didn't say anything at all; he just sat there. Finally, I asked him what he wanted in the house. He said, "Nothing particular, anything she wants." I realized he was used to not having much to say, so I asked him if there was anything that he especially wanted; for instance, a carport or a garage? He replied, "We have to have a garage." I asked why he

had to have a garage, since in that climate it wasn't necessary. He said, "Well, I have to have a garage because that
is where I have to have my power tools." I asked, "What
power tools?" He said, "Well, I do a little woodworking and
I like to have a place to work." I asked him if he would like
to have a shop instead. He said, "I never have had a shop."
So I asked if he would like to have a shop. He said, "Come
out to the garage and I will show you." We went out and
looked in the garage. It was a two-car garage completely
full of very good equipment: tools of all kinds—planers,
saws, all sorts of gadgets—and lots of storage of materials.
He needed the entire garage for his equipment. So it wasn't
until I went around about in a devious way that I learned
he did have something he wanted.

Lots of times you have to worm this out of people; you
have to find out what they really want and need. This goes
for colors, for amount of space, counter space, whether it
is intimate spaces, or open spaces. You see the continuous
present goes into this, too. You don't, any longer, have a set
of little boxes with doors and windows cut into them like
holes. You have spaces that are continuous. At least if the
space doesn't physically continue you like to feel you are
in the same house, don't you? You don't usually have one
room done in Chippendale, another in French Provincial,
and one in Egyptian, anymore. I guess that some people
still do, but not so much. Even the relation of the house
with the lot and the outside is more continuous, isn't it?
We have to have glass sometimes so we can see the garden
going on out, or coming in, or the walls continuing out,
the overhangs going on out—all sorts of devices where we
merge the inside with the outside more and make it more
continuous. That is why we say when you build a house
you don't build a house on a lot, you build a house with

the property and what is around it. That is what we try to do, no matter what kind of building it is. We try to think of our clients as continuing the design of the building; the actual life that goes on in it complements the design. That is why I hate to have you see these slides without the people in them. Sometimes the houses are noticeably empty if you know the people and you see the house without the people.

This bachelor, I did this pad for Joe Price (you can see the renderings of the house on the display walls) he had a party for fifty of my clients after his house was finished. Since he is a rich man, they all came: they were all dressed up in their Sunday best. He wore a one-piece terry-cloth jumper. They discovered when they got there that they all had to take their shoes off before they could come in. This cut them all down to size. After being a little stiff at first, they found it was impossible to be dignified in his home, so they began to relax and enjoy the occasion. They all had a very good time, but one of the curious things that happened was this was the first time I had ever seen all fifty of these clients together. I had always worked with them individually. I had never thought about how this one was in relation to that one, and so on. But here I looked at all these people and I thought, what in the world could they all have in common to have gotten me to be their architect. There didn't seem to be any kind of common denominator except me. They were all going around with the stock question, "What shape is your house?" The next time we do anything like this we will have a little badge that has the shape of their house on it. Each one of them came away feeling rather smug, that they liked theirs better than the others, and that Joe's bachelor pad was all right for Joe, but they would feel better in their house. Thank heavens. It would be awful if they liked another one better than their own.

Someone asked Joe what he thought of his house, and he said, "Well, all I know to say is that it has made me a better person." Which I thought was a very humble and a very nice thing to say. I don't guarantee that this will always happen, however. Sometimes a man and a wife will get divorced after they have built one of my houses and it is chalked up to the house, at least by the people who don't like the house.

If you do a house that people can use—one that becomes a part of their lives—they feel very close to it, and they love it, and they don't like to stay away from it. If they do go away from it, they want to come back. This is encouraging, but more and more I don't think we will have our houses as an anchor so much. I think that it will be something that moves around with us as our needs move around. Many people find that they have to have more than one house now, just like they need more than one car. Maybe the time will come when you will take the environment with you—not like a trailer, but in some other sense. Who knows, the sky may be full of strange things one of these days. It is very exciting to think about. There are all sorts of new inventions, new scientific developments that permit us to do many things. Sometimes the building codes prohibit this. Many times the inspectors try to be broadminded in administering the code by saying the code requires it, so at least put it in until I get through looking at it, then I don't care what you do. Lots of times you put in something to satisfy the code till the inspector goes, and then you can take it out. This adds to the cost, of course. Mr. Wright told me when he built the Guggenheim Museum in New York they had to pay out $80,000 in bribes to the city officials, which is a fair amount of money. Sometimes, that is part of the problem, unfortunately.

One of our biggest problems today, one of the biggest

obstacles in the way of accomplishing architecture, is a very strange one that most people don't realize exists. Even architects don't worry much about it, because very few architects do houses. If you do houses, you run into it immediately. This is the question of what can you build in a certain subdivision. Each subdivision that is opened up by real-estate developers has covenants and restrictions in the deed. It used to be just about costs, lot restrictions, setbacks, and so on, which are fair enough, normally. Now it has gotten into other matters. In most of them you have to have seventy-six percent masonry. Whether you want masonry or not is of no consequence. It has to be there, particularly in the front. They don't care so much about the back. You must have a certain pitch roof; many covenants specify you cannot use shingles, and others say you can't use anything but shingles. Sometimes they even specify the style of the roof: it must be a gable, or a hip, or a modified mansard. Then they have restrictions about where the garage is or the carport. Some have to be on the side or the back. They have all kinds of color restrictions. All this is supposed to be governed by a "good taste committee," which is appointed by the real-estate developer and controlled by him.

Suppose you don't want one of the hand-me-down houses that they build. Then they will say you are free to build your own house, but usually the builder is specified as part of the package when you buy the lot. He says he will build any house you want, show me your plans. If he bids, it will be two or three times too much. In that way, they try to force you into building one they have, and they will say it won't cost you so much because it isn't strange or different. He will say, we will build you a lot more house for less money. Well, some people get into this situation be-

fore they realize what they are getting into, and then they
are stuck with it. If they go ahead and try to build something different from the common duplicate-manor thing
that is supposed to be harmonious in this neighborhood,
then they run right smack into "the good taste committee."
There is the lady who lives across the street in a Connecti-
cut Cracker Box, or a Spanish Hacienda, or something like
that and she just can't stand your design. She gets up an
injunction and tries to get all the neighbors to back her up
and they cause trouble.

Not many clients have the fortitude and the guts to fight
all of this. Then they say we will go out further. Then
they go out further and find that the real-estate developers have bought a ring of property all around the area.
This is for future development, and future snob divisions.
Sunken Heights and Withering Arms and all of these kinds
of things. So where do you go? Well, you can go downtown
where the center of the town is rotting away and get some
old house and paint it pink, or charcoal, or something, to
jazz it up. Or you can go way, way out where there are no
schools, no churches, no shopping centers, or anything.
This is about what your alternatives are in most cities. This
is becoming alarmingly true in most places.

It isn't a free country at all, and don't think it is. *Democracy* is a word we bandy about and like to say we have, but
it doesn't work that way. People can control design just the
way they can control lots of other things. I ran into this recently in Kansas City. We had to appear before the tycoon
who was in charge of all the residential districts. They have
a czar for the business district, and a czar for the residential district—he was a stony-faced guy with no emotions
whatsoever; if he had any, they were carefully controlled.
He said, "You know we don't like to pass judgment upon ar-

chitecture, but we have a firm that works for us that has to decide whether the buildings conform or harmonize with the other buildings in this neighborhood. We have to do this to protect the other people that we have sold property to." He was reasoning this with me like I was a small child, you see. He said, "Now we don't care what you do inside. You can even have a round room if you want to, but outside it better conform."

This is the idea, more and more, that the only way we can have harmony is through conformity. Which is ridiculous. We have harmony in nature without this kind of conformity or duplication or monotony, you see. Even in the desert, where things are apparently monotonous sometimes, if you get to looking, they are not. There is always something that varies the monotony. One time in architectural school I asked a student why he did something that he did on a design that I didn't think belonged to the rest of it. In perfect innocence, he said, "I did it to vary the monotony." He wasn't kidding; it needed something, but I have never forgotten that because I thought it was a wonderful thing to say. We certainly need something to vary the monotony. Just by having all the buildings the same height, or the same color, or the same style, or the same kind of roof, doesn't mean there is going to be harmony, does it? Maybe and maybe not.

Because buildings are different doesn't mean there will be chaos, either. In nature you see different kinds of things together: you see rocks that are not like trees, and you see trees that are not like water, and you have water that isn't like flowers, and all sorts of things, and they all seem to get along together, don't they? We can't criticize nature. We have all of this variety and interest that is always changing, that is always part of the continuous present, and still the only way we think we can have harmony in buildings is to say that they all have to be the same height, or the same materials, or the same something else.

The city planners are guilty of this, too. They have decided, in many cases, that the only buildings that are worthy of being architecture are public buildings, like churches, or schools, or government buildings of various kinds, but there must always be background buildings. Who wants a background building, I would like to know? Why have a background? Painters have been trying to get away from backgrounds for years. Architects have been trying to get away from backs of buildings for years. Why have backgrounds? Why have stuff that doesn't amount to anything around behind somewhere? It all should amount to something. I think you will find in nature that things harmonize no matter how different they are, because each thing is honest itself and has integrity and a discipline in its design and its function, and no matter how much they might fight each other physically, they still are in overall harmony. It is always everlasting and ever changing. If we could only understand this in our cities and our buildings and our relations with each other, I think we would all be happier and function much better as human beings.

This is part of our job in architecture, to give people things as individuals—individual buildings for individuals—and still have everything of high enough quality so it will be able to exist in good faith with other things of value, you see. The things that don't get along are the things that don't have value. If everything has value, you will find that they get along quite well together. We don't want things that don't get along with other things of value. But it's what many times, in adjusting your building to a condition, where your design is an effort to tell the truth, or do something honest, you are up against the problem of an individual designer who may be with a group of design liars. They are all telling such whoppers that if you tell the truth it will seem strange. Lots of times you are the one that seems strange even if you are trying to do something you think is true. I don't think there is any problem in having buildings of quite different design and character together, providing that each one of them does have value, and is of the continuous present.

There is a lot to be done in architecture: our architectural schools are not doing too good a job. Because everyone wants to be a city planner, everyone is studying urban renewal, and this is tearing down some of our finest buildings in the name of progress. I suppose out of all this some good is bound to come, but I think a city has to grow just like a person does, or anything else, organically from within outward. I think that it assumes its shape because of its growth, rather starting in by saying I am going to make a city within a rectangle, or a circle, or something. You don't do this with a house. You don't start to make a circular house, or a triangular house, or anything like this. You may end up doing one, but this isn't what you start with. I think that this applies to cities, too. But this is another big question.

I think another problem is in teamwork. There is more and more emphasis on teams and a deemphasis on individuals. When you look back into history, what great work of art was ever done by a team? What great symphony, or what great painting, or novel, or play, or anything like this was done by a team? Someone had to have an idea—didn't they?—and they did it. Sometimes it takes a team to produce it: it takes a cast to create a play in actual life; it takes an orchestra to play a symphony; it takes a crew of builders to build a building. But someone has to know what it is all going to add up to. Someone has to give it direction and have an idea. I don't care how discontinuous the composition is, or how varied it is, or how unusual, or how usual, it still has to be directed by someone who knows what is going on. If it isn't, it's the same as "too many cooks spoil the broth," "neither fish nor fowl," and something that no one is happy with. We need architects badly who are willing to take a stand, to have ideas no matter how much they get shot at, to stay with the idea, be dedicated to it, to try to do something for people. People need it and appreciate it.

Seven

Music and Architecture

I used to hate music. It is hard to realize now that there ever was a time when I did hate it. But when I was just starting in high school, I had a notion that anything that was called classical music was longhair. The word *classical* had a stigma attached to it, in my way of thinking at the time, because I had already begun to find out there was an architecture possible that wasn't classical in the Greek sense, or Roman. It annoyed me to think that music would be classical, because I associated the word classical in music with the word classical in architecture. Naturally, I shunned any chance to hear music of any sort. About all I did hear was just the common, garden variety of stuff that you couldn't help but hear. In those days, they didn't have radio, so fortunately I was spared a lot of the hillbilly stuff, and so on. On the other hand, I didn't hear anything good of any kind of music.

There was a friend of mind in high school who was a music enthusiast [here Goff repeats the anecdote told in #1, March 1953—*ed.*]; in fact, he played the piano quite well. His name was Ernest Brooks. He played mostly Bach, Beethoven, Chopin, Schubert, and Brahms. He thought it was a shame that I didn't warm up to classical music; so he proceeded to try to educate me. He gave me sort of a course in music appreciation, but it worked just the opposite on me. The more I heard this music he played, the

Music was one of Bruce Goff's great inspirations. He listened to music at the end of every day, and it had a major influence on his philosophy of design. For this recording, made at a private session (January 27, 1954, on the third floor of the School of Architecture, Norman), I asked him what the influence of music was on his life.

more I disliked it, particularly when it was given to me as something that I should enjoy, whether I did or not. It was presented as something I should enjoy in order to be cultured. I didn't enjoy it, because it seemed I could always tell what was coming next in the music, for one thing. There were no surprises, and it seemed dull and uninteresting to me. I had no reason to know why then, but I did know it didn't appeal to me. I resisted all his efforts to overcome this block, and usually when he would play music for me, I was bored and disinterested.

Finally, the time came when the worm turned, and I did learn to enjoy music. It happened in a rather accidental way. Ernest had the habit of buying all the new piano records that came out by certain pianists that he admired. He would automatically buy anything that Alfred Cortot would record, because he liked him. He'd never heard the music; he would just buy it because Cortot played it. That was pretty safe in the early days, because they didn't record modern music. One time, he got a lemon, because Cortot did record *The Fountain*, by Ravel. When Ernest heard this piece he told me later he was puzzled and bewildered, because it didn't obey any of the rules of composition, or harmony, or melody, or rhythm, or anything else that he had been taught. Since he was baffled by it, he thought it would be a good joke to play it for me. He brought it over to my house and put it on just to see me squirm. But it had just the opposite effect: it was the first piece of music I ever heard that I enjoyed. This bewildered him all the more because he was not able to make any sense out of it all. But it fascinated me completely. I knew that I had heard music for the first time, and it opened up a vast world for me, just as seeing Mr. Wright's work in architecture for the first time.

I then became very curious about who Ravel was. I had

never heard anyone mention his name, and that seemed strange, because anyone who could create such a wonderful thing should be known. I asked Ernest, and he didn't know. And we asked his music teacher, and he didn't know. Of course, Ravel was still living at the time. I went to the library and looked into the music encyclopedias and there was no mention of him at all. It is hard to believe, but at that time no one seemed to know who Ravel was. This was about 1920.

I was determined to find out who this man was so I went to the librarian and asked her how I could find more about him. She suggested the magazine index, where I did find an article about Ravel in a magazine. This article mentioned him as the inferior of Debussy. This irritated me, because although I didn't know this man Debussy, I resented anyone saying my hero was an imitation of anyone. That bothered me considerably, and that's about all I could find out about Ravel at that time. So I decided to find out something about this Debussy, who was supposed to be so much greater than Ravel. I looked though books and magazines and could find hardly anything on him, either. He had only been dead two years so the word hadn't gotten around very far yet.

I did take the record catalog and go through it very laboriously. In those days they didn't list anything by composers at all. I took this thick catalog and searched through all the records they listed, not knowing the names of any of Debussy's works. I finally found three records in the catalog with his name. As I had done when I purchased Ravel's *Fountain*, I went without my lunch to buy the two dollar record which was recorded on one side only. It was quite a sacrifice for me to make in those days. I had about worn out *The Fountain*; I think I had played it about fifty times the first day I had it. I went down to the music store after saving my lunch money and bought the three Debussy records they had. I was afraid to listen to them in the store because they had an Amazon in charge of the store who would play about two grooves and say, "Well, do you want it or don't you?" I would never listen to it there, so I just bought the records and took them home. I was expecting to be as fab-ulated by them as I had been with Ravel's *Fountain*. When I played the records, nothing happened this time, for they didn't make me mad, or glad, but they seemed hard to take hold of. In fact, they didn't have sparkle or anything very dazzling about them as *The Fountain* had. I felt that I had made a mistake, at first, because the music didn't come out and get me. These three pieces were the *First Arabesque, The Girl with Flaxen Hair*, and the *Prelude to the Afternoon of a Faun*. All of these were acoustic recordings and very poorly recorded, so you could hardly hear them anyway. I put them on the shelf and went back to *The Fountain* and played it some more.

Still, I couldn't quite ignore the Debussy records. It seemed like I should like them, because they didn't sound like the classical music I had been subjected to. Every once in a while, I felt the urge to go back and play them again. Besides, I had an investment in them and I thought I should get something out of them. So I kept trying to understand them. I finally got to where I considered the *Arabesque* and *The Girl with Flaxen Hair* as very pleasant pieces, though they didn't thrill me as *The Fountain* did. The *Faun* eluded me completely; I felt like it was going in one ear and out the other all the time, and I couldn't seem to take hold of it any place. Some of this was due to the vague recording, of course. After a while, I became conscious of a strange thing happening. *The Fountain* was beginning to become familiar, so it was losing a little of its glamour, and the *Faun* was in-creasing in glamour. Even to this day, I can't say I completely understand the *Faun*, although I have heard it hundreds of times. It is still very mysterious, and very wonderful to me, and becomes increasingly more so as I grow.

This then made me very interested in Debussy. I could begin to hear there was more depth there, and even more mystery. I realized then, it wasn't the kind of music that came out and knocked me down, but I had to learn to grow into it. It taught me a very valuable lesson, because I would probably never have bought the record if I had heard it first, and I would never have had the benefit of that music if I had depended on a snap judgment. As it was, I have learned that I should never accept anything at face value or by snap judgment. My friend could hardly understand my enthusiasm for this music. Because of his having had a musical education, it bothered him considerably. It took some time for him to learn to like it, because he had to break down many older educational principles to understand. But finally he did, and instead of [his] educating me in music, I think I had a lot to do with his education in music, indirectly, by getting him to listen to the music as I was able to get the records. Fortunately for me, at the time there wasn't very much available on records that would be called modern music. I grew up with the industry, you might say, and was able to get a few records at a time, so that I could absorb it and assimilate it, as it was released. Now it is quite a problem, you have practically all the music of the world right at your doorstep. It is pretty hard to know where to start today.

I am naturally very curious and I wanted to know more about music—not technically, but just to enjoy it, and to find out who the modern composers were. I was interested in who the modern painters, architects, and so on were, and I began to realize there were modern composers also. So by watching the magazines and books and so on, as they came out, I was able to find out a little from time to time. Reading Paul Rosenfeld got me very interested in many names of composers and their works. Just reading his descriptions of the works made me anxious to hear them, because I felt that music that could excite a man to write as he did must be pretty tremendous. Time went along and little by little companies started bringing out music of more modern tendencies, and gradually I became acquainted with early works of Stravinsky, more work of Ravel, Debussy, Rimsky-Korsakov, Mussorgsky, Schoenberg, Bartók, and later Varèse. And the list keeps growing all the time, of course.

I also became very interested in exotic music, particularly from Africa, and the Orient. I could see that it was definitely related with their architecture and art. The same qualities that I could see visually seemed to exist aurally in the music. Then I began to wonder why it was that there seemed to be this fundamental relationship between sound, sight, smell—all of these correspondences of sensations. I also began to realize that the music that I liked the most seemed to be the most organic, which tied right in with what I was learning in architecture: the idea of the composition growing from the inside out, through the nature of the material as directed by a creative imagination. I realized, then, that the music of Debussy was much more organic, to me at least, than that of a formal composer, such as Haydn, because he [Debussy] didn't start with an outside form and fill it in with musical ideas: the musical ideas were the initial impulse and they grew into their own forms through the nature of the instruments and were disciplined into an organic whole that had its own order in each composition.

Naturally, music being so free by nature, many things could be done in a musical composition which would be difficult to realize in architecture, but which were, in many ways, prophetic of what architecture might eventually arrive at, because of architecture being a more unwieldy art. It takes a longer time to prove some of the ideas that exist in other arts through architecture. It has been said that architecture is the proving ground for any kind of art movement. If it can be realized in architecture, the movement is a very strong and healthy one. And it if can't, it is supposed to be a weaker one in the arts. It is true, certainly, that many of the same feelings that exist in music, at any given time, can be found in architecture slightly later, usually, because of this difficulty of the art.

Naturally, I got used to a great deal of freedom in composition through music, and through my own painting. I think I also found a sense of freedom through nature: my understanding of nature, and my close association with it. I spent many days in woods and swamps, in direct contact with nature as a child. I could understand nature as a very free composition, too. This all seemed to fit together and to belong together.

I could see in music, particularly in the best music, that we have the quality of mystery to hold it. The greatest music, of course, doesn't give up its secrets so easily and sometimes it requires quite a few hearings to really understand it at all. That is where listening to records is very helpful. More so, probably, than hearing these pieces in concerts, where you might hear them once under adverse circumstances and not get them at all, when the same piece could be heard on records any time you wished. Of course, the quality of records in those days was very poor, but they seemed adequate at the time and were very helpful. By listening and reading about the various composers who were doing these works, when I was able to find material on them, I realized that there were many composers in the world who had already died who had written music of unusual character. I realized that most of the classical music we call old is really not very old. The music of Bach is not old at all when compared with the music of the Orient, or the hymn to Apollo composed in 276 B.C. in Greece that still exists in a form where we can hear it. It took a lot of the austerity away from classical music for that reason. I also began to realize that much of the so-called classical music was like much of the building called architecture, where ideas were poured into forms instead of the forms coming from the ideas. It didn't matter a whole lot what instrument was playing which melody, because they could be tossed around to any instrument and not make much difference, really. In a contemporary piece of music, or a recent modern one like the *Faun*, the beginning flute solo in the piece is so perfectly conceived for that instrument and the qualities of the instrument, that even though it could be played on any number of instruments, of various characters, the whole idea of the music would be lost if it were played on even a clarinet or an oboe. The actual timbre of the flute is so integral with the quality of the melody itself, and vice versa, that they are inseparable. That is the same as it should be in architecture, or course, where it would be difficult to imagine the Johnson Wax Building built out of stone. You could build it out of stone, but it wouldn't seem right because the nature of the material is so important to the idea of the building. I think that is one reason I have been more interested in so-called modern music. By that I mean music roughly since Wagner.

Of course, native music has had this quality that I'm speaking of, of the suitability of the nature of the instrument and the musical idea, for many, many years. So it is nothing new. Just as they had it in their architecture. It is new to us today in architecture. After so much abuse, it took Mr. Wright and Mr. Sullivan to point that out to us. It took the music composers of recent years to show us that the instruments have something to do with it, too. I could then associate the development of the musical ideas with a closer regard to the medium and also a freer sense of composition; where musical ideas were not forced into straitjackets of form, but rather where the form came out of the growth of the musical ideas.

I am well aware that any of the older music was modern in its time. Beethoven's music was certainly very modern music for its day, and like any modern work that has real substance, whether it measures up to all our standards or not, what is really significant in it will hold, regardless of time. It is both timely and timeless. There is no doubt in my mind that Beethoven was a great composer. It just happens that my musical diet doesn't require his kind of music. I would never be so rash as to say because of that he is not a great composer, and the same would go for many of the now-classical composers who were once modern.

I think it is not a question of being modern: it is more a question of the music being organic and having a natural life of its own and growing in that way. I know that many composers in recent years have returned to classic formal ideas through neoclassicism, but they still can keep it interesting through more competent orchestration and more interesting ideas. I still value the music that grows organically more. That is probably why I am so bewildered by the genius of Debussy, who to me is the greatest artist of all in any field. In all the thirty some years that I have been listening to his music, he has never let me down. I have never felt that I have learned it or have known it completely. The more I hear his music the more mysterious and wonderful it seems, although I can tell you almost every note in many of the compositions, because of some of these reasons that I have been speaking of, and also because of his great range of feeling, and his ability to express it simply and directly through his music. This quality of range, I think, is one that we, as architects, or artists of any sort, should develop, so that we do have a real range of feeling and depth of feeling that isn't limited to just one brand, or two or three brands, as most people's are.

I have learned from Debussy that not only must we have a great range of feeling and depth of understanding, but we must also never do work that doesn't have a genuine creative impulse to start with. I also learned that each composition must exist in its own right, according to its own laws, and not be grafted one idea from the other, or be cut from the same bolt of goods. Many very wonderful compositions are, but it doesn't take much acquaintance with any composer's or artist's work to realize you are just hearing more of the same stuff, whether it is for orchestra, piano, voice, or what[ever], if it is the same feeling and the same general emotion just whacked off into little individual compositions. With Debussy, each piece, no matter how small or how large, exists with its own laws, and you are not necessarily required to know the other pieces of his to understand and enjoy the one that you are hearing then.

Many times, people have asked me why I listen to music so much: do I get ideas from it for architecture or painting or something of the sort? I can say right off that the main reason I listen to music is because I enjoy it. It is sort of a recreation and a pleasure to me, first of all. It also helps me a great deal in my work, indirectly, and I don't allow it to directly. I don't want it to influence my work directly. By that I mean I wouldn't listen to a piece of music and then try to paint a picture of it. First of all, the music moves so fast that you would have to paint pictures all your life just to paint all the images you might have in one composition, if you were trying to translate it into something visual. If you did, the chances are you would never feel the same way about it twice, anyway, because we never really hear the same piece of music the same, because our condition is changing within ourselves, not only in our experience, but what we require at the time. It is the same with food: there is a lot of food we like that we wouldn't want at certain times. I know as much as I like steak there are times when I wouldn't want to face one. The same goes for almost any other kind of food. You get the same kind of thing really when listening to music: sometimes you are not in the mood to hear something lively and fast, and it would only annoy you. Other times you require something very exhilarating, and if you are only hearing slow music then it would annoy you, too, probably, no matter how good it was. Through recordings we do have a chance to choose our musical diet according to the need we feel.

Going back to the idea of translating music into some other kind of art: I think that is not only dangerous from the standpoint of the composition changing so much in our understanding and feeling, but I don't like the idea of one art form grafted off of another. I like each art to exist in its own right, according to the same basic principles, perhaps, but each through its own medium, and means of expression, and one not so dependent on the other. When we hear a piece of music, we can understand the emotional content of it, or the feeling that's in it, or whatever you want to call it. Insofar as the mechanics of the thing are concerned, you could understand the rhythm, the harmony, the melodic lines, and the nature of the materials, or the instruments producing it, and the ideas of composition such as modulation, incident, terminal, and climax. The effect of tone color, the dynamics, the rests, the open spaces, the importance of counterpoint. All of these ideas are means of composition, which are basic in any kind of art. We usually talk about them more in relation to music because music has a more formalized language and study about them. Actually, architects, painters, sculptors, and other artists are using very much the same basic ideas, so far as composition is concerned. A rhythm, whether it is beat out on a drum or whether it is in a design, is very much the same proposition. Rather than try to translate those things we hear in music directly into architecture, by listening to music we can automatically store up impressions of many kinds within ourselves, and assimilate, and digest these experiences so that we can develop our rhythmic sense, for instance. By becoming more conscious of rhythm through music, and many qualities I spoke of, we can also be approached very directly through music. We then build up a sort of reserve of understanding of these things within ourselves, which we assimilate, and after having assimilated them, they are pretty apt to come through our work indirectly. Just as other experiences we have with nature, or other things.

Listening to music, then, is not just a matter of going into a trance, or losing oneself in an opiate world: it is a relief from being purely visual and tactile. After working with visual material so much, it's a nice contrast to be able to understand many of the same principles in sound. I think that, in that way, it becomes a form of recreation, as well as education, too. We also learn that the qualities of surprise and mystery, that I spoke of before, are in music. These qualities are valuable to us in that form as well as any other art form. I can see many parallels, probably more than I have mentioned, that do exist between the two arts of music and architecture, and other arts too, for that matter. In fact, I could almost say that I have learned more about architecture from music than I have from architecture, in spite of the debt that I owe Mr. Wright, and the great works of the past, and other works of the present.

I still feel that music has pointed out to me more clearly some of the basic ideas of composition than architecture has, because it seems more abstract, and I haven't had it tied down for me in an architectural solution. When I compose things architecturally, I don't think about music, or other architecture. I try to start with the problem, and my own understanding of these means which have been developed largely through hearing music. I think that is a much more valuable attitude toward music than to take a music appreciation course, which would usually end making one despise it, just as most poetry appreciation courses might. In those affairs, you are usually taught what you should and shouldn't like.

I also learned a great deal about criticism from music. First of all, I learned that most of the music that we think is great now was severely criticized when it first came out. The composers were almost always accused of being crazy, so far as being human beings might be concerned, because they were doing something different from what people were used to. It is hard for us to imagine, nowadays, that a major triad in music would be a strange sound to anyone's ears, but there was a time since the Greeks, and the early days of Western music, that people considered a major triad dissonant. Then later, fourths were considered dissonant, or fifths, and even sixths, and diminished sevenths, and ninths were considered impossible, and seconds still irritate many people's ears. I realized that practically our whole notion of music is rather strange, when you consider it in relation to the sound frequencies, because most of our musical system in the Occident is built on the way the Greek shepherds used to tune their harps. Our complete musical system is on a rather shaky foundation acoustically because of that.

Listening to the music of India, I have become accustomed to much finer gradations than our eighty-eight notes and what our keyboard on the piano permits. At first we are often puzzled by these apparently sliding sounds that don't seem to be very stable. We are often apt to say they missed a note, if it doesn't happen to fall on the one that is closest to it in our scale. We are apt to say they are out of tune. Actually, where we have a half step between E and F, in our scale, the Indians might have as many as sixteen tones in between those two half steps in very finely shaded Hindu music. They could be produced very accurately, too, and not just by accident. Naturally, the cultivated Hindu musician would feel that our music is very awkward and jumpy, and we are apt to feel that his is very slippery and slithery.

I began to realize then that even the music we have is not the end, by any means, anymore than the architecture we have is, or any other art. The possibilities haven't even been touched, particularly in relation to our modern means and materials. Just as in architecture, the composer today has resources at his command that have never existed before. These resources keep changing pretty much as the need of the composers of the time make them change. For instance, when Beethoven composed his piano sonatas, the piano that he had in mind was not the piano that was available on the market then. The sonatas didn't sound as good as they do today, because the pianos were not constructed to play what Beethoven demanded. He wanted a more or-

chestral sound out of the piano: a bigger sound than the
harpsichord. The puny sounding pianos that were first invented were not adequate in volume of sound to produce
what he wanted, and so he went ahead and wrote the music that he wanted anyway. Then the piano manufacturers
had to come along and produce pianos capable of playing his music. When Chopin came along with the feeling
he needed more subtlety, and pedaling, and shading of the
sound, there were very few pianos at that time that could
produce what he wanted. But by demanding it in his music, the pianos were finally developed that could produce
that quality. Debussy came along and demanded more subtlety of action, and also of pedaling, and tonal quality.
The pianos were finally developed to answer those requirements. The more recent composers like Stravinsky, Bartòk,
Schoenberg, and Prokofiev asked for more percussive qualities, so now a piano has to be able to take a beating and still
have the great subtleties that other music demands—just
as in building materials we stretch our limits many times
and materials are developed, such as the glass door. By demanding lighter and lighter frames around the door they
disappear entirely, and we have just the glass door, which
was considered impossible only a few years ago.

So we have changing resources in music. Nowadays, with
the explorations in electric sound, we have all sorts of vistas
opened up that are practically unexplored and unknown.
In fact, we are getting ready to go off on a new journey in
music which no one has ever experienced. This promises
to be as exciting as a trip out into space. Our whole idea
of acoustics in relation to music will change because of
this. Nowadays, with the possibilities of such things that
are being experimented with, we are still in a very primitive and embryonic stage musically, in relation to what will

undoubtedly come into being. A great artist, such as Debussy, with his range, will come along and be able to master
this great new medium, make it expressive, and give it real
qualities of art. The art of music keeps growing, and the
horizons are extended.

The same thing is happening in almost all of the arts.
Instead of having arrived at a summit, it seems we have arrived at a beginning. This beginning is exciting to think of,
and I think music is the first to discover this new spirit,
which we will eventually understand through other arts,
too. The artist, whether he is an architect, or composer, or
painter, or whatever, will have to have a much more scientific understanding of his art. By that I mean he will need
to be more familiar with the resources—at the same time
not to be limited by them, or hindered by them, just as
today architectural schools are much more aware of engineering, materials, structure, and so on, than the architects
were twenty-five years ago.

At the same time, we cannot consider any of these
things ends in themselves any more than we ever could.
It amounts to the same thing as learning to master our
medium in order to create works of art that have real value
and authority. In that sense, I think there is a great relationship between music and the other arts, because we have to
be able to approach all of this with a real scientific attitude,
which is also part of our time in this age of science. At the
same time, we must never lose sight of our relation with
nature and our own feelings. We must use all of this with
feeling that is genuine, and expressive of a direct, creative
impulse in the beginning of the creative work.

I think that, listening to music that is different from even
the so-called modern music, we are faced with the same
problem that the first people were that heard the so-called

modern music the first time. Recently, at a concert given for electrical instruments and mechanical means of producing music, the professor of music, who had been well seasoned with Bartòk, Stravinsky, and Schoenberg, jumped to his feet and demanded that this noise stop. He said that it was rubbish and offensive to the ears—the same sort of attitude that people had taken a few years ago toward these men that he appreciated.

It seems no matter when a change occurs, if it is a very drastic one, or seemingly so, that there is always a great deal of antagonism, particularly from the people who have just arrived and don't want to go any further. These people dislike the idea of being challenged to keep growing, because they feel they have earned where they are, at such a cost, that they would prefer to stay there a while. Just as in architecture sometimes, I have heard architects say, "Bruce, why do you keep muddying up the water? Why not sit down and rest awhile; we have gotten this far why not relax and enjoy it a bit?" Of course, that is all right for those who can relax and enjoy it a little bit, providing they don't care to go any further than they are right then. If you are possessed with the necessity to do architecture, you can't stop at any time. You have to keep growing. It is the same with everything we experience; the reevaluation of all we know has to keep going on. At the same time, we have to be discovering new things and have to be curious about what is part of our time in all the other arts, and other matters, too, for that matter.

Music that is called experimental, in the way experimental is usually used as sort of an apology, or else a left-handed compliment, I think that anything that is growing is an experiment. Some of the experiments come off and some of them don't, but usually any work of art that is any good has been an experiment at some time or other. It has usually seemed like that, too, when it was first done, particularly if it is anything that has any real quality of its own, or anything fresh to say.

It is surprising how rapidly we assimilate these things—particularly now with the ease of getting the word around, you might say, of music, architecture, and painting. For instance, it used to be in Bach's day he had to walk forty-some miles to hear compositions by a contemporary composer, Buxtehude. He was unable to hear Vivaldi's music played unless it happened that some musicians could get hold of a score, usually many years after it was composed. People had to travel long distances to get into a small hall to hear music and then only hear it once. Nowadays, we can hear it on the radio, and we can hear it almost as soon as the ink is dry on the manuscript. It is recorded, in most cases, and the word gets around pretty fast. We can assimilate pretty fast now. The same is true of our magazines, reproducing paintings and works of architecture. While three dimensional art, in printed form, is not entirely satisfactory, at least it is a clue to what is there. It is possible for us to have a notion of some of the work that is going on in other parts of the world, and still stay right at home.

With all of this avalanche of knowledge descending on us almost at once, we have to keep our bearings, and be receptive to that which is worthwhile to us, and at the same time try to forget it all when we do something of our own. It is necessary to use only what we have assimilated through our actual experiences. In that sense, I don't think we do attempt to recreate music through architecture. Naturally, the effect of it would come through it if we have really experienced music, just as any other vital experience would have its effect indirectly. When we do compose in our own art, we naturally draw from all of these resources.

That is why I think that architecture can benefit from as-sociation of other arts, because they all spring from very much the same fundamental source. At the same time, by understanding it in different guises, it helps us to under-stand it in our own, much more sometimes. I think then that the important thing is to always begin again and again in our own work and not try to graft our work off of mu-sic, or painting, or nature, or other architecture directly, but to bring it from our own experience and to forget what we have done, or anyone else has done, when we actually start to do creative work. The results of our experience will naturally show in what we do in some form or other, but I hope in a digested form. I don't think it is ever wise to try to confuse different arts with each other—to consider architecture as painting, or painting as architecture.

We have Ruskin's definition of architecture as being frozen music. In the first place I don't think there is any-thing frozen about architecture in the way we think of it today. Maybe, in the way Ruskin thought of it, it was a static and a dead sort of thing. We don't think of it as hav-ing rigor mortis any more, and to us a work of architecture has to be alive and vital through all of its parts, and singing at all times, and it is never really frozen or rigid. More and more we are working for more relaxation in our art, and more tension at the same time. It is very difficult to see any need to think of architecture as frozen music; it is more alive than that, and really much more musical than that in the sense that it is always a continuous composition.

The composer of music has the advantage of carrying us along with him and we can either get ahead of him or stay behind him if we are really experiencing the music as it pro-gresses. In the composition, he can lead us where he wants to, pull off his climaxes when he wants to, and the other tricks of the trade can be administered by the composer as he feels we should have them. This is very distinctly true of music and literature. Painting, architecture, and sculpture lay all their cards on the table at the same time. We are apt to anticipate the composer of these arts and jump to the conclusions of what we see most immediately, and for that reason we do not normally have the feeling of a composition growing as we go through it, as we do with music.

This is true in architecture mainly of the architecture of the immediate past. But nowadays in architecture we do have a closer relation to music, in that sense—that we think of it as something that we are experiencing as we move about in it and around it. We even have an advantage over the composer of music, in that sense: he can only have us follow through a certain path in his music. The architect can provide things so spatial that you can approach them from all sorts of ways, and discover different relationships. In a sense, most of the music we know has the idea of composition of the past, the present, and the future. That is, we have been somewhere, we are somewhere, and we are going somewhere. In the architecture of today, we have more a sense of the composition as continuous present; that is, no matter how we approach it or move about in it, we discover different relationships. It is much more impossible, in architecture, to see it as a sum of the parts in the same sense that we used to when it was merely a facade, or a very simple little room. Nowadays it is so complex that even if we took an aerial view of the building, we still only see the outside of it. If we are inside the building, we only see the part we are in. The design is moving on someplace else, usually. That is why it is so difficult to photograph architecture, because it is always moving, always changing, in relation to the viewer, and to the weather, the climate, the time of day, and all that.

Architecture is a continuous performance where music is probably a command performance. We don't expect music to run on continuously and just listen whenever we choose, but do expect architecture to exist day and night, any time of the year, in any place. I think there is a tremendous difference in these arts, but there is a parallel in the idea that they are moving at all times. That is why I resent the idea of architecture being called frozen music, because the main relation in that sense it has with music is its continuity and changing composition as it goes along. Actually, it is a less concentrated route than you would have in a musical composition.

In painting, of course, we can think of painting as a path, where we follow around a certain prescribed route as the artist draws our attention from one part of the canvas to another and leads us back to where we started. Just as in the old music you used to hear the theme announced and then some variations of some sort and then return to the theme, in the old buildings you used to go in the front door and walk around the home and come back to the front door. That was considered a pretty safe kind of composition, because you couldn't get lost. You were always brought back to where you started. Nowadays, we do not always have to be brought back to where we started, and we can wander through it in many ways and experience many surprises. In painting today, we no longer feel the necessity for a staked out route through the composition or path where we are supposed to go and never deviate. Instead, we can experience this relationship in many ways. This is making the painters less satisfied all the time with painting, because it is too static an art for them. More and more, there is the feeling for the need for movement and more flexibility and freedom than a fixed composition—even at its freest—can allow.

It is probable that a new kind of art will replace painting

gradually, at least as we know it now, because painting no longer needs to be the slave to representation. Photography has freed us of that. So what used to be a painter is now free to work with color, line, and form, and he can either fix it on some material or work with it in motion. Thomas Wilford wanted to do it with colored light, and he did some very interesting experiments with this method. He hoped for the day when people could have large concerts of colored lights in parks, where a number of light organs could be operating at the same time and producing tremendous compositions several hundred feet high where the play of light, color, lines, rhythms, and so on could give people a visual experience very much as they have musically in their aural senses.

I think there is a general sense of unrest among painters who have tried everything so much. They certainly have gone a long ways. I think the next step is going to be an expansion of the art through the development of its medium, just as I think it is with music. The composers have not exhausted the eighty-eight notes on the piano keyboard by any means. There are mathematically many more possibilities yet. We know, too, the same keyboard existed for Beethoven, and it existed for Debussy, and for Stravinsky and Schoenberg, and all have heard different things in that same keyboard. Many more will continue to hear different things in the same keyboard. There is also a straining at the leash by many composers who feel that our instruments are antiquated and who resent the idea of interpreters deciding how the music should sound in performing it poorly and incorrectly. There is the feeling for the need for more direct communications between the artist and the recipient in music as well as in other arts. Probably the new mediums that exist in electronics will do a great deal to develop this feeling into actuality. When the composer who is able to master all of this comes along, he will have the most direct means of expression that any composer of music has ever had. Just as the artist who can control it through light compositions, or color compositions that actually move, will be able to have a much more direct response from his audience.

Probably, in architecture, the same thing will eventually come about where architecture will cease to be so static and rootbound. It will actually have much more movement through it, some way or other. The uneasy feeling we have for free form is probably because the forms aren't really free, but look like they are free to move but are really frozen into position. If we know they can actually move, as they do in nature, they don't bother us. When we see them frozen into some solid shape, then we are uncomfortable about them.

So, probably, our medium eventually will allow us the same freedom of movement that exists in the other arts. At least our inclination is in that direction in all of the arts, to get away from the static thing and try to realize the power of movement as a very necessary force in a composition. In many cases, it is supplied by us as observers, that is, we have to sort of interpret it that way ourselves, even in static works that we recognize as having dynamic qualities in movement. Actually, the force that's in movement is a tremendous idea that can be unleashed through what is now painting and what is now architecture. I think that it is inevitable that someday even the freest composition we have now in these arts will seem very static, stodgy, and primitive to the artist who will be able to master such a new medium.

The idea of speed has a great deal to do with this, too. When people were just walking around, the building could be much more sluggish in design. A piece of music could be more sluggish, too. Now we are experiencing speed that is so rapid that the effects that we used to be able to pull off by walking by the building no longer count. Our whole sense of composition has to change along with that, too.

In music, for instance, we are arriving at sort of a musical shorthand through the work of Schoenberg. We no longer need the long, drawn-out sections of development and so on that used to be part and parcel of great symphonic works. Now we want to come to the point more readily, more quickly. Debussy's music is very timely in that sense, too, because it does say what it has to say and moves on. It doesn't get rhetorical, or bogged down with a lot of reiterations and repeated phrases and so on. People who merely manufacture music could take any one of those ideas and expand it into a whole symphony, if they wanted to stretch the material. There is a conciseness, and compactness, and directness about such music which makes it more valuable to us, because when we hear it again and again, as we are able to now, we must have substance there, that is very rich and rewarding all the time. We are not so anxious to go through long and laborious processes to arrive at the meat of the composition as we used to.

The same thing is true in architecture: long and endless colonnades are no longer the thing, because we want something to happen before that. The composition has to be alive all the way through: we are no longer satisfied with things happening every now and then, with long barren stretches in between making it big. No matter how small it is, or how large, we expect to have something interesting going on all the time, and that means the design is moving at a more rapid pace than architecture has formerly.

This, I think, we can learn from music, too—that the

speed of ideas in music can be assimilated, even in very rapid music. Whereas in architecture we are still pretty much in the horse-and-buggy stage for speed of ideas and design, because we aren't used to very much happening. In that sense, probably the architecture of India moves more rapidly than any of ours, because there is something interesting going on all the time that intrigues our eyes and never lets us down, or allows us to forget it. Whether we are close, or far, or inside, or outside, it is very close to what I am talking about.

The other thing about architecture that I would like to discuss in relation to music is what is called pure music and pure architecture. Pure music usually means that which does not tell a story, or symbolize anything, or try consciously to represent something. Pure music exists for the musical impulse itself—the musical idea as it is expressed through the material and through the medium, and ordered into a complete whole by the composer. It is self-sustaining and self-sufficient. That has been going on in music for some time. Music can, of course, serve a purpose. It can be made to dance to, or march to, or sing to, or tell some story in music, but it can also exist in its own right without attempting to picture or represent anything else.

In architecture we so far have always thought of architecture as functional, in the sense that we are building either a house or an office building, or a church, or a building for some purpose to be used. . . . Or it may be a monument to the unknown soldier, or something else symbolic. In any case, it always had to serve some function. Of course, if we accept the definition of architecture as being necessarily something that serves a function, by the same reasoning we would have to say that the only music worthwhile would be the music composed for specific uses. I think we know better than that in music, but we don't know better than that in architecture. If we examine what we call architecture closely, and we realize that a good building can serve these functions as well as architecture, then we realize that the qualities that make it architecture, more than just good building, is the amount of absolute architecture—qualities that exist over and above the call of duty in the building. These aesthetic qualities are sometimes by-products and sometimes aims, but they are the things that add up to what we call architecture as above just building.

I don't think that two hundred people a day go to see the Johnson Wax Building just because it functions well as a building—the way it works, and the way it keeps the heat in or out, and all of that. People take that for granted. The qualities of an aesthetic nature that exist in that building as a by-product, or an aim, are close to this thing we call absolute architecture, though the building is still serving the purpose—that is, the utilitarian purpose—as architecture has always had to do.

There are very few things existing in the world that do not serve some kind of purpose in that regard. Probably Sam's Towers, in Watts, California [Simon Rodia's—ed.] come a little closer to what I am speaking about now, as being an aesthetic experience through materials, not built for any particular purpose, nor to symbolize or memorialize anything, but to exist as something in its own right that has structure, material, and architectural quality. We may say, of course, they are merely large sculptures. Since sculpture no longer has to portray human figures, I don't see a whole lot of difference between sculpture and architecture, except in the matter of useful function. Of course, if we did build structures that existed as absolute architecture, with no strings attached, we could still argue that they are serving functions in that they are giving pleasure, and interest, to people who can experience them by going to view them and going through them. Of course, we meet many problems as to who would pay for such things. I feel if we can derive as much inspiration and pleasure from architecture that is chained to utilitarian purposes, then we could enjoy even more the qualities of architecture if they were absolutely free to exist for the purpose of enjoying and experiencing the designs more directly, firsthand, without the accompanying utilitarian reasons.

So in that sense I don't think we have ever had any architecture that is pure architecture in the sense that we have had pure music, or even pure painting. I know that many people would argue if we had that then it wouldn't be architecture. Of course, it wouldn't be architecture the way it has ever been understood. I don't mean that we shouldn't continue to solve problems through architecture; I think that is one function architecture can exert. I also think there is a great unexplored world in the other idea, too. We will eventually come to a point where we can require it and enjoy it, and we won't have to enjoy it as a by-product, as we do now.

It will be some time probably before this can come about. There is no reason though to not believe that some day we can have architectural compositions to experience, just as well as we have musical compositions that exist for themselves and for us, without any other reasons involved. When that happens, the architect's contact with the people will be as direct as it is in music, from the standpoint of his feeling being tuned into by correspondence with our feeling, and vice versa.

That is something worth thinking about and speculating on. I think it is a place where music is way ahead of architecture. Even painting is. Probably, we will eventually have it in a more controlled form than we see in Sam's Towers or some other isolated examples that approach it, where the architect would have complete charge of the composition from beginning to end and where the public could appreciate it through direct experience and not feel that it has to serve any other purpose. That is interesting to speculate upon. Architecture has always been a slave to something or other. It has had to serve religion, politics, industry, and almost everything else. I suppose it is to its credit that it has emerged from time to time triumphant over all sordid details. At the same time, in great cultures it has been allowed more freedom and development, even though it has served these purposes. I hope that someday we will have a culture that will allow it to exist in its own right.

Eight

Japanese Art and Modern Design

If we examine modern art, we find that there are certain common denominators which carry through all of the arts and seem to have a tremendous influence. With all of these common denominators, I think one of the strongest is that of the art of Japan, because it has influenced so many of our artists.

Goff had an extensive collection of Japanese prints, books, and music. This tape concerned his great interest in Japanese art and the influence of Japanese art on Western art and architecture. Recorded with just the two of us on the third floor of the School of Architecture at Norman (February 6, 1954), it demonstrates his broad knowledge and appreciation of oriental culture.

We find the influence carrying through painting, music, sculpture, industrial design, and architecture. I think there is no other one source that has been a healthier or stronger influence. Because of this, I think we should study the art of Japan with a great deal of care. The Japanese long ago achieved many of the things we are working for today.

The Japanese print has been one of the most influential mediums for our understanding of Japan. The Japanese prints were not considered much as great works of art as they were popular art. There was an artistic art of noblemen, rich merchants, and in the temples. Then there was the common, everyday art for the people.

Whoever invented the Japanese woodblock print was certainly one of the first to realize a true democracy in art, because here, great creative talents could be utilized to produce magnificent works of art at low cost so that almost anyone could afford to have them.

Japanese woodblock prints, in fact, were regarded as commonplace in Japan at that time, just as we would think of calendar art or advertising art today, but with the great difference that there was real quality in these productions.

The process of making the print from the artist's original drawing by cutting blocks of wood and printing the various colors by superimposition of one block with another became a highly developed art. It was an integral process all along, where the paper was not printed on as much as with. The colors and designs were stamped on the paper surely, but they stained the paper or dyed it through. The nature of the paper was never lost even after it was printed upon.

The character of the woodblock itself came through. The subject matters had to do with everyday life, the theater, legends, songs, but all abstracted in a very beautiful way. Even without our knowing about the subjects, we can appreciate them as great works of art. We find very few Japanese prints unworthy of our attention.

No wonder Frank Lloyd Wright was intrigued with them. Not only Mr. Wright but other great artists were quick to realize their value. As we know, Japan was closed for many years to foreign trade. Finally, the Dutch and Portuguese started importing mainly ceramics and china. They themselves did not usually realize the value of the Japanese works of art.

There is the story of a French artist who went to buy some cheese in Holland and found that they were wrapping the cheese in gaily colored wrappers of exotic designs—that is, Japanese prints. He was so amazed at their quality that he immediately bought all of the storekeeper's wrapping paper. The storekeeper had gotten these prints as packing wrapped around china that he had received from Japan. The storekeeper was amazed that anyone would want to buy his wrapping paper. The prints were smoothed out and exhibited and the French artists were wild about them. The artists were carried away by the strong compositions, the brilliant color, and what seemed to them designs that were modern, perhaps more modern, than any of theirs.

This discovery awakened a great interest in Japanese art. At that time, hardly anyone in the Western world knew who the great Japanese printmakers were, but they were quick to find out. Wealthy people found a new field for collecting and they sent art critics as buyers to Japan to see if they could find more examples of these remarkable prints. It wasn't long before great artists such as Monet, Manet, Whistler, Van Gogh, Gauguin, Renoir, and many, many others of the great modern European artists who are now classics were quite familiar with Japanese prints.

Van Gogh went so far as to copy them in his medium of oil, and when he wished to say that anything had perfection in art he referred to it as Japanese. I think if we study his brushstrokes and composition we can see that there is a great debt owed to the Japanese prints.

Another person who was strongly influenced by such work is Aubrey Beardsley. His work is traceable through many other European artists, so that we have a lineage coming down through him with the same influence. It is possibly stronger than most people realize. Whistler was another artist who was quick to appreciate the prints and even incorporate them into his paintings as part of backgrounds and so on. His sense for composition is in the painting of his mother, in *Carlyle*, and particularly in the nocturnes. His later works show a great deal of appreciation for composition which he undoubtedly learned from the prints. We know that he had a fine collection of Japanese prints.

We see the influence of prints coming through painting of the later part of the last century and the beginning of this century. This great awakening to Japanese art through the prints was spreading like wildfire all over the Western world. In this country, many great collections were made and are still being made. I think the finest collection of Japanese prints in the world is in the Boston Museum of Fine Arts. More and better prints are there than anywhere else in the world, even in Japan. The Japanese at that time were unaware of the importance of the prints. The prints were taken so much as everyday life that they didn't realize the great artistic importance of them. The Japanese allowed most of the finest examples to leave their country before realizing the prints' value. However, there are some great collections in Japan, too, but not the equal of those to be found in this country and France and England.

I think that is typical of people. In almost any culture, people do not realize what they have in the immediate vicinity; they become used to it. This was true in Japan. As soon as the printmakers found that this was a very marketable commodity at high prices, many bad reprints were made and many skillful forgeries. Even Mr. Wright, who had become somewhat of an expert, was fooled when he purchased some prints for the Spaulding collection. This is not so important to us now.

These prints, because of their freshness, their wonderful composition, and the organic method of the print rising out of the subject and the purpose for the use of the people, the character of the woodblock, the character of the painting, the character of the printing and the paper—all forming an organic and democratic kind of art—were most inspiring.

Then the Western artist became more conscious later of the great classical art of Japan—the more aristocratic type, such as paintings on silk, tokomonos, makimonos, horizontal scrolls, beautiful screens, sliding doors painted in temples and palaces. And they became acquainted with the names of great artists like Korin, Okio, and many many others. The tendency, at first, was to categorize all the artists together and say "those Japanese." And speaking of any particular feature of a work from Japan we would say, "Look how *they* did the tree," or, "Look how *they* did this or that"—when actually the artistic creation was the work of individuals, just as it always is in any country, and as important as individual work with the same great differences as we find elsewhere.

In Japan, the typical procedure for becoming an artist is quite different from that in the West. For instance, a young man will apprentice himself to a great artist and he will be called a *daichi*; that is, an apprentice, but meaning more than an apprentice. He will be considered more a son of this artist and he will live in the artist's house and will be very much a part of the artist's family. He will be allowed to share the experiences of many of the great pastimes of listening to music, walking together in the garden, or talking about art with his master painter. The master will work very hard with him to try first of all to perfect his technique and composition. The apprentice will study the works of the great artists of the past, not as imitation, but emulation. The apprentice will even copy some of the paintings mainly to try to retrace the steps that the great artist had gone through. At no time would he ever consider that his painting was worthy of him or that it was in any sense as good as the original until he was able to produce work of his own. The copying was more in the nature of exercise than as finished compositions as we would be apt to regard them. After his master feels he has done as much as he can with him, and the master feels the *daichi* is worthy, he gives him part of his name. We find bits of the master's name carried down in combination with the names of his pupils so that we can identify all groups of painters who came from some great artist-teacher. In this way, the art is carried on from generation to generation and is kept alive and meaningful for the people at all times.

This same method goes through the work of the print-makers and we find that there is a tremendous difference in the quality and the character of the work of these various artists. Hokusai is nothing like Utamaro, nor is he like Hiroshige. We are very much in error when we think that all of these men produced works that are imitative or that they are all alike. They are very different from each other and still there is a consistency which carries through their work which is remarkable. This consistency, I think, is due mainly to the fact that Japan had one of the great cultures of the world, where everything from the most common object used in daily life to the highest, most sacred object used in religious life was beautiful and of the same general culture. This included all things in life, such as the costumes, the food, preparation of food, and the way it was served on certain dishes because of the colors and textures. Just the serving of food is an art, the way it is composed on the dishes is an art. They way flowers are arranged is an art.

There was a custom every year of writing poems on the cherry trees so that the emperor would give prizes to people who could write the best haiku or seventeen-syllable poem about spring. These poems were tied to the cherry trees so they could blow in the wind and symbolized the poetic feeling aroused by the beauty of these trees. Then there would be national holidays where people would take off from work and go out and view the colors of the autumn leaves.

There was all sorts of interest in holidays and festivals, all with beautiful works of art, sometimes very inexpensive with paper and bamboo, toys that were inexpensive but still with a real artistic quality. Even the games were of that sort. The literature, music, the gagaku court music, and the popular music were all in character with this.

The gardens, the houses, the temples, the landscape, and the conventions of the people were all one. I don't know of any civilization where it so consistently reached such a high peak. Some of this was due to the fact that Japan was isolated from the world, and it was a small country of predominantly one race.

The landscape itself was so beautiful and the climate was relatively mild. With this appreciation for beauty deeply born in the Japanese, it was natural that everything the people did had this quality to some degree. Even the fisherman building a rack to dry fish on could do something that would not harm the landscape. The farmers harvesting rice had competitions to see who could stack the rice to dry in the most original and beautiful way. This was done by people who did not know the word *art* or anything connected with it as academic, but who felt it through everything they did as part of their everyday lives.

Tracing other influences of Japanese art, let us examine architecture. The three greatest architects today, Mr. Wright, Mr. Le Corbusier, and Mr. Mies Van der Rohe all owe a debt to Japan. I believe all do, or would, acknowledge the same. Way back as early as the seventh century, Japan was building buildings with the modular system, with prefabricated parts, with perfect relation to the site, not as imitative of the site and not as ignorant of it, but as working with it. Flexible planning was in every house; walls and screens could slide back and forth so the house could be separated into private units or open wide for the summer breezes. Materials were usually natural in color and very straightforward and honest in design. Craftsmanship was very high. Guild systems in various towns and communities worked out their own secrets of joinery. They guarded these secrets very jealously. We can appreciate that the craftsmanship of the guilds was of an extremely high order. This extended not only through woodwork but metals, paper, mats, tile, and gardening. It extended through practically everything connected with the building.

One interesting feature is that when a Japanese architect or head carpenter built a house, he was responsible for it as long as he lived. He would be the one to consult if anything went wrong with the house or if an addition or alterations were necessary. The owner would never dare to build something onto his house not done by the original builder. If the builder dies, he would will his rights on that house to his successor and his heir. By this method, a great deal of pride was present in regard to the work. The owners realized that their work was being taken care of properly by the man who had been in charge originally or by someone whom he appointed as one who would understand how to go on with it. In this way, very little damage was done to the work over a period of years. This also carried through the gardening and other features of the work.

We look upon the design ideas of open planning, flexible planning, close relationship with outdoors and indoors, light skeletal structure, translucent structure, transparency, natural materials expressed through the design, prefabrication, modular units, as new inventions today. But most of them were in actual application long ago in Japan.

One invention that the Japanese builders had, which Bruno Taut said would have been the savior for Western art, was the tokonoma, or alcove for art. Practically every house had at least one such alcove off of the principal living space, and larger houses had more. This tokonoma was the place where paintings were shown, flower arrangements and special works were exhibited. They were changed according to the occasion. At no time did they hang up paintings or put out other works of art and leave them indefinitely. The works of art were stored and used when the occasion seemed appropriate. For instance, if you had a literary guest coming to dinner, you would probably hang a poem in beautiful calligraphy that you would feel appropriate for this visit. There would also be a flower arrangement with it which would be symbolic. Your guest on entering would go directly to the tokonoma and stand before it in appreciation. He would probably not comment upon it, but would be quick to realize that it was placed there for him.

At other times of the year, for different celebrations or occasions, these exhibits would be changed. There was a continuous performance going on in the tokonoma of beautiful works of art. In that way, it was very close to the people in their living habits. I think this changing of the works of art kept the people from becoming immune to these works, they retained their freshness much longer than with our system of hanging paintings on the wall and becoming immune to them. They occupy space, and still we are hardly conscious of even the best ones after we get used to where they are on the wall.

The artist was fortunate in knowing about the amount of space his painting would occupy and something of the type of surroundings or environment it would be in. While he did not know exactly which tokonoma it would be in, he had a general idea that at least it would be a part of the whole scheme of life that was going on in this house or temple. The Japanese artist was part of all this in the sense that a Western artist who paints an easel painting can never be. No matter how fine a painting the Western artist can produce, there is no guarantee of where it will go or what company it will have. In that way, the Japanese artist was fortunate.

In Japanese music, we have very simple works that are not as simple as they sound, expressing naturally the nature of the instruments producing them. The voices may seem strange to our ears because there the possibilities of vocal production are explored and exploited, rather than trying to make everything soft and soupy as our Italian singers have taught us here. The harsh gutturals, the falsettos, the soft, low grunts, and so on, all are considered part of the Japanese vocal palette that can be used in connection with instruments integrally so that the voice itself becomes a sort of instrument. Western ears find this harsh at times, but if we resign ourselves to this we can learn to appreciate it as any other great music. The subtlety of the shading of flute tones, and so on, is in direct proportion to the delicacy and shading of the colors on silk. At the same time, the sensitivity never becomes sentimental. There is also a great vigor and dynamic roughness present in Japanese art. Many of the brushstrokes are brusque and many of the strokes on samisen are brusque. The range of feeling through all of this art in music, painting, poetry, and even in calligraphy is very wide.

In the finest calligraphy, the softer passages are written in very delicate lines, and the broader, louder portion is in more vigorous lines. The brush becomes extremely expressive of the nature of the thought that is being written. Probably this calligraphy, writing with a brush, did a great deal to develop an artistic skill in the people. In making these brushstrokes expressive and direct, without erasure, the people learned at an early age to be that way in their thinking and in their observations. Their expressiveness is a great release for the almost repressed conventions of their social lives. Lafcadio Hearn, the writer who lived in Japan most of his life, believes the reason for the great emotional content of Japanese art is because their emotions are held in reserve and their art becomes a great release from the restrictions of their conventional ways of living. It is highly concentrated in ways most Western art is not.

Another significant difference in the Japanese attitude toward painting, or any other work of art, is that the Japanese artist subordinates himself to the work. We find that instead of trying to interpret a tree the way he feels about it, he tries to interpret it the way it is—the real essence of the tree growing. The artist tries to understand the character of it such as understanding the sense of order in the willow tree as different from the sense of order in a cryptomeria; or the sense of order in a lotus differing from the sense of order of an iris. The artist has words to express these subtle differences. The word *edaburi* is used to refer to the formative arrangement of the branches of a tree. We have no such word in our language, and if we try to explain just what it means, it would take a small book to explain it. This word is in everyday use in Japan.

The nature of the thing always interested the Japanese. Even in the study of botany, which is scientific basically, they never regard it purely as such. In memorizing plants, flowers, trees, and so on they try to understand this aesthetic order which flows through the specimens. The design of them is thought of as much as other characteristics. I don't think many of our botanists are apt to feel that way about it.

In Japan, we have art as a closely related expression of

living in perfect harmony with the landscape, with religion, and with social customs. We have the honest use of materials and we have a consistency carrying through all the various kinds of art, such as architecture, landscape gardening, painting, sculpture, literature, music, dancing, and so-called everyday objects, toys, everything. All of these have unity and harmony as a whole with the people and at no time is there meaningless repetition. Even with all this consistency, there is an amazing variety and freshness of design. We are apt to hear many times that the Japanese are imitative people. I think that is false; they are no more imitative than other people, but when they are, it is with the purpose of learning how something has been done. They never lack the courage and the facility to go ahead and do something their way.

Today we are apt to look upon the Western influence in Japan as very degrading to them. It is particularly sad, since the Japanese themselves feel that they have to overcome medievalism in a very short space of time and live in a highly scientific world such as ours. This change is very rapid for them and naturally very disastrous to their culture because they have not learned as yet to assimilate the new things they are learning from us into their own spirit. We find European architects and artists having a tremendous influence on the Japanese. This is strange, because many of these influences are rebounding from Europe back to Japan where they came from originally. They are not learning the right things and the craftsmen are no longer wanted as they are being replaced by machine-made products.

Today, there is a great deal of looking around elsewhere in Japan, instead of within themselves. This feeling of inferiority in many of the Japanese artists is evidenced in their attempts to be little Picassos or little Le Corbusiers or little Mies van der Rohes, or someone else. It is too bad that their work suffers because of this great impact of Western art upon them. Whereas the impact of their art upon the Western world was so beneficial and so invigorating and stimulating. It seems that just the opposite is true when our work finds an audience there.

Maybe the Japanese people will be able to assimilate these influences and make them their own. It is true that they won't be able to continue living as they did back in the golden days of their culture in the same way; nor should they. They should continue to change and to develop their own spirit as they always did. We know that living in the world today is a different proposition than it was in the seventh century. The Japanese artist would not be honest with himself or his time if he tried to go back, anymore than any of us would be. He must try to realize that he has an inheritance that is much sounder and much more beautiful and much greater than most of ours—that is, in aesthetic matters at least. Rather than being ashamed of this, he should try to go ahead with it and realize it through the new materials and methods at his disposal. I think when he can do that, Japan will have a rebirth in art. I can't believe that all of this innate feeling for the beautiful can die so suddenly just because of the impact of Western civilization. It is a terrific thing for them to have to assimilate, and it will have to be done rather painfully at first. But there is a very good chance that in time these influences will be digested and will come out as something very great and very beautiful. At least, I hope so. Maybe in that way we can repay our debt to Japan by giving them new inspirations in return for all of the things that we have learned from their artists; something that will enrich them rather than destroy them. We have qualities, too, that I am sure could be constructive rather than destructive for them, if they understand which ones they are. It is very important for the Japanese artist to try to dig deeper than the surface in our work, too. I think that when he does he will find a great sympathy, no matter how new or how different many of our principles seem compared with his, which were so firmly established long ago. This feeling is so deep and so rich in Japanese art that it makes it almost impossible to find anything in really bad taste produced in the heyday of their culture. As I said, it enriched all of our arts and made us more conscious of principles which are way beyond any boundaries, geographical or racial or religious or time, even. We realize that certain principles, not only timely but timeless, are at work, and I think that they are most inspiring to us because we can see that here they flowered together so harmoniously. It shows that art *can* be of the people. We need to believe that very strongly, because today, with the ascension of science, we are apt to feel we do not need art—that it's a luxury or something foolish. I see no reason why science and art are incompatible anymore than why science and nature or art and nature or anything else that's great and good are.

We need to realize that sort of consistency in our civilization before we can have a culture. Our job is much more difficult than theirs because we have so many races, places, religions, complicated with commercialism and scientific endeavors. In addition, we have a much wider range of materials, methods, and many different conditions which make it much more difficult to find common denominators as the Japanese did. Through their example, we can find a great inspiration, and knowing that it is possible to accomplish—even though our task is greater—should do a great deal to encourage the creative artist in the West. It should make all of us realize that art can only be really authoritative and important when it is actually honest all the way through with its time, place, people, materials, and ideals.

Nine

Goff on Debussy

Of all the great artists of all time, I think the name of Claude Debussy stands out most clearly in my mind. I have been acquainted with his work for over thirty years, and I can honestly say it has never let me down. The more I learn about this remarkable man and his ideas, the more inspiring and wonderful he seems.

Many people are not aware that Debussy was a great thinker and had a philosophy of art which is very unusual and refreshing. For instance, he was able to say, "The struggle to surpass others is never really great if disassociated from the noble ideal of surpassing one's self, though this involves the sacrifice of one's cherished personality." I think Debussy, above all artists, was willing to sacrifice his cherished personality.

He never established a trademark and repeated it over and over like a pattern from a bolt of dress goods or by repeating his successes. He dared each time to let a composition have its own life and to go along with each work so that it was independent of his other works, or other people's works. Naturally, he had influences. It is easy to trace the effect of Wagner, Mussorgsky, Grieg, and others, including the old Gregorian modes, in his work. Certainly, all of this became his and was thoroughly assimilated. At no time was he willing to graft one composition off

In Goff's collection of more than five thousand records he had performances of all of Debussy's music. He was introduced to the music of Debussy in 1920, and it influenced him for most of his life (see #7 for details of his discovery of Debussy). Debussy was one of his favorite composers, and the music had an immense effect on his concepts of design and his view of the creative process. Goff must have had fifteen different recorded versions of La Mer, *and he listened to all of them. (Tape made at the School of Architecture, Norman, February 7, 1954, with just the two of us.)*

of another. He worked purely upon impulse because he had to. I don't think you will find very much manufactured music in his output. He was able to give us music that was direct through his wonderful technique from his depth and range of feeling. I don't think any artist that I know has ever had the terrific range of feeling that you will find in this man. He can make us feel as archaic as ancient Egypt or as modern as today. He can take us into the fields or into the forest or by the seashore. His understanding of nature was much deeper than anyone I know. He used to prefer to walk in the woods on Sunday, as he said, "When God is kind." He thought such a walk was much more beneficial to him than listening to Beethoven's *Pastoral* Symphony. He also preferred a few simple notes on an Egyptian flute to such manufactured works as we find in much of our music. His music came as a direct expression from his feelings. Just to glance at the titles of some of his work indicates the terrific range of his imagination. We have all sorts of feelings expressed; humorous, gay, solemn, sad, reveries, spontaneous flashes, brilliance, and all the feelings of the human emotions. What other document in art reaches into human feelings so deeply as *Pelléas and Mélisande*? We certainly cannot call this artist decorative, as many people did; nor can we any longer think of his music as being unmelodic. Once Debussy was given a banquet, and a man got up and gave a fancy speech about how he [Debussy] had abolished melody from music. He congratulated Debussy on this achievement. When Debussy had this interpreted, he rose up with a certain amount of protest and said, "That is not true. On the contrary, my music is aiming at nothing but melody." Today we can understand that it is extremely lyrical—singing and very melodic.

His philosophy has been expressed verbally through

many letters to his friends and in articles written in various French musical reviews. They have been collected together under the title of *Monsieur Croche, the Dilettante-Hater* [London, 1927]. This collection of writing, while extremely small, has a great deal of valuable information and principle for us to examine. He was rather clever in his invention of Mr. Croche, the character he could talk with, who can say the mean things about people that he doesn't want to talk about personally. In that way he can be very fair about the subject and argue all sides with this rather bitter and irascible creature, Croche, who had a sort of Edgar Allan Poe cynicism and dryness. He has Croche say things about music that he really felt deeply himself. I would recommend very earnestly that everyone should read this, not without a touch of humor, either.

Croche talks about how people despise music and he thinks they are preferable to the critics who don't understand it at all, even enough to despise it. He even favors the audience reaction of booing during the music as being better than the critic's reaction. He talks about various musicians and he seems to think of music as a picture sometimes. He says, "Music is the sum total of scattered forces." In another Croche comment that not only applies to music but to all forms of creative art:

> Who will discover the secret of musical composition, the sound of the sea, the curve of the horizon, the wind in leaves, the cry of a bird, who will register these complete complex impressions within us? Then suddenly, without any deliberate consent on our part, one of these memories issues forth to express itself in the language of music. It bears its own harmony within it. By no effort of ours can we achieve anything more truthful or accurate. In this way only does the soul, destined for music, discover its most beautiful ideas. If I speak thus it is not in order to prove that I have none, I detest doctrines and their

impertinent implications. For that reason I wish to write down my musical dreams in a spirit of utter self-detachment. I wish to sing of my interior visions with the naive candor of a child. No doubt, this simple musical grammar will jar on some people. It is bound to offend the partisans of deceit and artifice. I foresee that and I rejoice at it. I shall do nothing to create adversaries, but neither shall I do anything to turn enmities into friendships. I must endeavor to be a great artist so that I may dare to be myself and suffer for my fate. Those who feel as I do will only appreciate me the more, the others will shun and hate me. I shall make no effort to conciliate them. On that distant day, I trust that it is still very far off, when I shall no longer be a cause of strife, I will feel bitter self-reproach for that odious hypocrisy which enables one to please all mankind will inevitably have prevailed in those last works.

From that quote by Croche you can see that Debussy regarded art as something more than something for his own time. He has said, "I am always suspicious of the artist who is acclaimed by the public for fear that he will be too much a part of that same public."

Debussy said he strove in the early works to please the public. He wanted to write music that would give pleasure and enjoyment to people. As he continued to grow, he soon found out that the music he needed to express, in order to continue his growth, did not always give pleasure to the public immediately. He found that he had to go his own way and hope that some day the public would catch up with him. On the other hand, he felt that if the public did catch up with him then his music would no longer have that power to be above and aloof in regards to public opinion. He dreaded that time when he would become a household word and his music everyday fare.

Some of his earlier works now are in danger of being considered everyday fare. Everyone knows *Clair de Lune*, but how many know the works since *La Mer*? I think it will be a long time before we really understand the *Ètudes*, *La Martyr de Saint Sebastian, Jeux*, and the other remarkable works of his later period. He had the ability to find inspiration in all sorts of things—in nature or in cultures other than his own. For instance, at the Exposition of Paris, when the colonies of the French Empire were on display in Paris, Debussy was fascinated with the orchestras from these native islands, and particularly with the orchestra from Java. He used to stand and listen by the hour to this orchestra play. He was undoubtedly influenced considerably by the spirit, of the liquidlike compositions of the Javanese music where it all fits together easily without ostentatious climaxes. He was probably the only musician in Europe who could understand such music at that time. He has written about it saying, "There have been, and fortunately there still are, certain charming races who have learned to compose music as naturally as one learns to breathe. When we compare the sound of their percussion, and their delicate effects, with our music, we realize that ours is like the brash noise of a traveling circus band."

I think it would take a man of real perception to understand that difference in music. Particularly at that time, the world was under the yoke of Wagner's influence, including Debussy. He had a very difficult time shaking this strong hold of Wagner's music. Even so, he never lost respect for it, and contrary to many people's opinion, he admired Wagner's music tremendously, if disassociated from the poetic text which he thought was very poor, dramatically. He did admire Wagner the musician tremendously, but he knew that something else had to be done—that it wasn't enough to go ahead and repeat his work, any more than we should go ahead and repeat Frank Lloyd Wright's work, or any other great genius of our time.

Here Debussy was able, singlehandedly, to throw off this Wagner spell, and to enrich his art with many new technical innovations. The big, noisy orchestra of Wagner, which was pretty much a mass kind of orchestra, which had been given much more richness and expressiveness, by Richard Strauss, was thick with Germanic heaviness. Debussy was able to follow the clarity of Rimsky-Korsakov's orchestration and to develop it into an even more transparent and expressive orchestra. He was able, through his orchestration, to achieve much more subtlety and expressiveness.

I think that it is remarkable that one composer could work with so many mediums of music so successfully. For instance, he wrote for the piano extremely well. The piano was really a piano, and not an imitation orchestra. He was able to do one string quartet, which is still regarded as one of the very greatest of all, whereas Haydn and others wrote hundreds of them. He was able to do one big opera, and it is still regarded as one of the very greatest of all. This opera took him ten years to compose, and in all of that time he was growing by leaps and bounds. But he was able to sustain this creative effort for ten years so that the finished work does not betray what was done first and what was done last, but holds together as a complete work. That is a very remarkable feat in itself. His work for the voice was beyond comparison in the field of singing. He was able to follow the poems, to translate them into music; the accompaniment and the poem and the voice are so inseparably combined that they all add up to one complete experience. He always could write expressively for his instruments. I don't think we could ever replace the instruments in any of his orchestrations with others without losing the effect of the music, so perfectly has the timbre been considered in the tonal quality, the color, the sound, to give us exactly the shade of feeling he wished us to have. This honesty in the use of materials is a great inspiration to us as architects.

I think another most important thing about Debussy and his work is that he never did anything without a real creative impulse to start with. He preferred to wait until he had such an impulse before composing music. There is very little of his work [that is] manufactured or synthetic. Probably that accounts for the fact that he did not write as much music as many of our great composers have. It also accounts for the high quality of what he did do. I think that this principle of not doing anything without an idea is most important to all artists. Surely, if a man is clever, and has a good background, he can produce works of art, or seemingly works of art, quite easily, with a great deal of facility. The creative works that have real meaning and authority are the ones that spring from this inner necessity, that have to be. The artist is more or less a medium through which they materialize.

With Debussy's work we find each composition standing on its own feet and according to its own laws, its own sense of order. One is not grafted off of another, as I said before. I think that is most important for us to understand, because it is a truly organic approach to art, whereas many composers write music in set forms, such as symphonies, sonatas, and so on, where the form is the determining thing and the music content is poured into it and altered to fit. The organic approach, as we find in Debussy's music, is a free growth of musical impulses which are ordered by a great sensitivity, into a composition that is extremely disciplined. This freedom in design with music is often baffling to people who are used to signposts along the way. Sometimes the music is so elusive that it is not easy to grasp at first; often it refuses to give up its secret even after much acquaintance. The quality of surprise is there, but even stronger is the one of mystery. This sense of mystery is what holds our attention to his music for many, many years after we are familiar with it; it does not wear thin.

I think that this way of working is important for us to understand. It is significant to me that many of our contemporary architects and other artists who are working with formalism prefer music of older times, such as Bach, Haydn, Handel, and so on, because naturally they respond to that kind of formalism in their works. We hear a great deal said about the construction of this music, but compared with the construction in Debussy's music, and much that has followed, theirs is the A B C, post-and-lintel type, because it is not nearly so strong, light, athletic, and clear as the structure in more recent music, particularly in Debussy's. The structure is so perfectly assimilated into the musical content, and the means are so carefully considered in giving it expression, that we are not any more aware of the skeleton in the music than we are of the skeleton in a dear friend. We don't think of our friends as skeletons. We certainly know they have skeletons, but they are taken for granted, and they are part of our assumption that all of that is right because the result is right. I think that structure of that sense, such as we find in Debussy's music, is much more valid than the kind that stands out like a sore thumb. Likewise, in architecture today, the emphatic statement of the beam or column proclaiming to everyone that I am a column or I am a beam indicates a rather naive approach to engineering. It would signify that the architect is so much a novice in structure that he wants to make a big show of the simplest efforts in that direction. In music, a man who can write a composition in symphonic or sonata form is often apt to overdo the structure of it to be sure it stands out so everyone will say, oh yes, it has structure.

Debussy never wrote a symphony. He hated such forms and he said, "Most symphonies are built around themes that one heard as a child, and when we knock on the door, we find nobody home." I think that is often true of all sorts of things that are manufactured or concocted. Quite often they are not real and genuine, but something trumped up. If the artist is clever who is doing the trumping, we might easily be fooled into thinking that it is something. After we are acquainted with it, we find nobody home sometimes, and we realize that the qualities most necessary, such as the depth of feeling, are often lacking.

This tremendous range of feeling I spoke about earlier, I think, is most important to understanding Debussy. And I think it is another way we can be greatly inspired. With most artists, if you analyze their output, you will find that they have about three or four tricks up their sleeve. They have a certain solemn vein, a certain humorous vein, a certain playful vein, and so on, and they stick with it pretty much. The rest is very much like a variation on a theme. They can pull out of the mothballs any of these effects when they want to use them. It is sort of a musical yardage which can be brought out when the occasion demands. There seems to be a fear of getting into the unknown in music, just as there is in other arts. Most composers, if they do have very deep feelings, are often afraid of them and prefer to manufacture things where their feelings are absolutely cut and dried.

This is particularly true today, I think, with our International style going on in music, just as it is going on in other arts. We seem to be looking for shelter under the cloak of anonymity, and we are trying to make a virtue of the fact that something is not personal, that something is manufactured and has a trademark, is commercially acceptable. We find many artists who at one time showed a great deal of daring and promise who have fallen into ruts that are well worn in line with the International style. We find all sorts of little men in art today copying the big men who have just taken their stands. Picasso one time, when he was asked what he thought of the younger generation in painting, said, "There are many of them who are admirable, but what a pity they don't rebel against me as I rebelled against my predecessors." That takes a big man to say that because most men are flattered with imitation. Picasso is enough of an artist to know that only through change can art be kept alive and that a mere imitation of him is not enough. I think any great artist would realize that and perhaps be secretly flattered by emulation and imitation, but I think they would know, deep in their hearts, that each man has to fight his own battle, just as they have done.

Having this wide range of feeling and sensitivity to all sorts of things is so important to an artist. The artist draws from this, as Debussy said, "I didn't know just where it was coming from," because he had assimilated those experiences. Just as we have assimilated what we had to eat or drink or breathe into our physical selves. We are not conscious of what we had for dinner a week ago but we have assimilated some of that into our physical being to be kept alive; and, likewise, we have to assimilate these experiences and arrive at the sum total of these scattered forces in what we do.

Another point I think that we should talk about is clarity. Stravinsky has remarked that Debussy's music is white music because it has so few black notes on the page. This, I think, is interesting because Stravinsky's music, particularly something like the *Rite of Spring*, is almost black with notes on the page. Stravinsky knew that the work of Debussy had clarity. It was clean, simple, direct, and every note counted.

That is another point we should realize in any kind of art: that everything does count, even the silence and the voids or the resultant forms or spaces. Everything is important; there is no background. When Debussy writes a song, the piano or the orchestra is not just a background for the song, but it is so skillfully interwoven with it that everything becomes inseparable. It is all done with a clarity and economy of means that only a really great artist has at his command. Debussy once said, "How much we must first discover, and then reject, to arrive at the naked truth of inspiration." We do strive a great deal to find out new and different ways of doing things. We go in for all sorts of strange, exotic, and unusual ideas. I think that is healthy, but in discovering all of this we have to discipline it then. We need to simmer it down and reject a lot of what doesn't apply in order to arrive at the few simple things which do.

Another time, commenting on this, Debussy said, "Discipline must be sought in freedom and not in the outworn traditions of the past; give ear to no man's council, but listen to the wind, which in passing tells the story of the world." I think that he has made it clear that because an artwork has freedom doesn't mean that it should lack discipline. In fact, the discipline should come from freedom, not from the traditions of the past; not through formalism, but in the sense of freedom itself. Each artist must learn to discipline his own freedom. I think that is another very great thought Debussy has left with us to work with.

We have this great understanding of nature, of land, of science, all sorts of things, all finding expression through the work of one man. He was a very simple and wonderful person who had to withdraw from the world a little bit in order to understand it. Just as Stravinsky said in recent days, "The best way to escape Hollywood is to live there." So Debussy lived in the world, and he escaped the world, and found the world within the world, in which he could understand the one we call the real world better. This is not an ivory-tower isolationism, but an effort to get a better perspective on things. He was able to understand people better that way than by mixing with them all the time. A few select friends were enough for him. The great love he had for art and nature allowed him to complete the cycle, and give expression through his own work to the widest range of feeling.

Ten

The Design of the Garvey House

In working out an idea in architecture, of course, we usually have to do this for a client for a specific problem. As an example, not long ago Mr. Garvey came to me and said he wanted a house. I happened to know that he is a musician and his wife is also, and that they have two children, and an English bulldog, and that they owned a piece of property between two houses in Urbana, Illinois. Mr. Garvey is well acquainted with modern music, playing the viola in the Walden String Quartet. He knows a great deal about music, old and new, which has taught him that there is such a thing as new ideas in music, and, therefore, he assumed there could be in architecture. After seeing some of my work, he was convinced of it and asked me to do his house, even though he is quite a distance from where I am working.

At the time of this recording, Goff was designing the first Garvey House (which I considered one of his finest designs). A house designed for a typical midwestern neighborhood, for a musical family of four, it introduced a revolutionary architectural concept for a residence. For the recording (made on the third floor of the School of Architecture at Norman, January 17, 1954), I asked Goff how the idea evolved, and he responded with a complete discussion.

I was involved with the first Garvey House. We had hoped to get a manufacturer to participate because of the publicity that could be generated, and at that time I had a contact who was a senior administrator with Kaiser Aluminum. Kaiser wanted to furnish aluminum spheres, structural members, doors, and so on for the house, but, with working drawings complete and Kaiser preparing shop drawings, my contact left the company. The new people were not interested, and this first design was never realized.

Mr. Garvey said he would like to build a house that is more than just a house—that he would like to have me experiment. He wanted to do something that would give me a chance that I would never have with most clients, who had pretty cut-and-dried ideas of how far they wanted to go. In other words, he was willing to go a long ways, so long as it could be accomplished within his financial means. So, I suggested then that, inasmuch as his financial means were not enough to allow for a great deal of experimentation, or taking chances, that we might proceed with the idea that certain materials in it would be donated by manufacturers to further the cause of their materials and through the advertising that would inevitably result from the character of the building. The manufacturers would gain from it, and so would Mr. Garvey. So the house was not planned for Mr. Garvey's limited budget, but would include the advertising appeal it would have to the manufacturers of such modern materials as aluminum and plastic, and so forth.

Then the problem was not necessarily to start out to shock anyone, but to see if the problem of the house couldn't be approached differently from the usual attitude toward one. This normally consists of a series of boxes of various kinds, loosened up more or less, but still pretty much according to established patterns.

The design started then with the idea that we wouldn't be trying to do it in the way any other house was ever done, but that we would try to solve all of these problems of the Garveys' way of life in as fresh a way as we could in relation to this particular environment.

It seemed, first of all, the problem of the way they would live in it had to be met. Not only were they going to live in it as a family, but they also conduct a semipublic kind of life by having concerts and evenings of music, and discussions and so on, with many friends participating. That means there would be many people coming and going to this house. It also meant that the house would naturally be so different from any other house that the owners had to be protected from the curious public. The public is apt to think that anything that is new and different is public property and would want to take over. One of the first considerations, then, was how to handle the public in relation to the design. We certainly didn't want to build a spite wall, where they couldn't see anything of the place; rather, we wanted the house to present an attractive appearance to the street and an inviting one, rather than a hostile or retiring one. At the same time, we wanted to keep the public from coming onto the property unless they were invited there or had a reason for being there. That called for some sort of fence. The fence, instead of being a solid wall as it used to be, is now a transparent plastic wall through which you can see but do not enter unless you are invited through the gate.

The principal means of approaching the property would be almost always by car; very little is done by pedestrian traffic anymore. The car entrance is an important item in the plan. I think it is very bad when, inside a lot plan, you have to drive the car up the driveway and then back out, because of children playing in the neighborhood. It is very dangerous with the children and because of the cars driving on the street. It is much more advisable to drive around and see where you are going, than to back out. So this naturally called for semicircular sort of driveway where you could enter and park by the gate under a covered canopy and then drive on out without backing. There was not enough frontage to allow for a lot of parking for guests and friends, which might amount sometimes to ten cars. And the street was narrow and fairly crooked, so it wasn't right to wish all of this parking problem onto the neighbors. I widened the driveway enough to accommodate the cars of the friends and screened it with some planting so it will not look like a parking lot.

We go through the gate and enter the house through a revolving door. We used revolving doors so they could always be closed. With the children running in and out, that is always a problem keeping the cold air from rushing in, or the hot air, whichever it might be, as well as the dust and the dirt. But the revolving door solves that problem, and beside, the kids can have a lot of fun running around in them.

This circular motion established by the driveway and the revolving door seemed to indicate a circular feeling that might be carried through as an idea. The next thought that came into it, about this point, was the need for separation of the living accommodations for privacy and also for sound. In this particular case the sound problem was very important, because Mr. Garvey likes to practice his viola, and Mrs. Garvey gives piano lessons. The children would need to have their own kind of sound, too. It made it necessary to separate the elements of the plan sufficiently so that each member of the family could have his own kind of music or sound, and have a large enough space where they could get together for musical events. That seemed to indicate entirely separate units that could be soundproofed easily. These could have all been arranged around some sort of a court. The court, of course, could have been any shape: it could have been square, or rectilinear, or triangular, or all sorts of ways. Still, the right-angular pattern of traffic is not a very natural one, so a circular arrangement seems more desirable again.

Now they could have been all on the same level, too— all opening off of an interior court, or hall—but it seemed to me that each one would have more identity and privacy if they were on slightly different levels. Mr. Garvey wanted his study as remotely located as possible from the other activities of the house, and still close enough so that he didn't have to walk a mile to get to it. That led to the consideration of some kind of stepping-up arrangement of the rooms so there wouldn't be a first story or a second story. Mrs. Garvey had to keep control of the situation of the children all the time—many times while she was giving piano lessons. So a second story was not very feasible, and a one story that was all stretched out was not very wise either because she would not be able to control the house very well. By arranging the units around a circular pattern, and stepping them up, we could achieve the control and the privacy that we wanted with the least amount of space involved. The rooms could have been reached by steps, but seemed a little awkward when you needed to go around it so much all the time, and a little dangerous, perhaps. The idea of the low, easy ramp came in then. When we enter the house we entered so that we step onto the ramp and we can go down a short distance to the music room, the largest interior space that is enclosed, or we can go up this ramp, which is low and easy, to the various units, such as the kitchen, the children's room, the bathroom, the owners' room, and Mr. Garvey's study. Going around this circular ramp we are going around an interior garden, which is advisable because, in this particular climate, outdoor living is not very good—as it might be in California, where much of the time you can actually be outdoors. In this particular location, many times the climate is not satisfactory for outdoor living, in summer or winter. So we created an interior garden, which can be air-conditioned and maintained at a temperature that will be comfortable in winter or summer and where the children can play inside in inclement weather without feeling cooped up in some little room.

The problem of sound-insulation was handled by lining the interiors of these cabins—each unit seemed to turn into sort of a cabin—with cork. That became the interior finish as well as the sound-insulation and the heat-and-cold insulation. In working the rooms, then, as separate units with space in between them around the circular ramp, we needed to maintain the temperature in the ramp to go with the rooms so there wouldn't be a sudden hot and cold change going from one place to another. So the ramp is enclosed also with a tube of cocoon-transparent plastic, so you can see through it into the interior garden and, at the same time, maintain the temperature that is in the individual living rooms.

These rooms could have been almost any shape, even if they were arranged around this circle: they could have been square, or hexagonal, or all sorts of shapes, but I followed the same circular theme, not only in plan but in section, making them spherical in shape. When you are looking around these rooms, you don't have the feeling that they are blocking your view as they would if they were squares, probably, or triangles, in plan. This way you can see around them, and under them, and over them much more easily, and the space moves much more freely around them that way. And the spheres are places half in half out of this big plastic cylinder which encloses the interior garden. The spheres could be heated at a warmer temperature than would be necessary for the indoor garden.

The problem of enclosing the interior garden, then, was managed by a plastic wall around the cylinder. When it came to the roof, we could have had some sort of truss, or suspended roof, or something like that. But I wanted the sky to enter into the interior because the view out was not particularly good from the inside, looking out onto the neighbors or out onto the street. It seemed best to open it up to the sky, as much as possible, but still we have to have protection. If we had put some kind of a glass roof, or transparent roof, on, we would have the problem of heat and also structural problems that are complicated. We would also have the problem of heating a great volume of space inside in cold weather.

Also the sense of space. If it were just a big cylinder with the ramp running around in it, it would not be as interesting as if there were something within the space which helped to define it. This led to the series of arches that were springing from the center and spanning out to the exterior wall of the cylinder, resulting in a form of the roof that is like a morning glory. These steel ribs could be covered with chicken wire and sprayed with transparent cocoon plastic to keep the weather out and the sun could come through. It would be possible to see the rain and the snow through it. To insulate it without losing this vision, we have a water pipe running around the circumference of the circle at the top of the roof which allows water to trickle down in the summertime to a pool at the base of this funnel. The evaporation of the water is helpful toward insulation, just as water that stands on roofs made for that purpose in other cases. The water will also wash off the surface, so it will always be clean and not covered with dust or other debris. The problem in winter could be handled by letting the water flow down on cold days and freezing, so that the ice itself would act as an insulation, very much as it does in the Eskimos' igloo. We would be able to circulate this water in the summertime so that the water loss would not be too great, and the whole interior opens up the sky in this way.

In the interior garden, they can feel that they are screened around the outside with a translucent screen which doesn't actually shut out the life around them, but it minimizes it to the effect of the sky and the weather, which can actually be experienced at all times, day and night. I think it would be very pleasant to be in there and have the feeling of the rain coming, of the lightning, or the moonlight, or any other natural condition where we would be living in it more than considering nature as an enemy that we have to run and hide from. This may take a little adjustment to get used to—not so much the clients as other people who look upon a house as a cave or a shelter. I feel it will be such a pleasant experience that it would not be too great a difficulty for them to do this.

The garden area inside has a water garden that is shallow enough for children to play safely with, and there is a sand area where they can play in the sand, and they can run up and down the ramp. At the high part of the ramp is a slide that goes down into the sand pile, and a kind of jungle gym so that they can climb up and run down the ramps so it gives them plenty of exercise space inside that they can have fun in when the weather is bad outside.

In the circular order that was established from the beginning and followed through in section and plan, I felt we needed to sense that these spheres were inside as well as outside of the main cylinder; the cylinder, being translucent, would not give us quite enough sense of that. Besides, we would want to look out someplace around the outside, anyway. The idea was to provide a clear plastic ring of some sort around the spheres so we could look out and could sense from inside or outside that the sphere was penetrating the cylinder. That led to the ring windows of transparent plastic that run around the spheres in the cylinder. They could have been circular, also, but I felt they would be too parallel with the spheres, and that we needed another element in the design. A square seemed to be too awkward at the corners for the circular scheme, and the circle was too parallel with the sphere. The natural thing, then, seemed to be something that had the merits of both, which would be what is called a Chinese circle, or more in a slang phrase, a *squircle*. A squircle is a square circle, where it is almost a square and still has no straight lines, but the sides are slightly curved and the corners are curved so that it moves with a little more of a jerk than a circle, but not so much of one as a square. This avoids being parallel with the spheres, which gives a more interesting counterpoint. The divisions in the plastic are radiating around the spheres, which tends to remind us that the radial idea coming out of the center of the sphere had something to do with this particular window, too.

Arches extend out all around the cylinder to form sort of an eave, or protection, from the weather, and the chicken wire, which covers the roof, is allowed to hang unevenly around this eave, with plastic in part of it, and vines in other parts of it, to soften the design so it won't be too mechanistic in effect. This irregular, free pattern that is caused by the hanging chicken wire and plastic around the eaves also moves freely with the breeze and gives motion to the design, which keeps it from being static as usual.

The materials are kept free from wood as much as possible, or any material that requires maintenance. The aluminum can be left as is, and the plastic, too, without painting or other upkeep. Wood is not used at all, in any way, structurally, or as little as possible. The ramp is covered with rope for traction, and underneath the ramp the section is circular to allow space for heating pipes and wiring conduits, which run up and feed all of the spheres ranged around the ramp. The whole thing is sealed against the dirt and wind and the outside and still there would be plenty of fresh air inside, and it could be maintained at any temperature which would be comfortable for the occupants. Each person in the family has their own sphere, literally, to live in. Mr. Garvey says that he requires a study where he can leave his things out. His wife is a neat and orderly person, and she dislikes seeing a lot of clutter on his desk, so we put him in the top sphere so that no one has to walk past his room. He can leave his books, scores, and everything out if he wants to, and only he, or whoever he takes into the space, will see it. On the other hand, everything is compact and efficiently laid out so that Mrs. Garvey can keep her very strict sense of order and discipline in all of her parts. The children have been provided for in play areas inside and out and the fun they could get from living in such a structure.

The house is insulated against the neighbors with planting all along the sides of the yard. With the plastic screen around the driveway in front, the public is kept at arm's length. It provides the maximum of privacy for the occupants, which is quite a problem when one builds a house that is very different from other houses, because of the curiosity of the public about them. We do have to recognize that problem, and I do think it has been solved in this design.

The production method of the house has been considered, so that it can all be shop fabricated, with very little foundation work. The rooms can be assembled, the spheres can be made up and delivered to the site and hoisted into place with a minimum of time and effort. All the materials in the design can be shop fabricated, so that very little site work is required.

I think that more and more we have to face the fact that shop fabrication is infinitely better than job fabrication, because of the weather and the tools and equipment needed to work with new materials. Also, it is an advantage when you are building anything as different as this, because the longer it takes to build it the more it costs, and the more public curiosity and resentment is apt to be stirred up. People will often like an idea after they see it complete, but in the making they are apt to be very opposed to it or very startled by it. So the sooner you can bring all this about the better it is for the public and for the owner both. Those are some of the physical reasons connected with the house.

I have felt for some time that architecture needs to be more of our time by being less rooted to the ground; I think that our time is less rooted to the ground. That doesn't mean we are getting away from nature, because the air is nature, too, and water is nature; the sky is, and I think a dragonfly is just as much part of nature as a rock. In this sense, these people would not live a life of calm repose in the house. They are active and engaged in music, they are people who are interested in new developments. I couldn't see a house that was very earthy, rooted into the ground for them. It seemed to me that here was a chance to explore some of the possibilities of lightness and new materials and to play the translucence and transparency idea more than the solid and the opaque. The solid and opaque idea is recognized in the shapes of the spheres, but the nature of the material, like aluminum, would have so much reflected light that there would be the effect of the translucence of light even with these solids.

I feel the Garvey House is a step toward a more athletic and lighter understanding of architecture. I don't mean that architecture should be only light and airy, and never heavy, because I think there are times and places where the other qualities are desirable. It seems to me that it is one way to enlarge our vocabulary and to have a wider range in architecture. It is possible now to think in this way, too, which is made possible now through the materials and methods we have at our disposal. In this particular case, it seemed an opportune time to try some of these ideas.

I hope that over and above the physical solution of the problem, the relation of the scale of the building to the environment, and the abstract qualities that have gone into the design, the way it works, and all of that—I hope that it achieves something more than all of that, too—that will help to extend the boundaries of architecture, at least in some direction toward translucency and transparency and toward a more flexible notion of space.

I think our sense of space in architecture has grown tremendously in the last fifty years, but our consciousness of it has been in existence long before that, of course. In most interior space, we feel that it is a static kind of space that stays pretty much within certain limits. In the Garvey House, I tried to activate this space more, to make it feel like it changes all the time without any abrupt sudden changes of floor levels or anything of this sort, but a continuity of change that would carry on.

In this sense, I think it is related to the Bavinger House there in Norman, Oklahoma, which is also an effort to have a continuous space which is ever changing. The Bavinger House has a spiral, starting broad and low and narrowing into a greater height so that nothing is parallel anywhere. In the Garvey House, the sense of space is moving up and down through the ramp, around the core of the translucent structure of the interior garden, so that you can have this very open feeling of space, or you can have a very snug feel-

ing of going into the spherelike cabins and being as cozy
and enclosed as you wish to be.

Probably the real importance of the Garvey House would
be, not only its use of new materials, but this idea of
lightness and more athletic design where ornament is not
applied but where it is gotten out of the structure and the
design of the plan itself, with the color and textures. In addition, the sense of the living space is active and varying at
all times.

Eleven

The New Geometry in Architecture

I don't know whether I have a right to be here in this meeting or not, being just an architect. I think that we are all engaged in research of various kinds; certainly, I have been all my life.

First of all before we get started on this I would like to qualify, somewhat, the title of this talk that is given in the brochure you have. It is noted in there as "The New Geometry in Modern Buildings." I would like to change that to "The New Geometry in Architecture." I would like to make a distinction there. I don't think that modern buildings are always architecture, but I think that architecture is necessarily a good building. We could have a good building that is physically functional that would do its job, but I believe that in architecture it has to be more. It is this class that we are particularly interested in this morning.

In regard to geometry, I have never felt I was a specialist in geometry, be-

This lecture was recorded on October 28, 1953, at the Illinois Institute of Technology (IIT) in Chicago, where Mies Van der Rohe was head of the School of Architecture. This was a delicate position for Goff, since he was considered to be a renegade, undisciplined designer by the IIT group. The conference to which he was asked to present his lecture was a technical-scientific conference on new geometry in building, but Goff quickly changed his talk to "New Geometry in Architecture." He was well received by the group.

cause math has never been one of my long suits. I know that of all the different mathematics, it is the one that seems closest to what we are involved with in design and in aesthetics. So far as the new geometry is concerned, I am not so certain that it is new; probably, it is more a case of reevaluating many principles that have been in existence for a long time. Certainly, there has been a change in the attitude toward architecture that has come about because of a looser or more varied sense of the use of geometry. By geometry, we mean the theory of space and of figures in space. In that sense, I think there has been a very definite change in architectural concepts of space and figures in space. Probably all the geometry we use in design could have been proved by the Chinese many thousands of years ago. Every time we think we have thought of something new, we find that they beat us to the draw. I do believe that one of the most significant changes in the concept of space and figures in space is due to our increased desire to have the space inside and outside more continuous, more flexible, more dynamic, and more active.

In the past, architecture was much more sedate—but it was something that had repose, in a quiet sense, because life was comparatively quiet. Excepting for wars that are eternally with us, we have had a rather peaceful and quiet period in history. Every once in a while there is a sudden burst of activity, energy, and new life coming into being which demands more freedom and flexibility. We have had it in structures; we have had man's continual desire to free interior space—to get away from obstruction, to get more room, to make the room more serviceable, and more active with the functions in the room. In this respect, we find that we are no longer concerned with interior spaces as separate little boxes with holes punched for doors and windows, with an especially ugly hole for the main entrance. That was often the case in the past. We do feel the need for more continuity, more plasticity and flow in design of space and materials.

We are not satisfied anymore with just a box, no matter how nice the box looks. We can use nice materials; we can use good proportions, colors, textures, and all the tricks in the book—and still it is apt to end up as a box in feeling. The parallel planes we get with floors, ceilings, and walls create a feeling of a static kind of space.

I think that many of our leading architects today, particularly our most outstanding ones since 1900, have been working with this problem in their own ways. We are apt to think of them as all rugged individualists who have nothing in common. It is very hard for some people to understand what these great men could have in common while working with architecture—and, particularly, when they don't get along with each other. Architects are proven to be prima donnas, just like other artists, you know. We have certain ones who won't speak to others, and so on, but with the great men we do have certain common denominators which carry through all of their work. This will become clearer as the battle dies down and the smoke clears away and we realize what they were really up to and not what they were just saying. I have no trouble at all, in my own mind at least, in reconciling principles that seem so opposite as those of Frank Lloyd Wright, Le Corbusier, Mies van de Rohe, and Antonio Gaudi. I believe in many ways they are working for similar things. They are facets of a different kind of many of these basic drives that are at work in our societies.

In thinking of geometry, we have been used to the usual things, such as the square, the rectangle, the circle, polygons of different kinds. All through history we have had architects working with all of these figures. I think they are not only true in architecture but they are true in painting and other arts as well. Of course, there is another approach to art—we are speaking of architecture as an art, now, as well as a business and a technology. I see no difficulty there and I can reconcile those different aspects of architecture.

We feel, also, a need for a very free approach. As individuals in a democracy, where a man has a right to be an individual, we feel the need to explore, not only geometry but other ways of doing designs, in the way we feel that it should be done. Some of us are not content to leave geometry the static and quiet sort of thing that it has been many times. Some of us want it more active, more alive—not just a background for activities. Some of us feel a building should be expressive of what it is, more than just geometry. Geometry, all by itself, certainly isn't enough to make it architecture; any more than structure, all by itself, is— or any other one part of architecture. It is all necessary to add up to something we would call architecture, as over and above just good building.

Sometimes we feel the need to go to the other extreme and to develop a very free approach to try to emancipate ourselves from geometry, you might say. Geometry has been a pretty good crutch for an artist, because no one can criticize a circle, or a square, or a triangle. They are pretty good. I don't know who invented them; I don't know if anyone invented them: they were probably principles that were there before they were discovered. We are pretty safe if we stick close to these simple forms and don't deviate very much from them. Then we are on safe grounds. If we start moving these things around, if we start making them go in another direction, and at right angles, or for instance if we have a circle and we do anything with it besides extrude it into a cylinder, or revolve it into a dome, or a sphere, or an arch, or something, then we are apt to be suspect, because it might have a little different look.

Gaudí tried geometry in motion in much of his work— particularly the great cathedral in Barcelona, which has never been completed. As a result of his efflorescence of this idea of geometry in motion, the first impulse for most people, critics particularly, is to think of it as the work of a madman—of someone who is insane. The cathedral is considered a great architectural sin by many people. I know Wright deplores it, but Sullivan thought it was the greatest flight of the creative spirit of our time. So we have diametrically opposed ideas, even from men in basically the same camp. One thinks it is sinful and one thinks it is great. I don't think it makes very much difference what anyone thinks about it, as an individual, because its true quality will survive public opinion, whether it may be favorable or unfavorable, if it has vitamins and real quality. I think probably it does. There is no reason why we can't understand this in the Barcelona cathedral of Gaudí or understand it in Le Corbusier's work in his very fine new church in Ronchamp or in the work of other artists.

Many times we have architecture and the public who feel that they must take sides in architectural styles. In the schools of the past we had the old eccentrics, who taught that art died with the Greeks, or the Romans, or the Renaissance, or the Gothic. As students of architecture, we were not permitted to have any ideas of our own. Just as we had that old kind of eclecticism, we now have the new eclecticism in education today which takes sides with certain more contemporary movements of an architect's work. We learn in one school that there is no god but so-and-so, and in another school that there is no god but their so-and-so. The creative growth of an individual is still squelched in most cases. The students are taught to follow, not books any longer—because books don't move fast enough—but magazines, which are much more serviceable. In following the magazines, the young architects should remember that many other people subscribe to these magazines, too, besides architectural students. It is getting now so that the real-estate man, the engineering companies and builders, and all sorts of people have the key to the situation and can produce the same kind of copies, as good, or better, than some of the architectural students.

I think it is very important that we learn, in architecture, not to follow just because something is good, or something is great, or because it is in style, or no matter what it is. I think we need very much to look into it and to enquire into what we can do with it and study the principle—to study architecture as a big principle, bigger than anyone, or any place, or any time. To try to reevaluate this concept always in terms of our materials, our methods, and our civilization that we are a part of, just as it has always been done in the past. In this sense, I don't think we could say that it's particularly a new idea, the use of geometry in buildings, or anything else—but we are reevaluating it, always. We are reevaluating it now. We have men who are not even trained as architects who are very concerned about developing new kinds of structures. We have architects more and more interested in structure.

There was a time, not too long ago, when architecture was just design; structure and materials were something else, and they were considered incompatible. Each thought the other was off his rocker. The engineer thought the architect goofed up his work, and the architect thought the engineer was always getting in his way, and usually it was true on both sides. More and more we have the desire to work together and to make it all of one thing. We know that structure isn't everything, any more than aesthetic design is everything, or that materials are everything, or geometry, or any of the other parts of this thing that makes up architecture.

I believe that just inventing a new kind of structural system, as valuable as that is to the architect, and as necessary as it is, is not to be confused with architecture with a capital A. Sometimes it is like developing a new hat without anything else to go with it. We may have a nice dome, or a nice vault, or a nice roof, or something, and still not have the pants and the vest and all that goes with it. I think that we have some cases of that kind, but I don't deplore them. I think they are necessary in the way of research and experimentation. I am happy to see men working on these various approaches to structure and design. Things are moving so fast, it will take some time for these new structural forms to be absorbed into the entire consciousness of our architects. But more and more they will be part of it.

Geometry, I think, doesn't mean necessarily to stick to the rigid forms that we usually associate with geometry. I think that we can conceive of space and of forms as one. I hear Mr. Wright quoting from Lao-tze, "The reality of the building is the space within it," but I don't think that is entirely true. I think that is certainly an integral part of it, but there is more to it than just the space within: there is the space without it, and there is the design itself—the material and the structure of the design itself. I believe that geometry is naturally involved in all of these thinking processes. The void and the volume, the negative and the positive, all the parts that go to make up the complete design should be in this.

It is rather strange, to me at least, that when an architect does try to experiment or to extend the horizon of his field, he is apt to be considered sinful. People worry about his influence. I hear people worry about the influence of Wright; I hear people who worry about the influence of Corbu and Mies. Some people say, "Build a better Mies trap and the world will beat a path to your door." Some people say, "It is better to be a little Wright than all wrong." You hear all sorts of things about all of them. Personally, I like them all. But I don't see why if we like roast beef we can't like ham, too. I don't believe that other fields in the building business get the same raking over the coals. If a man is working on a new kind of heating system and there are some bugs in it they try to improve it. It isn't a matter of national calamity about his evil influence. But the minute an architect does something new, he is in for it, particularly the nearer to something his work is. It seems that the nearer to perfection anything becomes, the more we notice its flaws. John Dalks's building, here on the IIT campus, is just a building; it can have a roof leak and no one will notice it; they will fix it. But just let the roofs of some of these men I have been talking about leak, and it will be written up in *Life* magazine. It is a matter of public concern.

I heard the story about Corbu one time and that one of his roofs leaked and the lady called him out to the job and said, "Look at this big puddle of water in the middle of my living-room floor. What are you going to do about it?" Corbu pulled a piece of paper out of his pocket, and she thought he was going to make some important calculations, or something real technical, and he starts folding it up. After folding it, he came out with a little paper boat that he put down in the middle of the floor and said, "Now you can have fun."

I happen to know of a job of Mr. Wright's where the lady was showing me through the house and the roof was supposed to be flat, but it wasn't. It sagged a little. The roof was holding water because it had just rained. She said, "Wasn't it thoughtful of Mr. Wright to provide this lovely birdbath for us on the roof." I agreed with her. Other people wouldn't be so broadminded as that.

I think an architect has to worry considerably about the technical aspects of his building. It has to stand up under something that you can't figure. You can figure wind loads, live loads, dead loads, stay within the code and costs and all that, all the physical functions, and still, I think, the one thing you can't figure is the criticism. You are sure going to get it, too. The building has to be doubly good if it is good architecture: it has to be a good architectural concept and it has to be well built, because it does have to stand up under criticism. And after all the laughing and ha-haing and everything is over, there has to be something there, if it is going to be architecture. Criticism of architecture is nothing new: it has been going on for thousands of years and I think that most of the architects who are trying to grow in their art are willing to accept it and to learn from it and to try to improve their work all the time.

I do believe we shouldn't look upon the work of these advanced architects who are pioneers—they are not followers—as sinful. There was an old Tibetan philosopher and poet who lived a pretty rugged life. I understand he was a real bearcat in his younger days and he did everything he shouldn't do. His mother taught him witchcraft and how to burn down people's houses and everything; he was terrible. Then he saw the evil of his ways and became just the opposite—a saint. He lived as a hermit for a long time up in the mountains until finally one of his students murdered him. On his deathbed, when you are supposed to say something very important, Milarepa summed up what he thought was his whole life experience that might be valuable to others. He said, "Do what you will—that which may seem sinful but helps others—for that is truly pious work."

Advancing Architecture

I have been invited to talk about architecture and the problem of advancing architecture. I have talked to quite a few AIA groups over the country and it interests me that the AIA is more and more interested in talking about something other than just fees, although that's very interesting. But there is a real search and a real interest in architecture for something besides the business part of the practice of architecture. In almost all of these meetings over the country, I have noticed a general question that comes up, and that is: What are we going to do to enlighten the public about the architect? How is he going to know about us, and how will we wise him up about how good we are and why they need us, and so on. Of course, we know the AIA has been sponsoring radio programs and television soapbox operas about what happens to the person who builds a house without an architect—but, of course, they don't tell what happens to some of them who have architects, but that's just between us.

This tape was made when Goff spoke to the Wisconsin state chapter of the AIA in Madison in 1956. The hotel ballroom was decorated in the worst possible taste, using stripes, mirrors, and classical plaster decorations. Although his subject concerned educating the public about why architects are needed, he developed his material in such a way that it became advice to the architects on how to become architects in the greater sense.

It is interesting, though, how there seems to be a genuine concern everywhere about educating the public about architects. At one of the meetings I attended, the advertising manager of this particular group had to give a report. And he got up and said, "Well, we have been doing a good job: we have gotten several spots on radio and on TV, and had articles in the papers—practically everything but dropping pamphlets from airplanes." Then he said rather meaningly at the end, "But, after all, you fellows have to do something." I thought there was more truth than he realized in what he said, because we do have to do something.

The way we can make the public the most conscious of the architect and architecture is by doing architecture—it's very simple. We do need to advance the understanding of the public about architects and architecture, I grant you, but we also need to deliver. And the thing we have to deliver is architecture, and that will do more to convince them than anything else.

Now I speak of architecture as something separate from what is usually called architecture—that is just building. We are used to referring to many things that are built in this country as "architecture". We could even hear someone refer to the "architecture" of this room. That would be farfetched, of course. But it has been done. I think if there had been a Watusi standing by the wall when they painted this room, they would have had the stripes go right across him, too. Anyway, this was supposed to have been architecture at one time, I suppose, with a capital A.

We have had all kinds of ideas about what architecture is. And this word "eclectic", which Mr. Sandstedt hated to talk about, in the dictionary doesn't mean anything particularly bad, but we use it as a cuss word. Because not very many years ago, the architectural schools, without exception, taught that architecture had all been done and that the most we could possibly do was to follow suit. And different schools specialized in different suits. If you wanted to be a good little "Greek," you went to a certain school; if you wanted to be a good little "Gothic," you went somewhere else; and if you wanted to be a Renaissance man, you could specialize at another one. But you would never dare have an idea of your own.

At that time, engineering was a bad word in architectural schools. We were supposed to consider the engineering a necessary evil that had to be covered up. And the engineers considered the architects as the people who plastered over all their work with this meaningless stuff you see around you. Naturally, they learned to hate each other.

I'm sorry, but that was the atmosphere I was brought up in and many of you, I am sure, saw it. Mr. Wright was working, and Mr. Sullivan, and other people were doing things both in Europe and here, but they were regarded as odd specimens, entirely out of the realm of good sense, and they were strange and fantastic, and so on. People wouldn't take them seriously at all. And so, a young person starting out in architecture had to follow along in those lines or else. When he questioned professors and asked "What about these men?"—"Oh, they're crazy."

I remember, if you'll pardon a personal remembrance, when I was just a youngster starting in the office as an apprentice, the old man of the firm told me that I should learn the basic principles of architecture first, and he knew what they were because he had some plates with the Greek Orders on them. It was my job to trace those in ink on tracing linen. I didn't know why, except he said to, so I did, without any particular enthusiasm, and I saved the worst until the last, the Corinthian one.

One day I was working on that one and feeling very despondent and wondering how I got tangled up with this stuff anyway when the engineer of the firm happened to be going through. I wasn't allowed back in the drafting room where all the work was going on. He said, "What's wrong with you?" And I said, "Oh, I hate this stuff." He asked,

"Then what are you doing it for?" I said, "The old man told me to." He said, "Well, you don't always do everything you're told, do you?" Those were seeds of revolution. So I said, "Well, I have always been told I should." He said, "Well, you'll never get any place that way. What do you care what the Greeks did. Why don't you find out what is going on now?" I was inclined to think that sounded like common sense. So I went into the drafting room with him and he gave me a table. Everyone was too busy to notice me. I was too little to be seen then, anyway. They gave me a table at the back of the room, and the first job he told me to do was to design a house. I asked what kind of a house and he said, "Oh, any kind, just make up one." I had never heard, at that time, of Mr. Wright or other architects, so I thought I was originating a house. But it was probably influenced by things that had been influenced by things that had been influenced . . . I don't know. Anyway, it was very low and spread out, had casement windows, and low chimneys, all the tricks, you know. Finally, the draftsmen in the office got curious about what I was doing. They came over and looked at my design and they said, "Hmm, that looks like some of Frank Lloyd Wright's stuff." I felt rather chagrined and asked, "Who's he?" They said, "Well, he's a crazy nut up in Chicago." So I thought, Well, there's something strange about this. If it looks like his work, and he's crazy, what does that make me?

It didn't happen just once, it happened a number of times. The material salesmen used to come through the office just like they do now, and when I could find one from Chicago, I'd nail him and ask if he knew an architect named Frank Lloyd Wright. "Oh boy, do we!" They thought he was crazy, too. So I was wondering about this business of this man. It took quite a while to find out who he was. All I could hear is that he was crazy.

I noticed, though, that the head of the firm, when he designed something, used to go and unlock a little cabinet by his desk and pull out an old, dog-eared magazine. He would rather furtively look around to see if anyone was watching, then he would look through the magazine and get to something and look at it real hard. Then he would put it back in the cabinet and go and draw like mad. I wondered what it was he kept looking at and he seemed to be very secretive about it. One day I watched my chance, and he forgot to lock the cabinet. I got into the jam when he went out for lunch. It was the March, 1908, issue of *Architectural Record*, which was about ten years old then, I think. That was the first time I ever saw any of Mr. Wright's work. I was knocked out. Here was something that looked like something I wanted to see. I was so interesting that I even forgot to eat lunch, which is amazing if you know me. So when Mr. Rush came back and caught me looking, I thought this is where I get the air. He smiled and said, "I knew you'd find that sometime." I think now that it was a plant.

From then on I could only eat, sleep, and think Frank Lloyd Wright for a number of years. It took me quite a while to find out that there were things going on other places. In the meantime, one of my first house designs got built. For me a very important thing happened with that house. It wasn't anything very remarkable in the way of a house, but I didn't realize in my ignorance that there was any question about this business. I thought you just did your job and that was it. After the house got up, I went out there one day feeling rather proud. It was the first thing of mine that had gotten built, and you know how you feel about that. Some people were going by in a car and they started laughing at the house. There were saying, "Look at that ridiculous house, isn't that a scream? Isn't it funny?" I couldn't see anything so darn funny about it. But I thought maybe I am not seeing just like they are. After they drove away, I went up to the house and took a real good look and I thought, "What is it that is so funny about it?" I knew it was different, but I didn't think it was a freak. It worried me quite a bit, for as you know young people hate to be laughed at almost worse than anything. So I went back to the office, and this engineer knew again that something was wrong. He could read me like a barometer. He said, "What in the world happened to you?" I told him about this experience. He was a preacher's son and he said, "Oh, hell, don't let that worry you. Just remember that as long as you're in the trenches doing what everyone else is doing no one will notice you and you'll get by. You can be thought of as just like everyone else. The minute you get out into no-man's-land, they are going to start shooting at you from both sides. And brother, the way you're headed you better get a good tough hide." Truer words were never spoken. I didn't realize how true they were right then. But from that time on, I have never really worried much about it.

I think that was a wonderful thing that happened to me at a time when I could easily have chickened out. From that time I have never worried about that, but on the other hand I have never tried to shock people in spite of what people think. And if I ever did, I could. But that wasn't my purpose and it isn't my purpose and never will be my purpose. If it does shock someone, I can't help it. I hope sooner or later people will understand the reasons that I try to have in my work.

Now, to get back to this idea of advancing architecture. It is the responsibility of the architect, not just to advance himself in a business way, but I think we need to advance our art, just as a medical man advances his profession. Many times we lose sight of this and we are not always as inquiring about the things we work with as we might be.

We take an awful lot for granted sometimes. Even in basic things, such as matters of aesthetics, we are apt to take for granted and do intuitively or instinctively many things we need to think about more as architects. The thing that helped me most in this respect was having to teach. I had to talk about some of these things, and I had to try to bring them out of people.

Such a basic thing as rhythm in architecture, for instance. We take it for granted, but it is still one of the life-blood elements of our art, just as it is in music and poetry. We are so apt in architecture to just take rhythm for granted, and the result is that in most of our architecture we have as deadly a monotony of rhythm as we have in our popular music, which is pretty bad rhythmically. Our rhythms are running along in fence-post style if they're fast, or in telephone-post style if they're slow. There is never a surprise in a carload. I think more and more our rhythmic sense is getting monotonous and even and uninteresting. Partly responsible for that is our module system. I think we often get stuck with it and have "moduleitis." The module system is a very useful one and a very good one; I am not saying that it has no merits, because the Japanese proved that back in the seventh century and we are just finding it out. At least they knew when to change it. One time I asked a student why he varied something in his design, why he changed it, and he said, "I did that to vary the monotony." I thought, well, after all, that is a good reason. So rhythmically I think we need to vary the monotony sometimes to at least have a break in it occasionally, because it gets pretty deadly.

Another thing that we need to consider is proportion. Too many times we take the stock material, a four-by-eight sheet of plywood or a stock-size acoustic tile, or something of that sort, which is all done on the module now, and we are too apt to accept ready-made or hand-me-down proportion. Certainly, the great architects of the past, and the present, are very conscious of proportion, and very personal in their use of it. I don't think there are any valid rules for proportion, but I do think it's something that we need to be highly sensitive to as individuals and to try to feel and understand the order of proportion that goes through a certain job.

It pains me when I see poor imitations of Mies, who is a master of proportion. You see a slab wall made out of Sheetrock and Chem-toned. It doesn't come off, not only because of the Sheetrock and the paint but because it doesn't have the sophisticated feeling for proportion Mies has. And many of the imitations of Mr. Wright's work fall short there mainly because the proportion hasn't been considered, really. It's just something that happened out of stock materials—or out of certain modules or some preconceived dimension.

We can go through all of these things; we can talk about balance—formal balance and informal balance. We can talk about color and texture, and we can talk about materials. There has been a great deal of emphasis on materials— maybe too much. That is a natural reaction from a time when materials were not materials, and that wasn't very long ago. You don't really know, in this room, whether this is plaster or wood, but it really doesn't matter very much, either. At least you aren't aware of it as material or as an honest expression of material. From that state of affairs, we are apt to go to the other extreme and get too self-conscious about it, and we say a brick is a brick brick, and a board is a board board, and a glass is a glass glass, and so on. We rattle it all off and we think we are being just as honest as hell if we don't paint the wood. Then we have the feeling that we must never cover anything and that it is a sin to have paint on something or to finish something with another material. You have to have all the materials show, and then we get all kinds of reactions as to whether materials are honest. We get a very moral point of view about that. I think that is good to a certain extent if it isn't overdone. Certainly, it was necessary, but I think that the architects are entirely too self-conscious about it now, and that we need to use it and to assimilate this rather than trying to make it an end in itself.

Actually, don't you feel when you walk into a material yard, or walk out on the job and see a pile of cement block, or brick, or lumber, [that] it looks better then than anything we ever do with it, usually? It's just like a blank piece of paper, it's hard to beat. You can imagine all sorts of things that could be done with it, but to do it with it is another matter, isn't it? I think that too often we get stuck with our materials and we don't carry beyond the materialistic stage. That is, we're pretty physically-minded about them.

I think in great architecture the material is always honestly used, but the feeling of the design of the building, the character of it, and all, transcends the material. Just like the person who may be a good skeleton, a good set of muscles, and nerves, and so on, that doesn't interest us too much, does it? We expect them to be a little more so. We expect architecture to be a little more than just the bread-and-butter materials that it is made of, although we do want the material to be honestly used, of course.

Another thing we are awfully self-conscious about now is structure. Here again we have reason to be, but as a result we have bent over backwards to be structure-minded.

316 Goff on Goff

Some people feel that if you have a good-looking structure that is about all you need and they stop too soon. We get all kinds of domes figured out, like hats to wear, but we have to have something to put under them. We have all kinds of domes, and I am glad that Bucky invented his domes, but we need to have something to wear them with.

Then we get very involved in different systems of structure, and that's fine. We should always keep an inquiring and experimental mind toward all of this, of course. Still, the skeleton isn't enough either, and I don't think very many of us would enjoy sleeping with a skeleton. We need a little more than that. Just as we need it in people, we need it in buildings. We do want a beautiful skeleton, of course, and we hope it's beautiful—it should be beautiful all the way through the whole building to be architecture.

We could go on and we could talk about these things such as texture, color, ornament. The whole feeling for ornament and detail in architecture is changing rapidly on account of the way we live. It used to be in the old days, when people just walked places, they had time to sit down and rest and look at things and study the fine points of the game. People in the Alhambra could sit there by the hours and trace these intricate geometric arabesques out. They didn't have TV, so they had to do something. They could look at all these interesting floor patterns and other details. When they got to riding around in horse and buggies, and so on, there was less time to look at all of this, so there was less of it to look at. Then with cars and airplanes speeding things up, our sense of detail in architecture has practically gone out the window. And ornament has, too. We are more inclined now to regard a whole building as an ornament rather than to think of spots of ornaments, and bands, and borders, and panels. They used to say in architectural schools, "When in doubt, panel," so there must have been an awful lot of doubt. Now they say, "When in doubt, plant." Quite often we have the pyred aregled [sic] water plant thing happening—it's really modern—but more and more we have less time to really look at things. We go by them fast; we have to get instantaneous impressions. We are in an awful hurry to get someplace so we can go someplace else, but in the meantime it seems to be passé to have anything that requires much time to look at or to listen to, to read, or anything that requires any period of concentrated attention.

I am not saying this is good or bad but it is something we are faced with. Besides, it's very expensive. Very few people can do these things anymore. Even draftsmen who can detail Gothic tracery are worth their weight in gold now, because very few can.

We are changing our perspective on all of this. At the same time an interesting thing is happening: while there is less and less of this detail and breaking down into fine scale in buildings and in architecture, there is more and more of it in the scientific fields. Where we used to just see a tulip, say, as a pretty thing just to put in a vase, now we can see X-rays of them. We can see all sorts of microscopic photographs. It seems that the more we go into them the more mysterious they become. Very exciting and very interesting. We have fine movies showing the plants growing, crystals forming, and all these things that we never used to see at all.

On the one hand we are speeding up our vision, and on the other had we are able to examine things even more closely. I believe our sense of hearing is developing considerably. While our sense of rhythm is deadening, in general, our sense of hearing, I understand, is improving considerably. That is helpful, but not so much to the architect now except he has an awful lot of problems acoustically he didn't used to have to worry about. Mr. Wright sold us on the idea of opening up interior space and getting it all free and nice and flowing; now these darn radios, and televisions, and hi-fi sets are making us close it up again, so that people will have the proper privacy acoustically. It isn't moral privacy they require so much anymore as acoustic privacy. I can remember when it was considered very bad architectural planning to have to cross a hall to go into a bathroom. If anyone saw you go into a bathroom that was very bad, because no one was supposed to go in them. Anyway, they had all kinds of little make-believe screens and things that you were supposed to hide the doors behind, never to be seen by the eye of man going from one place to another. Now it's not so bad that way, but it is a problem acoustically, isn't it?

Now we have lots of other problems to consider, like the problem of depth. In design we need to understand more and more that depth is not a matter of thickness but a matter of spatial relationship of planes and items of interest in our scheme. That would get rid of a lot of the two-dimensional facade thinking that we find in many buildings if we could get this concept of depth more.

We need to understand counterpoint as a composer of music understands it—particularly in architecture where you have many things working together and many ideas carrying on at the same time—how to weave those together and make them come off at certain places. We need to have incidents in our compositions. We need terminals to terminate these things, or periods, at places; have climaxes that would come off, and anticlimaxes if we want them. Those are all tricks of our trade, and why don't we use them? Why don't we understand them and try to reevaluate all of these things? The problems of site relation, I think, we are more conscious of as contour planning than we are as the spirit of the site that we are working with.

So we do have all these things to think about, and many, many more, of course. Problems in space. Mr. Wright is fond of quoting Lao-tse saying, "The reality of the building is the space within it." I think that's very true, but that's not the only reality, because there is also a space without it and the thing that separates these spaces, too. They are all working together; it isn't just one or the other. And all with the way we live, and work, and all that, of course.

The architect has a pretty big job on his hands, just thinking about matters of this sort without business and mechanical equipment and plumbing and all of these things. Often we wonder whether one person is capable of handling all of this. I think that probably there never was such a genius. But I won't say there never will be, but it's not very likely very soon that we would have a person equally versed in all of the mechanics of a building and the aesthetic considerations and all the others, equally at least. But there has to be some guiding force, some imagination at work, some person that's cooking the broth—as the saying goes, "Too many cooks spoil the broth." I think in architecture it can very well be the same thing: too many people can spoil the building by having too many kinds of ideas in the building rather than to discipline it into some big idea, some big scheme.

The architect, of course, would be the man who could work with these problems, solve his client's problems, as an individual solution each time. He would not be a follower. Genuine articles are not followers—not even disciples. But they are originals in the sense that they are people who have been inspired by other men in their works either past or present, and who have tried to work out something of their own, for their own time and place and people and materials and methods and so on.

Not long ago, I was invited to speak to the Houston Architectural Society. Several of our students went to the talk and one of the questions that these people asked the most of our students was, "Who do you follow—Mies, Frank Lloyd Wright, or Goff?" Our students were amazed at this question, because that isn't a concern in our school—who do you follow. They don't even think about that. They were dumbfounded that such a question would be asked. I think there is entirely too much following and too much taking of sides. One side calls the other names. I have heard Mr. Wright blast Mies, and I have heard Mies followers blast Mr. Wright. It seems that there is no honor among us. It's so foolish, and then it all changes.

Someone said [something] not long ago to Mr. Wright and referred to Mies as an enemy and Mr. Wright said, "He's not an enemy; he's a disciple of mine." I didn't get Mies's side of that but I am anxious to hear what he will say about it. Anyway, there is a tendency to pit one against the other and to take sides just in the same way that the eclectics used to take sides about whether it was Gothic or Renaissance or Greek. They used to have pretty hot arguments about that, too. Now it's whether it is Mies, or Corbu, or Wright, and it couldn't be anything else.

It is just as impossible to think of having some idea of your own now as it ever was. And just as dangerous. You are just as suspect. About the biggest compliment people can give you is to say that doesn't look like you, because that means they already have an idea of what you look like.

Speaking of that, I think many times I'm amused when I give talks people say, "You don't look anything like I thought you would." You wonder what they thought. I know what a lot of them think. They expect you to come in with a plastic helmet and some copper antennas sticking up and to have Varèse music coming from your lapel or something and to talk in an unknown tongue. That would not surprise them nearly so much as that you were just like anybody else. That is the thing that surprises them the most—and I guess we are, we are all human beings anyway, more or less.

The thing that I think we need to understand the most is that so long as we are following, so long as we accept the magazines' editorial policies dictated by their advertisers, of what is all architecture, what's the thing they are doing now, the more dangerous ground we are on, because they change all the time. If you look back in the magazines in this country for a few years—go in the library and look at the architectural magazines—you can see the ring around the bathtub where things changed right away. What was it that changed them from the old eclecticism to the new? Why was it that the *Architectural Forum* never published a single building of Frank Lloyd Wright's until 1938? He had done some pretty good ones before that, but not a single one was ever published in one of the leading magazines in this country before 1938. That is one reason Mr. Wright says, "I knew him before it was fashionable."

It is true that these magazines change; not long ago it was the Cape Cod Fish House, the little hot box, and now it's the Ranchburger. There will be something else next year. If we are just depending on copying those things, we are going to have to keep pretty busy just finding out what they are wearing this season. We can't tell what they will do. It might be that with the Indochina wars there might be a sudden interest in Burmese architecture. Then where would we be? Because there are very few books on Burmese architecture. Then we would have to get busy and get some—just like the schools and the architects did when this modern thing came along.

I remember the architects were caught with their T squares down because all of a sudden people wanted modern buildings and the modern designer was worth his weight in gold then. There weren't so many of them at first. Magazines hadn't started publishing much of the modern designs. It didn't take long before they did, but remember you don't have to be an architect to subscribe to these magazines. The lumberyard man, and the real-estate man, and the engineer, and everyone can take the same magazines, and some of them can crib the stuff as well as we can. So what do we have to offer? We have only what we as individual architects can give when you get right down to it, if we are going to do architecture.

If we are going to do buildings, we can do very good buildings that will keep the rain off and the heat in or out, whichever we are trying to do, and serve the purpose and look pretty good—not bad, maybe, but that's all. No one is thrilled and no one is mad and no one is glad; the building is just there. There is an awful lot of building going on like that—when you consider that last year, I understand, only ten percent of all the buildings in the United States were done by licensed architects. Out of all that little bit, how many were real architects with a capital A? You see, there isn't much being done, really, in comparison with the great volume of work that is going on.

So there is a real demand for architects and a real demand for architecture. No wonder that people don't know what an architect is; no wonder they are so astonished when they see architecture. It scares them; it frightens them; it makes them laugh; it moves them. You should see them: they really look at something as though it came from another planet.

I bet you could go into any town in the United States where it's unfamiliar and rebuild the Robie House that Mr. Wright did in 1908, and it would still be considered a very curious specimen in almost any community. Things have changed a lot since then, too. There is a real shock value in architecture, even when you don't mean it to be. It astonishes people because it's unfamiliar; they are not used to architecture meaning something. I don't think it is always an unpleasant shock; sometimes they get over it.

I am not condemning the public, because I think that the public is much more ready for architecture than is realized. I think that they want it, and require it, and need it. It's our job to give it to them, and by doing that I am sure that they will learn to respect an architect and they will learn to have more judgment about architecture. I've never doubted the people. I'll trust their judgment anytime after they get over their initial hee-hee's and ha-ha's. I'll trust them anytime to many so-called enlightened people.

Not long ago, I moved my office into Mr. Wright's Price Tower in Bartlesville, Oklahoma, and I am coming into very close contact with architecture there. I got skinned-up several places when I ran into it: the walls are painted with plastic and there is sand blown on so you better stay away from them. All kidding aside, I have heard lots of people damn it and praise it, but one thing interested me very much. One day I was walking down the sidewalk and an old grandma walking by—she didn't know that I knew the building or knew anything about it—stopped me and pointed to the building and said, "Isn't it pretty?" That was nice, because she wasn't trying to be arty about this—it was an honest response.

I had another response like that once from an old grandmother—they seem to have lived and be willing to let live—with this rather strange design I had done. This particular job she had gone through with fifteen thousand other people in two days. It is a very strange house, you know. After she got through it she came over and said, "Young man, are you the architect?" I said, "Yes." She said, "Let me congratulate you. This is the most fun I have had since my first ride on an elevator." I like that response, too.

I think these incidents are interesting. Another I am very fond of was when the church I designed a long time ago for Tulsa, Oklahoma, was regarded in its initial stages as a trip to Mars, as most of my buildings are. But, anyway, when it was completed I heard an old black woman talking to the woman she was with and she said she was late because that morning she had been walking down Boston Avenue and the sun was shining on the top of the Boston Methodist Church tower and she had to stop and look at it "because it looked so beautiful, like it came right down out of heaven." That had much more meaning to me than someone saying something very scholarly about it, because it was direct, you see, and a real response.

That is what architecture is for and who it is for—the people all around us, and we should never forget that. I don't mean by that we need to sell down or bring down to the public, to try to get down and wallow with them, as they say, but I do think if the design has something it will eventually win their respect. I am very convinced of that, no matter how frightened or how amused they are at first.

So we have lots of fun. When we built the Ford House in Aurora, Illinois, there were all sorts of comments; people worried because we used coal. They said, "Coal burns." We know that, but so does wood and no one worries much about that. All kinds of strange stories got out. It was round, so therefore it revolved. One lady asked Mrs. Ford if she knew if the house revolved and she said "It better not." The lady said, "Well, I heard that it did." And Mrs. Ford replied, "I'm sorry, but it doesn't." Not long after that I went by to see Mrs. Ford and she had merry-go-round horses out on the screened porch. "What in the world are you doing with those things out there?" Mrs. Ford laughed and said, "Everyone thinks the house revolves so I thought I would give my grandchildren a honk."

Another funny incident happened there. Before the glass was put in you could walk in almost any place, and on the garden side particularly, but there was a small opening where I didn't want to run the coal wall into a wood wall, so I separated it with some translucent glass. It was an opening about eighteen inches wide and a little lower than a table: it wasn't a window, but it was used to separate these materials. Mrs. Ford went out one day and she saw what looked like some old rags stuck in this hole. She thought they looked very unsightly and she was just ready to jump on the contractor about it when the rags started to wiggle: she realized she was looking at the "posterior of some large babe." She was very curious what anyone would be trying to crawl in that little hole for; then she heard cries coming from inside. "Help, help. Get me out of here. I'm stuck." Mrs. Ford ran around and into the room and there was the front half of the lady struggling to get through. Just then, another lady came around the corner and said, "They must have two dogs. There's one just like it on the other side." So Mrs. Ford said, "Is she a friend of yours?" "Yes." "Well, let's get her out. You go outside and get her feet, and I'll take her arms, and we'll try and twist her out of here." So they struggled—this would have made a good Mack Sennet comedy, I'm sure—

and they finally got her out. And she got up and dusted herself off, very annoyed by this, and she said, "Well, I still don't see what those are for." And Mrs. Ford said, "Obviously not entrances." I am sure that the lady went away and told her friends that was the craziest house—that you couldn't even crawl into it. These are the kinds of things that happen, and that is where the tough hide comes in handy, of course. You get to where you can take it.

Seriously, all this is what happens when you try to advance architecture: you are going to get it, but it's worth it. I think that in order to advance architecture we need to advance ourselves. We need to keep an open, inquiring mind—need to realize as Debussy said, "Within every beautiful idea there is something that seems absurd to fools." Expect people to laugh sometimes. Why not? On the other hand I think we need to be curious and to try to extend the horizon of our art and not to be chauvinistic or to take sides and say this is right and that is wrong—this fellow is the only one who knows what is going on, and all that. We can learn from all the great architects today. When we think of our short half-century, so much has been happening and we have had great architects like Gaudi, Sullivan, Wright, Mendelsohn, Mies, Corbu—all of these men and many, many more. We can't be said to be architecturally impotent.

But architecture has to keep growing; we can't say that it stops with these great men anymore than we say it stopped with anyone in the past. It is very much like the story of Brahms and Mahler, the composers, when they were walking by the seashore one day. Brahms pointed to the waves coming over the sea, it reminded him of Beethoven, and he said, "Beethoven was the last great composer." Mahler replied, "Yes, and there is the last wave." Mr. Wright once said, "There need not be another Frank Lloyd Wright for five hundred years." Some people hope there won't. Why should there be? Why should anyone feel that architecture stops with anyone? It needs to go on, and it will. It is going to change and it is going to grow and it will be different all the time. Each work we do will change and be different if we are actually solving our problems.

There is a lot to do: stop calling names and get to work and do some good architecture. I think it will pay off every way under the sun. Even the public will realize there are such things as architects.

One time, not long ago, Mr. Wright addressed a group in Arizona. People had come there from miles around to hear him speak and he said, "Is there any person here who can ask a single intelligent question about architecture?" No one wanted to be the guinea pig, so no one said anything. So he said, "Well, I guess we might as well go home."

Index

Absolute architecture, 204, 252–54

Abstraction: in architecture, 33–34, 48, 50, 294; in Japanese prints, 256; in music, 239; in painting, 159–60

Aesthetics: building materials and, 252; commercial expediency and, 150; Japanese, 265, 267; knowledge about, 117; reconsidering, 313; skyscrapers and, 118–19, 128

African music, 232

American Institute of Architects (AIA), 201, 307

Arabesques (Claude Debussy), 24, 25, 230

Architects: commercial expediency and, 149–50, 153; conflicts among, 299; dropout rate of, 75–76; education of, 30–31, 207, 242, 301–302, 308–309, 316–17, 320; plan factories and, 150–52

Architectural Forum, 321

Art nouveau, 101

Atterberg, Kurt, 135–36

Bach, Johann Sebastian, 244, 278

Background buildings, 223

Balance, 32, 202, 314

Balinese architecture, 206

Barcelona cathedral, 300–301

Barnsdall, Aline, 138

Bartók, Béla, 232, 241, 243

Bathrooms, 318

Bauhaus, 22

Eugene Bavinger House (Norman, Okla.), 4, 184–86, 192–94, 294

Beardsley, Aubrey, 257

Beauty, 67

Beethoven, Ludwig van: Claude Debussy and, 272; originality of, 167, 214, 235; piano design and, 240–41, 248; reputation of, 326

Berlin, Irving, 97

Boston Avenue Church (Tulsa, Okla.), 6, 28, 212, 324

Boulez, Pierre, 195

Brahms, Johannes, 326

Brooks, Ernest, 22–23, 227–29, 231

Building materials: circular design and, 211–12; cost of, 123; design philosophy and, 28–29, 36–37, 84, 137, 138, 173, 215, 234, 241, 252, 291–94, 298, 302, 314–15; diversity of, 169; donations of, 283, 284; honesty in, 277; Japanese, 262; manufacturing art from, 57; ornaments and, 48; shop fabrication and, 292–93; truth and honesty in, 111, 114–15, 117, 125–27, 131, 136, 277, 315

Buxtehude, Dietrich, 244

Calligraphy, 264–65
Camp Parks, Calif., chapel, 28
Cantilevers, 79–80
Carlyle, Thomas, 77, 143
Carson Pirie Scott Building
    (Chicago, Ill.), 121–22, 123
Change: continuous present and,
    106, 195, 202, 203–204,
    206–208, 214; feeling and,
    100; progress and, 83, 95, 96,
    195; resistance to, 243; spaces
    and, 294–95, 298; tradition of,
    94–95
Cheney, Sheldon, 6
Children, space for, 207–208,
    287–88, 290, 292
Chopin, Frédéric, 241
Circular design, 48–49, 211–12,
    286–95, 325
Circulation, 36–37, 111, 114,
    154–55
City planners, 223, 224
Clair de Lune (Claude Debussy),
    274
Clarity, 54–56
Classical art forms: design
    concept of, 194, 195; Japanese,
    258–59; in music, 198, 227,
    234, 235
Clients: code restrictions and,
    219–22; conflicts with,
    139–42, 215–17; continuous
    present and, 203–204,
    208–209; design philosophy
    and, 34–36, 218–19, 283–93;
    experimentation and, 138–39,
    192–94, 284; FHA limitations
    and, 146; modernism and,
    82–83
Cocteau, Jean, 170

Code restrictions, 219–22
Cole House (Park Ridge, Ill.), 27
Collaborations with artists, 69–72
Colmorgan House (Glenview, Ill.),
    27
Color, 88
Common sense, 113
Communication style, 11, 191
Community colleges, 6–7
"Composition as Explanation"
    (Gertrude Stein), 11, 33
Condict Building (New York,
    N.Y.), 121
Conformity, 222–23
Continuous present: in art, 194–
    95; careers and, 191; change
    and, 106, 195, 202, 203–204,
    206–208, 214; communication
    style and, 11, 191; design
    philosophy and, 33–34, 37–38,
    212, 215, 217–18, 224,
    246–47; in music, 195–96,
    198; in nature, 197, 223
"The Continuous Present"
    (Gertrude Stein), 11
Coonley House, 166
Le Corbusier, Charles: five
    architectural points of, 55;
    Japanese art and, 261, 266;
    leaking roofs and, 304;
    reputation of, 22, 299, 303,
    320, 326; Ronchamp church
    design of, 301
Cortot, Alfred, 23, 228
Courtyards, 286
Craft guilds, 262
Creativity, 3, 79, 236, 277
Criticism: of cutting-edge
    architecture, 20–21, 60, 79, 83,
    167–68, 192, 201, 204,

211–13, 293, 301, 303–305, 311–12, 324–26; honesty in, 134–35; of music, 239–40, 243, 273
Crystal Chapel (Norman, Okla.), 4, 179
Cubism, 159
Cultures, 168–69
Curiosity, 24, 74

Dalks, John, 304
Dana House (Springfield, Ill.), 5
Da Vinci, Leonardo, 89
Debussy, Claude: on cherished personality, 41, 163, 271; on criticism, 213, 273, 326; on discipline and freedom, 42, 281; feeling and, 236, 272, 279; inspirations of, 275, 281; isolation of, 282; on his musical career, 191; nature and, 91, 272; order and, 43–44, 198, 277–78; originality of, 94, 165, 167, 230–32, 235–36, 242, 250, 271–72, 274, 276–78, 281; piano design and, 241, 248; on public approval, 213–14; Maurice Ravel and, 24–25, 229; on symphony compositions, 109, 279; on truth in design, 112, 134–35; writings of, 272–74
Democracy: building restrictions and, 221; horizontal design and, 123–24, 130; Japanese prints and, 255, 258; new geometry and, 300; verticality and, 27, 46, 120, 123, 130; Frank Lloyd Wright and, 47, 51, 130

Depth, 318
Design philosophy: building materials and, 28–29, 36–37, 84, 137, 138, 173, 215, 234, 241, 252, 291–94, 298, 302, 314–15; clients and, 34–36, 218–19, 283–93; continuous living spaces and, 31–32, 36–37, 294–95, 298; continuous present and, 33–34, 37–38, 212, 215, 217–18, 224, 246–47; drawing tools and, 107–108; experience and, 84–85, 162; feeling and, 28, 32, 98, 100, 104, 170–71, 242; innovation in, 82, 84–87, 90, 92–93, 101–102, 106, 250–51; modernism and, 86, 322; music and, 227, 236–39, 244–46, 251, 271; science and, 32, 98, 100; speed and, 250; truth and honesty in, 112–14, 117, 125–27, 130, 132, 134–36, 145–49, 223–24, 268–69
"The Devil in the Belfry" (Edgar Allan Poe), 80–81
Discipline: absolute architecture and, 204; Claude Debussy and, 42, 281; freedom and, 169; order and, 42, 55, 56, 68, 170, 201–202
Domes, 106–107, 316
Doors, 46–47, 241
Draftsmen, 151, 317
Drawing tools, 107–108
Driveways, 35, 46, 212, 285–86

Eclecticism, 118, 308, 320, 321
Education: of architects, 30–31, 207, 242, 301–302, 308–309,

316–17, 320; of Japanese
artists, 259–60
Education of public about
architecture, 307–308, 323,
324
Effect, 56, 134–37, 163, 204–206
Egyptian art and architecture:
historical authority of, 94;
influence of, 122; order in, 64,
68, 72, 172
Einstein, Albert, 74
Elevations, 107
Elmslie, George G., 83, 100
Ernst, Max, 166
Études (Claude Debussy), 275
Excuses, 77
Experience: design philosophy
and, 84–85, 162; nurturing
talent through, 158–59,
161–62, 170–73
Experimentation: clients and,
138–39, 192–94, 284; criticism
of, 166; limitations on,
136–39; in music, 243–44; in
structural forms, 303
Expressionism, 159

Feeling: Claude Debussy and,
236, 272, 279; design
philosophy and, 28, 32, 98,
100, 104, 170–71, 242;
honesty and, 111, 116, 117,
125; in Japanese art, 264; order
and, 50–55, 57, 66, 72, 74;
principles and, 89–90
Fences, 285
FHA, 139, 146–48
First Arabesque (Claude Debussy).
See Arabesques
First impressions, 25–26

Floor plans, 107
Flying, 88–89
Ruth Ford House (Aurora, Ill.), 4,
15–16, 182, 183, 324–26
Formalism, 278
The Fountain (Maurice Ravel),
23–25, 228–30
The Fountainhead (Ayn Rand),
209–10
Freedom: absolute architecture
and, 204; discipline and, 42,
169, 281; geometry and,
300–301; of movement, 249;
nature and, 233; order and, 42
Free form, 86–88, 91, 109,
154–55, 249
French art and architecture, 137
Fuller, Buckminster, 106, 316
Furniture, 211
Futurism, 159

Gardens, 287–88, 290, 294
John Garvey House (Urbana, Ill.),
4–5, 187–89, 283–95
Gaudí, Antonio, 87, 299,
300–301, 326
Gauguin, Paul, 257
Geometry, intersecting, 82
Geometry, new: design
philosophy and, 32–33,
300–301, 303; development of,
297–300, 302; free form and,
86–88, 91, 154–55
The Girl with the Flaxen Hair
(Claude Debussy), 24, 25, 165,
230
Glickman, Mendel, 10, 125, 136
Goodhue, Bertram, 153
Gothic style: expertise in, 317;
honesty in, 130, 153; in

skyscrapers, 122–23
Greek art and architecture: effect
    in, 204–205; influence of, 119,
    122, 309–10; music and, 234,
    239, 240; order in, 39, 72,
    195–96
Greene, Herb, 178, 185, 187–89
Grieg, Edvard, 271
Grinnell Bank (Grinnell, Iowa), 5
Group work, 67–73, 224–25, 302,
    319
Guggenheim Museum (New York,
    N.Y.), 219–20

Hallway gatherings, 14
Handel, George Frederick, 278
Haydn, Franz Joseph, 214, 276,
    278
Hearing, sense of, 317–18
Hearn, Lafcadio, 265
Hiroshige, Ando, 161, 260
Hoaxes, 135–36
Hodges, Jerri, 9
Hokusai, Katsushika, 62–63, 161,
    165, 171, 260
Honesty: in building materials,
    111, 114–15, 117, 125–27,
    131, 136, 277, 315; in design
    philosophy, 112–14, 117, 125–
    27, 130, 132, 134–36, 145–49,
    223–24, 268–69; eclecticism
    and, 118; feeling and, 111,
    116, 117, 125; order and, 131–
    34; realistic requirements and,
    143–45; truth and, 111–16,
    130–32, 143, 145, 223–24
Hopewell Baptist Church
    (Hopewell, Okla.), 5, 180, 181
Horizontal design, 123–24, 130
House Beautiful, 90–91

Howe and Lescaze, 124
Howell and Hood, 123
Humility, 60, 63

Iannelli, Alfonso, 192
Ideas: building materials and, 234;
    combining, 162–63, 318;
    discarding, 112–13, 121; group
    work and, 224–25; innovation
    in, 102–103, 108–10, 320; in
    music, 83, 95, 97, 167–68,
    234–38; obligation and,
    104–105; order and, 38, 39,
    42–44, 61–62, 157, 162,
    169–70; perfecting, 164–65;
    style and, 41; technology and,
    89; trademarking, 163–64;
    truth and, 135; Frank Lloyd
    Wright and, 39, 54
Illinois Institute of Technology
    (IIT), 297, 304
Imagination, 133, 138
Imperial Hotel, 66
Impressionism, 159
India, 240, 251
Infinity, 199
Information desks, 47
Inorganic principle, 93
Inspiration: Claude Debussy and,
    112, 275, 281; individualizing,
    164; music as, 227; mystery
    and, 200; nature as, 171; Louis
    Henri Sullivan and, 121, 128;
    truth and honesty in, 131
International style, 279–80
"In the Cause of Architecture"
    (Frank Lloyd Wright), 20
Intuition, 99–100
Invention, 93, 99
Irrationality, 56, 62

Itō, Jakuchū, 161

Japanese art and architecture:
  alcove display areas for,
  262–64; classical, 258–59;
  cultural pervasiveness of,
  260–61, 264–66; modernism
  and, 255, 257; modular system
  of, 261–62, 313; music and,
  264; nature and, 91; order in,
  39–40, 41, 62–63, 68, 72;
  printmaking and, 255–58, 260;
  training in, 259–60; Western
  influence on, 266–68
Javanese music, 275
Jeux (Claude Debussy), 275
Johnson Wax Building, 39, 45–49,
  66, 136, 166, 234, 252

Kaiser Aluminum, 283
Kandinsky, Wassily, 26
Kansas City, Mo., 221–22
Kewanee, Ill., 5–6
Klee, Paul, 69–70
Klimt, Gustav, 71
Knowledge, 102, 103, 244
Korin (painter), 71, 165, 259

Lao-tse, 303, 319
Larkin Building, 39, 45–54, 66,
  166, 196
Leacock, Stephen, 42
Ledbetter House (Norman,
  Okla.), 86
Licenses, 151–52
Living rooms, 208
Louis, Pierre, 95
Luxfer Prism Building, 124

McHugh, William, 8

Mahler, Gustav, 326
Manet, Édouard, 257
Le Martyre de Saint Sebastian
  (Claude Debussy), 165, 275
Marx, Groucho, 77
Mass production, 56–57
Materials. See Building materials
Matisse, Henri, 166
Mechanical approach, 91
Mendelsohn, Eric, 22, 72, 326
La Mer (Claude Debussy), 165,
  198, 271, 275
Midway Gardens, 66
Milarepa, 305
Millard House, 139
Models, 107
Modernism: book collection on,
  13; clients and, 82–83; design
  trends and, 86, 322; Japanese
  influence on, 255, 257; in
  music, 23, 24, 231–32, 235,
  242–43; order and, 40, 56; in
  painting, 24, 26, 40–41, 71;
  plants and, 317; Frank Lloyd
  Wright and, 58–59
Modular systems, 261, 313–14
Moldings, 48
Monet, Claude, 257
Monsieur Croche, the
  Dilettante-Hater (Claude
  Debussy), 273–74
Monterey, Calif., 6–7
Monumentality, 27
Morris, Vere, 7
V. C. Morris Shop (San Francisco,
  Calif.), 7, 148
Movement, 249–51, 300–301
Murals, 15, 69–71, 177
Music: abstraction in, 34; clarity
  in, 55; competitions, 135–36;

continuous present in, 195–96,
198; criticism of, 239–40, 243,
273; design philosophy and,
227, 236–39, 244–46, 251,
271; development of
appreciation for, 22–26,
228–32; experimentation in,
243–44; expression in, 115–16;
freedom and, 233; ideas in, 83,
95, 97, 167–68, 234–38; as
inspiration, 227; instrument
design and, 240–42, 248–49;
international style in, 279–80;
Japanese, 264; mass
production in, 56–57;
modernism in, 23, 24, 231–32,
235, 242–43; mystery in, 233,
238–39, 278; nighttime
concerts for students, 13–14;
orchestration of, 96–97; order
and, 43–44, 57, 232, 277–78;
pure, 251, 253; rhythm in,
202–203, 313; speed in,
250–51
Mussorgsky, Modest, 232, 271
Mystery: Claude Debussy on, 213;
in music, 233, 238–39, 278; in
nature, 199; surprise and, 90,
199–200

National Insurance Building
(Chicago, Ill.), 124
Nature: continuous present and,
197, 223; Claude Debussy and,
91, 272; in design, 91–92, 171,
290, 293; freedom and, 233;
harmony in, 222–23; looking
into, 198; mystery in, 199
Neoclassicism, 235
News Building (New York, N.Y.),
123
"The New Sensation" (Pierre
Louis), 95–96
New World Architecture (Sheldon
Cheney), 6

Oak Park, Ill., 209
Objectivity and order, 73–74, 75
Obligation, 104–105, 162
Office buildings, 45–54
Okio (painter), 161, 259
Opposites, 29–30
Order: clarity and, 54–56;
definition of, 67; democracy
and, 47; discipline and, 42, 55,
56, 68, 170, 201–202; feeling
and, 50–55, 57, 72, 74; in
Greek art and architecture, 39,
72, 195–96; group work and,
67–73; honesty and, 131–34;
ideas and, 38, 39, 42–44,
61–62, 157, 162, 169–70;
Japanese concept of, 39–40,
41; modernism and, 40–41; in
music, 43–44, 57, 232,
277–78; personal sense of,
73–74, 75; social and
architectural reflections of, 61,
64–67, 72; style and, 41–42; in
traditional works, 43, 64;
Frank Lloyd Wright and, 39,
45–54, 65–66, 74–75, 166
Organic principle, 92–93
Oriental art and architecture:
artistic method in, 160–61;
inspiration and, 93; music and,
232, 234; organic nature of, 22;
rhythm in, 203. See also
Japanese art and architecture
Ornament, 48, 50, 295, 316–17

Painting: displaying, 263–64; early explorations in, 26, 27; form in, 196, 248; freedom and, 233, 248; imitation in, 280; modernism in, 24, 40–41, 71; movement in, 249; music and, 237; order and, 57, 63, 64, 265; squircle in, 5; styles of, 159–61; viewing, 247–48

Paneling, 317

Parrish, Maxfield, 69

Parking, 35, 285–86

Parthenon, 204–205

Pelléas and Mélisande (Claude Debussy), 272

Perfection, 164–65

Perspective, 107

Phidias, 205

Photographing buildings, 198–99

Picasso, Pablo, 280

Plan factories, 150–52

Poe, Edgar Allan, 80–81

Pollock, Jackson, 64

Practicality, 143

Prairie School, 5

Prelude to the Afternoon of a Faun (Claude Debussy), 25, 116, 165, 230–31, 234

Joe Price studio, 5, 218–19

Price Tower (Bartlesville, Okla.), 323

"Pride of the Prairie," 3, 8

Prints, Japanese, 255–58, 260

Progress, 83, 95, 96, 195, 224

Prokofiev, Sergei, 241

Proportion, 314

Quonset ribs, 4, 15–16

Raglan, Lord, 211

Rameau, Jean-Philippe, 170

Rand, Ayn, 209–10

Ravel, Maurice, 23–25, 228–30, 232

Religious space design: French, 137; of Bruce Goff, 4, 5, 6, 28, 69–71, 179–81, 212, 324; of Eric Mendelsohn, 72; of Frank Lloyd Wright, 50–54, 166

Renoir, Jean, 257

Rhythm, 202–203, 238, 313, 317

Ridged bents, 86

Rimsky-Korsakov, Nikolai, 232, 276

The Rite of Spring (Igor Stravinsky), 85, 203, 281

Robie House, 323

Rodia, Simon, 252

Roman art and architecture, 122, 195–96

Ronchamp church, 301

Roofs, 288–89, 304

Rosenfeld, Paul, 232

Vernon Rudd House (San Mateo County, Calif.), 14–15, 177

Rush, Endacott & Rush, 17–21, 311

Ruskin, John, 245

St. Mark's Building, 124

Sam's Towers (Watts, Calif.), 252, 254

Sandstedt, Mr., 308

Savings Fund Society Building (Philadelphia, Pa.), 124

Scale, 46, 47

Schoenberg, Arnold: originality of, 60, 85, 167, 168, 243, 250; piano design and, 241, 248

Science: art and, 242, 268; design

philosophy and, 32, 98, 100; detail in, 317

Shop fabrication, 292–93

Sibelius, Jean, 213

Site relation, 318–19

Skyscrapers, 118–29

Small-house problems, 145–49

Soundproofing, 286, 288, 318

Spaulding collection, 258

Specialization, 97, 98, 104, 151

Square form design, 49–50

Squircles, 5, 190, 291

Stairways, 46

Stein, Gertrude, 11, 33, 106, 195, 206

Strauss, Richard, 276

Stravinsky, Igor: on critics, 213; on Claude Debussy, 280–81; on Hollywood, 282; originality of, 85, 167, 232, 243; piano design and, 241, 248; rhythm and, 203; work method of, 112

Structure: design philosophy and, 302–303, 315–16; knowledge about, 117; science of, 98, 100; truth and honesty in, 111, 115, 126–29, 131–32, 136, 278–79

Style, 41–42

Subdivisions, 220–21

Subjectivity and order, 73–74, 75

Sullivan, Louis Henri: Barcelona cathedral and, 301; democracy and, 130; on native influences, 235; originality of, 103, 309; ornament and, 19; on principle, 142; reputation of, 5, 83, 100, 326; skyscrapers and, 120–23, 124, 127–28

Surprise, 90, 238–39, 278

Surrealism, 160

Talent, 157–59, 162, 172–73, 200–201

Taliesin (Spring Green, Wisc.), 5, 6, 7, 19

Talmidge and Watson, 5

Taut, Bruno, 262

Teaching: of aesthetics, 313; commitment to, 31; of creative design, 3–4; criticism in, 113–14; hallway gatherings and, 14; hands-off philosophy of, 10–11; music and, 14; team projects and, 73

Teamwork. See Group work

Technology, 89, 98–99

Three-part form, 196

Thurber, James, 129–30

Tract builders, 211

Trademarks, artistic, 163–64

Triaero House (Fern Creek, Ky.), 28

Tribune Building (Chicago, Ill.), 122–23

Truth. See Honesty

Unity Temple, 39, 49–54, 66, 166

University of Oklahoma School of Architecture: design trends at, 86–87, 112; displays at, 9, 13, 108, 178; lectures to, 39, 79, 111; reputation of, 11, 101, 110; stadium location of, 68–69; teaching methods at, 8–14

University of Santa Clara, 12, 191

Unseth House (Park Ridge, Ill.), 27

Urban renewal, 224

Utamaro, Kitagawa, 260

Utilitarianism, 115, 116, 251–53

Van der Rohe, Mies: apartment building design of, 125, 127, 128; Illinois Institute of Technology and, 297; inorganic principle and, 93; Japanese art and, 261, 266; plan factories and, 150; proportion and, 314; reinforced concrete design of, 128–29; reputation of, 34, 299, 303–304, 326; Frank Lloyd Wright and, 320

Van Gogh, Vincent, 257

Varèse, Edgard, 232, 321

Verne, Jules, 89

Verticality: democracy and, 27, 46, 120, 123, 130; Louis Sullivan and, 120–23, 127–28

Viewpoint, 142–43

Vivaldi, Antonio, 244

Voltaire, François-Marie, 59

Wagner, Wilhelm Richard, 167, 234, 271, 275–76

Wainwright Building (St. Louis, Mo.), 120–21, 127

Walker, Della, 7–8

Walker House (Carmel, Calif.), 7–8

War of the Worlds, 92

Welch, Philip B.: Bruce Goff and, 8–16, 91; Frank Lloyd Wright and, 3, 6–8

Whistler, James McNeill, 257

Wilford, Thomas, 248

Windows, 52, 290–91

Woolworth Building (New York, N.Y.), 122

World War II building restrictions, 28

Wright, Frank Lloyd: Architectural Forum and, 321; Barcelona cathedral and, 301; buildings designed by, 5, 6, 39, 45–54, 65–66, 124, 136, 138, 139, 196, 219–20, 323; culture and, 105; democracy and, 47, 51, 130; on end of architectural epoch, 89, 150, 326–27; on experience, 84–85; on feeling, 170; on The Fountainhead, 209–10; on free form, 87; freshness of, 101; Mendel Glickman and, 10; House Beautiful and, 91; idea and, 39, 54; on ideals and excuses, 77; imitations of, 314; inconsistency of, 30; influence on Bruce Goff of, 17–24, 27, 30–33, 36, 228, 239, 310–11; Japanese art and, 256, 258, 261; modernism and, 58–59; on native influences, 235; nature and, 91–92; order and, 39, 45–54, 65–66, 74–75, 165, 166; on principle, 202; reputation of, 83, 100, 103, 147–48, 209, 276, 299, 303–304, 309, 326; on space, 303, 318, 319; style of, 41, 59, 128; Mies van der Rohe and, 320; Philip Welch and, 3, 6–8. See also Price Tower